**Reflections on
American Foreign Policy
Since 1945**

Reflections on American Foreign Policy Since 1945

Christopher Coker
Lecturer in International Relations
London School of Economics

St. Martin's Press
New York

© Christopher Coker, 1989

All rights reserved. For information write:
Scholarly and Reference Division,
St. Martin's Press, Inc., 175 Fifth Avenue,
New York, N.Y. 10010

First published in the United States of America in 1989

Printed in the United Kingdom

ISBN 0–312–03991–3

Library of Congress Cataloging-in-Publication Data

Coker, Christopher.
    Reflections on American foreign policy since 1945 / Chrisopher Coker.
       p.   cm.
    Includes bibliographical references.
    ISBN 0–312–03991–3
    1. Unitted States—Foreign relations—1945–   I. Title.
E744.C63   1989   89-37315
327.73—dc20   CIP

'We have the past behind us, the future before us. We don't see the future, we see the past. That's odd, for we haven't eyes in the back of our heads'
Eugene Ionescu, *Fragments of a Journal*

'And that,' put in the Director sententiously 'that is the secret of happiness and virtue – liking what you've got to do. All conditioning aims at that: making people like their inescapable social destiny'
Aldous Huxley, *Brave New World*

'Like all mystics. . . he is baffled, a child before the real now, happier out of it, in a narrative past, or a prophetic future, locked inside that weird tense grammar does not allow, an imaginary present.'
John Fowles, *A Maggot*

Contents

Preface	ix
1: Auguries of innocence: the past as the key to US foreign policy	1
2: Not the end of the world news: the United States and the origins of the Cold War	36
3: Rite of passage: containment and the legacy of George Kennan	54
4: Squaring the error: the lessons of the Vietnam War	87
5: Living with Caliban: The United States and the Third World	104
6: Intimations of mortality: is the United States in decline?	128
7: Present at the Fall, or the death of history	148
Bibliography	163
Index	177

Preface

I have been teaching American students for many years. It is enlightening for a British academic, looking in from the outside, to appreciate how much Americans of all generations are captive of a past which is more vivid than that of any other country with the exception, perhaps, of the Soviet Union, a parallel which many Americans would doubtless find disconcerting.[1]

The 'past' offers not an ideology, as such, but a sense of purpose, which derives from one of several mythical histories to which the republic's politicians have constantly reached back in order to commune with the nation. Like their constituents, they are all part of a historical flow, in touch with their forebears, acutely conscious of their obligation to posterity.

This study is not a work of history, still less a comprehensive account of post-war US foreign policy. It was once said of the lectures of a Harvard Professor of the History of Art, 'drop your pencil and you have missed a century'.[2] My case is worse. I have chosen to drop several themes, such as the United States' relations with Europe, or US policy in the Middle East. As the book's subtitle suggests, it is a set of reflections about some of the key developments in the post-war period, anchored to an interpretation which if not original has not, perhaps, been stated before so explicitly: that the past continues to inform the present.

History is not myth. The past is. The essence of mythology is to state by means of analogy or metaphor an experience which transcends history. There can be a history of myth, but not a history based on myths as part of its structure of meaning. The United States has three myths with their own distinctive metaphors, from manifest destiny to Kennedy's New Frontier, and Jefferson's Beacon of Light. As Dean Inge wrote 50 years ago:

When the mind communes with the world of values, its inevitable language is the language of poetry, of symbol and myth... Philosophy has to deal with a number of irreducible surds which cannot be rationalised. Our reason... has reached its limits. We are driven to mythologise, confessing that we have left the realm of scientific fact.[3]

Ultimately it is salutary to remember that many US leaders – although aware that the past offers no answer to the predicaments of power – have not always shown much concern about the fact. As Jefferson wrote to de Marbois in 1817, 'my theory has always been that if we are to dream, the flatteries of hope are as cheap and pleasanter than the gloom of despair'.[4] US Presidents have not only found themselves preaching to the converted, but to a nation that needs to believe, to cling to a faith at any cost.

Whether the United States is the protagonist of this book, or whether the protagonist is a country seen through my eyes subjectively, I could not say. Opinions may also differ on the question of whether it is to be considered as a historical enquiry, or a political one, or an account of a country's foreign policy charged with historical meaning. For me it is all three.

Christopher Coker
London School of Economics (January 1989)

NOTES

1. The 'convergence' theory of US and Soviet post-war history as propagated by Huntingdon and Brzezinski in the mid-1960s was based largely on economic and political determinants – namely that both countries had spawned imperial bureaucracies pursuing essentially the same limited ends. As early as 1977 Ronald Steel argued that like two generals of mutinous armies the superpowers were becoming aware of the fact that although they were on opposing sides the problems they faced were strikingly similar, and that what advantaged one side did not necessarily disadvantage the other (Ronald Steel, *Pax Americana*, Penguin, 1977, p. 47).
2. E. H. Gombrich, *Means and Ends: reflections on the history of fresco painting*, (London: Thames and Hudson, 1986) p. 32.
3. Arnold Toynbee, *A Study of History*, vol. 12: *Reconsiderations* (Oxford: Oxford University Press, 1965) p. 40.
4. Saul K. Padover (ed.), *Thomas Jefferson on Democracy*, (New York: New American Library, 1939) p. 29.

1. Auguries of innocence, the past as the key to US foreign policy

'The Past is never over. It is not even past'
William Faulkner, *Intruder in the Dust*

'Nations are like infants; they are what they are taught to be'
Joel Barlow, A letter to the National Convention of France, 1793

Academics have done a great disservice to the study of US foreign policy by treating its problems as interesting abstractions to read about and from which occasionally to draw lessons which may have wider application in other fields. Studying foreign policy is not at all the same thing as understanding politics; it does not even equip people for high office. As long as political scientists continue to be obsessed by quantitative data, or dry-as-dust theories of rationality and groupthink, the study of foreign policy is likely to remain marginal to an understanding of the political process, or why particular options have appeared particularly attractive over time.

I have written this book in the hope that the balance can be redressed in favour of 'cultural politics'. There are no studies on this precise theme, although many contain some reference to ideas, or American ideology, to explain a role or particular mission.[1] The excuse for a more involved treatment of culture, of historical myths or images, is that they have played a far more significant role in US foreign policy than societies with a longer and more complex cultural heritage. It is a means by which an often rootless society has managed to retain its own identity. In *The Grapes of Wrath* John Steinbeck paints an especially vivid picture of the uprooted Okies who, when told that there is no room for their souvenirs in their enforced passage to California, refuse to leave them behind; 'How will we know it's us without our past?' they plead.[2]

De Tocqueville foresaw that in a democracy a sense of community might quickly dissolve: 'Not only does democracy make each man forget his ancestors, it hides his descendants from him and divides him from his contemporaries: It continually turns him back into himself and threatens at last to enclose him in the solitude of his own heart.' Without a historical frame of reference de Tocqueville saw that humanity would meet at the point where it was most irrelevant; where it exchanged money, not ideas, where men worked not together, but in factories as 'machines'.

Crevécour's famous question, 'What is the American, this new man?', has been answered by travellers to the United States for two centuries. They have always returned to the past. In 1952 Crevécour's 'new man' was still being defined as new kind of hero – 'an existential adventurer', wrote William Barrett, on the margins of new and unlimited experience, a hero who needed the past as a sustaining frame of reference by which to define himself, or 'find' himself as a later generation would say.[3]

The men who reach positions of power, the men who remain faceless in Steinbeck's novels, are the most clearly moulded by the past. They exercise power in accordance with the ideals of the Founding Fathers; they draw sanction from the past for their deeds. In no other country are political speeches so resonant with references to history. Reagan's invocation of the United States' rendezvous with destiny recalled Tom Paines's vision of a nation 'great enough to begin the world all over again'.[4] His insistence two years earlier that the United States had been born out 'of the one true revolution in man's history' suggested that every other revolution had simply been a pale imitation of the 'first'.[5] Far from being a lone voice, Reagan was merely the most recent President to appeal to the past, to add authority to his public utterances and policy decisions, as the historian Steele Commanger once put it – to try 'to imprison in an ideological strait-jacket the turbulent tides of [American] history'.[6]

This is a study of that strait-jacket, of a political culture which is unyielding in its forcefulness and all-embracing in its scope. It is an attempt to explain how great a part historical myths, images and metaphors play in US political life, consciously, and often unconsciously as well. Truth, as Nietzsche once put it, is a 'mobile army of metaphors . . . which poetically and rhetorically intensified become transposed and adorned, and which after long usage by a people seem fixed, canonical and binding on them'. Later he adds that truths are worn-out metaphors, 'coins which have their obverse effaced, and are now no longer of account as coins but merely metal.'[7]

The central theme of this study is that the past has been used consistently as identity, affirmation or escape according to the needs of the moment. Its lesson is straightforward enough; if Americans could be weaned away from their atavistic attachment to a past that has been largely invented, they might be able to face their own history more honestly with results that might help them better appreciate their less-than-fairy-tale present.

The past, alas, is not necessarily an accurate reflection of US history. It is a past which Americans have not lived but which they have manufactured, like most former great nations, who having fallen into decline have rediscovered their real history only when it is too late to make it. Real history, of course, is a relative term anyway since all historical 'experience' is necessarily subjective. 'Man is a history making theatre', wrote Auden, who can neither repeat the past nor leave it behind; at every moment he adds to and thereby modifies everything that had previously happened to him. Hence the difficulty of finding a single image which can stand as an adequate symbol for man's kind of existence. If we thing of his ever-open future, then the natural image is of a single pilgrim walking along an unending road into hitherto unexplored country; if we think of his never forgettable past then that natural image is of a crowded city built in every style of architecture in which the dead are as active citizens as the living ... Everyman is both a citizen and a pilgrim.[8]

To write about the past since the end of the Second World War is to write of two generations of public and elite opinion, an elite which has made an appeal to the past to win public support for its actions, a public which (to paraphrase one English historian's description of Churchill) has paid the price for reading history too avidly.

In looking at the public I shall be looking at 'informed' or 'attentive' opinion – not those few thousand people who read history books after the ninth grade, nor the works of contemporary history which pass by the name of political memoirs, a now sadly debased trade. I shall be looking instead at the hundreds of thousands who have responded in the period to the speeches of politicians, or the popular moods of the moment – those who have expressed their views in opinion polls, or voted in elections, who have drawn inspiration from the past evoked by their political leaders, a past which has given meaning and resonance to their own lives as 'pilgrims' journeying towards Whitman's unknown destination, 'citizens' – who, to quote Sartre (*Les Mots*), are condemned to carry the past on their backs all their lives, as Aeneas did the aged Anchises on his flight from Troy, those 'invisible parents astride their sons for all their life'.

The Americans did not know about the 'significance' of the expanding frontier until the mid-nineteenth century when manifest destiny became the prevailing wisdom of the hour. They did not know they were a 'special people' fighting a war to end all wars until Woodrow Wilson reminded them of the historical obligations conferred on them by the Founding Fathers. They did not know of their responsibility for defending the Free World until Roosevelt and Truman, in respect of very different enemies, appealed to the spirit of redemptionism which the first Puritan settlers had left the thirteen colonies as their enduring (or unendurable) legacy.[9]

The past has provided the United States with a frame of reference without which its history like the Bellman's map in *The Hunting of the Snark* would be 'a perfect absolute blank'. It has sustained the United States' resolve in crises, and given it the self-confidence to tackle tasks which would have defeated most other nations. As late as 1981 when the United States narrowly voted in Ronald Reagan, four out of five Americans still believed the United States had 'a special role to play' in the world, a measure of how successfully they had imbibed the past and its 'lessons'.[10]

The United States is not the only society to have resorted to the past to explain, justify or even rationalise its actions. The use to which it has put its own past, however, differs considerably from the sense of imperial destiny which the Whig tradition created for the British in the nineteenth century and which sustained them, possibly for the last time, in the dark days of 1940. It differs even more from the historical dialectic propagated in the Soviet Union, which has legitimised the control of a single party that has remained in power for 70 years. It is not a national myth as von Treitschke would have understood the term in the 1890s because it is not a racial code, nor even a nationalist one, although the United States unlike Wilhelmine Germany has the distinction of being the only power whose history is precisely coterminous with the history of nationalism itself.[11]

Unlike each of these powers the United States has not one past but three. As a unique country the United States had little to offer the world, and no obligations towards it. As a country founded by Protestant fundamentalists it inherited a historical mission to redeem mankind from tyranny, whether imposed by eighteenth-century monarchs or twentieth-century commissars. As a country blessed more than any other with resources as well as political liberty it had a duty to show the world that freedom can produce efficient government and economic growth.

If the present is subordinated to the past, the past gives meaning to the present as well. The nearest we can get to this concept perhaps is Auden's definition of art as parable and escape. Escape art is just what its name suggests; parable art is 'that art which shall teach man to unlearn hatred and learn love' (1935). That is not a political function, of course, but a highly moral one. It too is the meaning of America's past.

De Tocqueville once said that the misapplied lessons of history were more dangerous than ignorance of the past. Unfortunately, knowledge of the past seems to be no less dangerous if for different reasons. Americans have expected too much of their past and made too many demands on it, by putting it to too many questionable uses. It has had to serve as a source of folklore, myth and political sanction. It has also had to serve as a substitute for political theory. As a people the Americans have exhibited a singular indifference to dogma or political values. The meaning of their experience has been derived almost entirely from history: 'The American Clio has been placed in the role of a sacred oracle of events from which the pathway of the future is periodically sought.'[12]

In this respect, history has been reinterpreted or rewritten to gell with whichever 'past' is most appropriate to the age. It is a practice which goes back many years to 1787 when the Federalists had to blacken the public memory of the first constitutional government simply to rewrite the constitution; or earlier still to 1776 when the Founding Fathers found it necessary to rewrite the history of England's contact with the colonies. Such instances show that the United States is a profoundly ahistorical (not historicist) culture that is inevitably attracted to the messages of its two greatest twentieth-century historians Charles Beard and Carl Becker. Becker's maxim 'Everyman is his own historian' and Beard's doctrine of 'History as an act of faith' gave the United States a Protestant right to commune with the past without the intercession of professional historians.[13]

The unique problem the United States now faces is that the 'parable past' has begun to lose its appeal. Having lost its authority in Vietnam, the elite has also lost its ability to use the past to legitimise its aspirations – in short, the past has lost its hold over the popular imagination. As the same time history has been unable to liberate the Americans from their past as the historians of the early 1970s hoped now that history is in terminal decline in the schools. Beard and Becker had at least written as historians for a public to whom even their most abstract speculations did not appear alien, even less alienating. Their successors are inclined to speak as experts only to other experts. What the language has gained in technical precision it has lost in general appeal.

For the first time the past even as interpreted by historians may be about to fail the republic, intellectually and politically; a question which raises the larger issue of how in the years to come the Americans will define their culture, and what they will choose to exclude.

EXCEPTIONALISM

'A fig for your feuds and vendettas! Germans and Frenchmen, Irishmen and Englishmen, Jews and Russians – into the crucible with you all. God is making the American'.

Israel Zangwell, *The Melting Pot*

One of the United States' central beliefs is that its success is not for export. The American historians of the nineteenth century took Calvinism and secularised it. Bancroft, Motley, Prescott and Parkmen were all examples of historians who portrayed the United States as a country apart, destined to stand alone, as an inspiration to those who were denied freedom but could not obtain it because they were not yet members of God's elect. As Plumb writes, they were not historians but manufacturers of a past that had particular resonance among a Puritan people. They were the banner carriers who lost sight of everything but their own dream – the dream of a special divine (Calvinist) dispensation, a land where nature bred a tougher, purer, more sterling individual – the American.[14] Fenimore Cooper and Henry Longfellow even saw the first native Americans – the American Indians – as noble savages, superior to the 'uncivilised' races of the Old World. No one alas could find a place for the American blacks. Sold into slavery they carried with them the taint of the white man's sin; they were best ignored, if not forgotten.[15] The belief that the American Revolution was not for export dates back to the end of the eighteenth century. It was the American ambassador to France, after all, who informed the French that, try though they might to remove every vestige of the *ancien régime*, they would never succeed. 'They want an American constitution', he wrote home rather dismissively, 'without realising that they have no Americans to uphold it.'[16]

The 'perfect constitution' has cast a spell on the Americans ever since, something which was perhaps, most obvious to the foreign visitor during the bicentennial celebrations of the 1787 Philadelphia Convention when any suggestion that the constitution might be seriously flawed, or even partially irrelevant for a late twentieth-century state, met with frank disbelief. In 1776 when the Americans drew up the much earlier Declaration of Independence, they already imagined themselves to be a unique people, forgetting, as Bryce remarked in his comparison of the different Western democracies, that they were really 'an old people, the heirs of many ages'.[17]

The Declaration of Independence was not a truly revolutionary document, in part because it was never considered for export by its authors. If its language may have been universal, its application was not. If it appealed to the 'opinions of mankind', the appeal was highly selective. Only those in a state of grace could comprehend its message. 'God the Educator', as one historian put it, had already replaced 'God the engineer'. Jefferson, egalitarian though he was, lived in an age when the unbending truths of an earlier age were giving way to the idea that God might have timed his revelations by staggering the stages of man's understanding. The thirteen colonies were the first country to find God's truths 'self-evident'.[18]

That is why the Founding Fathers never once referred to their actions as 'revolutionary'. Why should they? Throughout the eighteenth century the term 'revolution' referred to a change of power within a state, not the creation of a new one. It was not until the publication of Noah Webster's *American Dictionary* in 1828 that the American Revolution arrived; by then the word had gained its present meaning. In the Declaration of 1776 Jefferson and Maddison offered themselves not as revolutionaries but heralds of a new age – a *novus ordo saeclorum*.[19] In other words the fact that they chose not to call themselves revolutionaries was not an expression of their conservatism, but their innate belief that they were charting a new course through history, one which they were far from convinced others could follow.

Even in their appeal to the right to happiness the Founding Fathers were treading entirely new ground. It was a right that would have been meaningless in any society but the United States. Happiness is at the core of the US constitution – an inalienable right, even if it involves a perpetual quest. Most Europeans at the time, indeed ever since, have accepted that human progress is impossible without an element of discontent; that happiness if attainable would produce an atrophied, apathetic society, conservative to the core, so self-satisfied that its members would be unwilling to improve their condition. Even Kant who saw the striving for progress as irrelevant to happiness (in his belief that the noble savage was much more content than the European) accepted that in a civilised society progress and happiness were connected by insisting that man's happiness had to be 'created by his own reason' which, in turn, through enlightenment would lead inexorably to progress, or the betterment of his lot.[20] The United States' belief that it could achieve a state of happiness once independence had been won was entirely American – a national conceit, not a natural right, which divided the New World from the Old with its permanent discontents.

Even in the nineteenth century when the English Utilitarians came nearest to promoting happiness as a political end they departed from their US colleagues by talking of the *'felicifer calculus'*, or what Bentham called 'the greatest happiness of the greatest number'. For Bentham however, happiness was a key not to progress, still less to equality, but to security or order, a very English preoccupation.

Not only did the American version of happiness clash with the Utilitarian concept of progress, it also found itself at odds with the standard European view of the social contract. In social contract theory the individual agrees to enter society only to secure life and property. In *Civilisation and Its Discontents* (a highly significant title) Freud provides a very Hobbesian explanation for the growth of different cultures and countries, wistfully remarking that for the individual himself 'it would be better perhaps' if he could achieve happiness without having to experience the alienating process of socialisation which inevitably makes happiness an impossible goal.[21]

In sum the American preoccupation with happiness or more strictly social contentment has puzzled European opinion for two centuries or longer. Commenting on Dickens' first trip to the United States, Chesterton observed: 'He was quite prepared to be pleased with America. He would have been better pleased with it if it had not been so much pleased with itself.' Later he added that Dickens 'was annoyed more with its contentment than its discontents', in particular its exaggerated sense of patriotism. In the old days, Chesterton continued, the word 'patriot' meant a discontented man. In Britain a 'courtier' meant a man prepared to uphold the prevailing social order, for fear of the consequences of its collapse, a man, in short, who was easily pleased. In other nations such as France the word 'patriot' meant a pessimist. The Americans were living in an unreal world – complacent, ignorant of those outside, on the road to total self-absorption and madness.[22] It would never have occurred to any American except the few like Ezra Pound and T. S. Eliot that contentment was in fact a psychological malady, a social malaise from which they both chose to escape to the continent from which their ancestors had emigrated in search of greater contentment.

How far has this belief in exceptionalism translated itself into US foreign policy? Isolationism in the inter-war years derived much of its legitimacy in the eyes of the American people from the wish to keep the country's virtue intact. Unable to expand any further once the frontier had been reached, unwilling to follow up Theodore Roosevelt's imperial mission which for a brief moment in the United States' history had extended the frontier into the Pacific, the Americans felt 'trapped in time'. In this supreme moment of introspection, of 'sectarian withdrawal', many Americans felt the need to maintain their exceptional standing by contracting out of a corrupting world which had little or nothing to offer the United States, or the American people.[23]

After the Second World War the majority of Americans no longer felt isolationism to be a legitimate response to their predicament. For Reinhold Niebuhr, one of the most persuasive exponents of the providential school of US history, the United States might indeed be unique, but it could not wilfully turn its back on the world as it had done in the 1930s. As a member of the international community the United States had a moral responsibility to help its neighbours and allies, a responsibility which the inter-war interpretation of exceptionalism had wantonly obscured.[24] Where he remained true to the exceptionalist tradition was his belief that no social institutions, no countries or societies could be 'reformed' or redeemed by the United States, any more than an individual could be redeemed by the church or the rule of the saints. Historical fulfilment (as God intended) would be realised not by the United States, not even through historical events, but through moral enlightenment of the kind the Americans had achieved through God's dispensation, and which the rest of the world would realise over time.[25]

Disillusioned after 1950, George Kennan also turned to the United States' past to find in it the key to a better understanding of how the republic might act more effectively. In his memoirs he recalls that his father came from a long line of pioneer farmers, the outstanding characteristic of whom was an 'obdurate, tight lipped independence', a reluctance to become involved with other people outside their own community (the church), a wish to fight clear of any association that might limit their individual freedom of choice.[26] In the course of time Kennan found inspiration and confirmation of the need for a return to Fortress America, the need to turn its back on European allies whom it had allowed to become welfare dependants, a recognition that the United States could not communicate its success by actions or deeds, only by its example, that possibly its success could not be repeated at all.[27]

Kennan was not alone in finding in exceptionalism an argument for changing some of the ideas he had propagated when in office, or the policies associated with his name. George Ball was another. In a book published ten years after he had resigned as Undersecretary of State at the height of the Vietnam War, Ball argued that the United States should not force its allies to fall into line, or suborn erstwhile enemies to follow its own example. If it was ever again to lead the Free World as decisively as it had in the 1950s it must once again discover a belief in itself, in its uniqueness as a nation. 'A nation illiterate in its own history is incapable of unity', he wrote in 1976, conscious of how disunited the nation had become during the Vietnam War and its immediate aftermath.[28]

For Ball, manifest destiny conveyed the message that the United States needed to expand, not this time to fill space or overcome physical distances, but to span the imagination, its spaciousness of spirit, an imagination which had made possible the Marshall Plan. Before any further actions could be taken the young would have to re-find their social moorings, the shared values that had given the United States 'its special distinction'. The purging of corruption through 40 years or more in the wilderness which the isolationists had demanded in the 1920s in response to the 'futility' of another war, General Pershing's, not General Westmoreland's, gave Ball's message an isolationist resonance, although he was no isolationist himself.

At times exceptionalism has made the United States question whether a nation that is unique has really anything in common with others, in particular whether it should accept the authority of laws and rules drawn up by other states. Examples include its long debate whether to join the International Court of Justice, its refusal to join the League of Nations, or the United Nations Human Rights Committee in 1948. The historian Moorhouse Millar's criticism of the League serves as a good example of that concern, Acheson's criticism of the United Nations is another. 'If America is to serve the cause of peace', Millar wrote in the 1920s, 'it will only be by a clear and generous proclamation of her own true principles and not by bartering them for an international security based on mere utilitarian expediency.'[29] Twenty years later Acheson argued that the United States could not be governed by the United Nations – if it ever looked to the Security Council to formulate policy, then it would have abdicated responsibility for its own history to a body that could not possibly comprehend what its history was about:

How fortunate were the American colonies in 1776 that there was no United Nations confronting them. I need hardly remind you that our constitution had nothing to say about adult universal suffrage but did have a few pregnant paragraphs concerning the institution of slavery.[31]

Even the United States' initial reluctance to sign such United Nations resolutions as the Genocide Convention of 1981 stemmed not from its hostility to the organisations or resolutions concerned, but faith in its own uniqueness. 'We have a unique development of legal history', declared Senator Jesse Helms, 'the result of our traditions, our religions, our moral and ethical values and our experience.' He for one could see no 'justification for submitting this tradition to the judgment of the world'.[32]

It was a sentiment echoed many years later by President Reagan's Secretary of Education William Bennett: 'Strictly speaking the United States did not simply develop; rather the US was created in order to realise a specific political vision.' Referring to the role of history in US schools Bennett went on to maintain that 'today, as in the past, it is the memory of that political vision that defines us as Americans'.[33] The threat to the United States' 'past' posed by membership of organisations such as the United Nations, which might make the American people doubt their uniqueness as Americans, was a price he was unwilling to pay.

In American literature the assertiveness of the American traveller when abroad and his belief in the superiority of all things American have a long tradition. We find it in Henry James's *The American*, in which Newman, the self-made American traveller without antecedents and quite unaware of the United States' own traditions accepts Europe for what it is. 'It had come back to him simply that what he had been looking at all summer was a very rich and beautiful world and that it had not all been made up by sharp railroad men and stockbrokers.' Babcock, on the other hand, the Unitarian minister from Boston who has also come to Europe for self-improvement, ultimately turns his back on the Old World. As he admits in a final letter to Newman:

I feel as if I must arrive at some conclusion and fix my belief on certain points. Art and life seem to me intensely serious things and in our travels in Europe we should especially remember the immense seriousness of art.

Art was so serious, in fact, that it had to be authentically American if it was ever to have meaning to an American himself. The United States had to create a culture superior to that of Europe in keeping with its social and political traditions which were necessarily non-European by being 'unique'.

Lest we dismiss Babcock as a philistine, and his conclusion as entirely self-indulgent, we might recall Kenneth Clark's introduction to Ruskin's *Praeterita*, a work written some years before James's novel. Clark explains Ruskin's passion for propagandising art and imparting its 'eternal verities' as a natural position to take, given that Ruskin himself never doubted his Calvinist upbringing which had instilled in him the supreme confidence that he was one of God's elect. Writing of his youthful reaction to the grotesque passages of Protestant millenarianism in Taylor's *Natural History of Enthusiasm*, Ruskin had written that he already had the advantage over the author of knowing when he saw them 'sincere art from lying art, and happy faith from insolent dogmatism'.

Perhaps, Clark concludes, this Messianic confidence is contrary to reason, but no windows are opened, no horizons are enlarged, no spirits are set free by 'wise indifference'.[34] The one thing exceptionalism gave to the United States was expanding horizons and liberation of the spirit. It was to this land, which Cyril Connolly was to call 'richer in incident and opportunity' than any other,[35] that British writers like Auden and Isherwood fled in the late 1930s. Indifference was impossible. For the non-redemptionist, however, it did not necessarily dictate political action.

REDEMPTIONISM

'America is a bad experiment conducted by Providence. At least I think it must have been Providence. I should hate to be held responsible for it.'

Sigmund Freud (1925)

The second historical sanction of the United States' past is by far the oldest, that of redemptionism. Redemptionism and exceptionalism have never been mutually exclusive. For Zbigniew Brzezinski being 'historically relevant' and military powerful were both mutually reinforcing. The former encouraged positive change; the latter created a framework of stability that could absorb it.[36] As Brzezinski observed in his last year at the National Security Council (NSC), 'We can help history along by positive deeds'.[37]

As one of the United States' leading historians, Arthur Schlessinger helped to shape the memory of a nation, using the theme of redemption, a theme as old as the United States itself. Through the speeches he wrote for John F. Kennedy he hoped to give direction to the idea of the past as a 'regulative idea' and source of hope.[38] On the 200th birthday celebrations of the Declaration of Independence twenty years after Vietnam and Watergate, Schlessinger, now a much more chastened man, advised the United States to abandon its mission to redeem a sinful world, to accept that no nation is chosen by God for any task, however unimportant or significant, that the United States was 'part of history' not outside it,[39] an ordinary country, not part of a morality play in which it had all the best lines. To judge from President Bush's inauguration speech, Schlessinger's warning has gone unheeded.

The redemptionist theme in US history has a distinguished heritage. It is true that James Adams removed a sentence on Providence and America from an essay he had written before the Revolution. By the 1780s he refused to accept that Providence had any role to play in US history. John Quincy Adams thought otherwise, while his own son rescued the passage his grandfather had cut out, calling it 'the most deserving of any to be remembered'. Within a generation the secular idea of experiment began to yield to the mystical idea of national destiny – the redemption of man.[40]

In its absurdity this version of the past has been taken to extreme lengths. In millenial Puritanism the Calvinist preachers and politicians caught a glimpse of the future outside history, even its end. In 1778 Joel Barlow compared the United States' new birth to that of the Nativity and the eagerly anticipated Second Coming.[41] If Mark Twain thought he saw in Queen Victoria's Diamond Jubilee parade 'a glimpse of the Second Coming',[42] Reagan's first Environment Secretary James Watt took little interest in the environment itself because he believed Christ would be reborn in his own lifetime.[43]

In its more subtle manifestation redemptionism has influenced American thinking far more than many non-Americans may imagine. Under his administration Truman told the American people in 1952 the United States had finally stepped 'into the leadership which Almighty God intended us to assume a generation ago'.[44] It was no accident that his last Secretary of State Dean Acheson should have entitled his memoirs *Present at the Creation*, at the birth of a world which the United States tried to reconstruct and save at the same time. Many years later Acheson recalled how his father, 'widely read in theology and Christian doctrine', aimed at the salvation of his soul, 'salvation by works, performed with charity and humour as well as zeal'.[45] It was a description which might have applied to the Truman Doctrine or the Marshall Plan. If the Americans received little thanks for their efforts Acheson was not particularly disheartened. His own belief like his father's was stoical. Much in life could not be changed, only mitigated or borne, preferably without complaint.

The Eisenhower administration was similarly obsessed with America's mission. As the President told the American Legion in 1955, the most basic expression of Americanism was recognition of God – without God there could be no American form of government, or an American way of life.[46] Dulles provided the gloss. In a book written before he became Secretary of State he argued that the severest test for the United States was to redeem the world after having redeemed itself. The United States had been founded as 'an experiment in human liberty'; its institutions reflected the Founding Father's belief that the country's destiny lay in God; that it could not survive unless it showed men the way to a better life.[47]

Dulles was the most 'fundamentalist' of all the United States' Secretaries of State, the one who believed in redemptionism most consistently. His speeches at times had the authentic ring of a sermon, especially when he urged that the world abandon materialism and seek the kingdom of God.[48] His contempt for the non-aligned nations of the Third World was typical of a man who believed the lowest circles of Hell were reserved for those who refused to stand with God or against Him, those who refused to make a choice.[49] One of his favourite quotations was Woodrow Wilson's 'Our civilisation cannot survive materially unless it is redeemed spiritually.'[50] Ultimately, he believed that the United States had the moral authority to lead because it had chosen the path of virtue before seeking power.[51] Political balance, of course, requires a politician with a fine eye for the shade of grey. Dulles saw politics in terms of sharply defined antitheses and antagonisms.

Even William Fulbright, who was different from Dulles in every conceivable respect, was nevertheless a redemptionist for whom the past offered a guide to the present. In his early years, far from condemning 'the arrogance of American power', Fulbright believed the world could be redeemed by the United States provided the latter used its power boldly, not timidly. He supported the Marshall Plan, the Truman Doctrine and the Atlantic Alliance as international organisations that offered Washington scope to pursue its ends. As late as 1966 he believed 'our own human nature does not allow us to give up the game in advance.' The United States' obligation was to feed the hungry and cure the sick,[52] if not perhaps, to aim so far as to resurrect Lazarus; Lazarus, who – Peter Ackroyd once observed – probably never forgave Christ for bringing him back from the dead since death was the only important event he had ever experienced.

More recently the redemptionist theme has been associated with the political Right, especially with the neo-conservatives who originally gave Ronald Reagan their unequivocal support. Fulbright himself finally renounced it in *The Arrogance of Power*, insisting that the United States should return to exceptionalism, that the government should think of the nation as a society whose primary responsibility was to itself and the happiness of its own citizens.[53] Yet redemptionism still survives on the Left, among those who have been all the more insistent in their criticism of the establishment for failing to keep its covenant with God by its exploitation of the Third World overseas, and its exploitation of its minorities (largely of Third World origin) at home.[54]

Jimmy Carter specifically tried to return to the more liberal version of the United States' historical mission when he originally chose for his inaugural address a text from II Chronicles 7:14, which exhorted the Americans to turn from 'their wicked ways'. At the urging of his aides who felt that he would be accused of condemning all Americans as sinful, he inserted another biblical passage instead, Micah 6:8, 'What doth the Lord require of thee, but to do justly and to love mercy and to walk humbly with thy God.'[55] In his personal copy of a book on Niebuhr's life the President underlined the following quotations: 'faith in God's forgiveness makes possible the risk of action'; 'there must be a passion for justice'; 'man's capacity for justice makes democracy possible; man's inclination to injustice makes democracy necessary'.[56]

The past to which they all alluded was Calvinist in inspiration, part of the United States' Puritan tradition.[57] If only a small number of Americans were Calvinists by the mid-eighteenth century, the Puritan tradition none the less influenced their lives more vividly than they might have been prepared to concede at the time. William Penn's *Laws, Concessions and Agreements for the Province of West New Jersey* provided the basis for the Virginia Declaration of Rights which culminated in the Declaration of Independence. As Perry Miller wrote in 1963:

Any inventory of the elements that have gone into the making of 'the American mind' would have to commence with Puritanism...among these traditions Puritanism has been the most conspicuous, the most sustained and the most fecund . . . without an understanding of Puritanism there is no understanding of America.[58]

In the seventeenth century Puritan preachers were dealing with the psychological problem of a dissatisfied minority. Their purpose was to inject moral purpose into men who felt lost in moral confusion, the minority who had fled the Old World, a world where by definition their existence had lacked meaning.[59] Men who have assurance of entering heaven, Haller adds, have a way of taking possession of the earth. The Puritans wished to create a godly world, in the image of God who had made them the elect. Only the elect were called upon to do good works, not to save their souls which were already saved, but to honour the divine Creator. Bacon transferred this certainty and purpose to science when he argued 'not to try is a greater risk than to fail'; not to try would be a failure to press God into the service of man.

In a strangely discordant coincidence the Soviet Marxists' 'faith' in the historical dialectic mirrors almost exactly this early Puritan view. 'We cannot wait for favours from Nature', the Soviet scientist Michirin wrote in 1951, 'our task is to wrest them from her.'[60] For the Puritans their role was clear; convinced that God was with them, fortified by faith confirmed by events, they were fortified in their ambitions as well.

The New World offered then a *tabula rasa* to which they had escaped from Europe. At the Second Coming, Bunyan said, men would be asked if they were doers or talkers only.[61] It was not sufficient to know what they were against, they had to declare what they were for. It was not enough to trust to God for one's ends; men had to supply their own means; not just to enlist God's support, but to earn it as well. To neglect the means was to presume on God, to expect him to help man in time of trouble, brought about by human wilfulness, by the refusal of men to help themselves.

Since the first Americans were living in a pre-industrial society in which God's help was necessary to change the world, the need to help oneself required a knowledge of God's purpose. Hence the stimulus that Puritanism gave science, the study of history, above all politics. The extension of intellectual horizons was predicated on unlocking the mind. The New World was receptive to the scientific revolution of the seventeenth century, as it was to the theories of Locke, for science like politics was not a pure but an applied subject. To unlock God's secrets was to advance His cause.[62]

The Puritan tradition was 'Americanised' in a number of ways which created a redemptionist past. First, it survived as a political force long after it dissolved into sectarian oblivion in Europe. As Alan Heimert argues, Calvinism reached a dead end in the eighteenth century. It was no longer a liberating force as it had been in New England a hundred years earlier. It was rescued – if only just – by the new formulas propounded by Jonathan Edwards, developed by Joseph Bellamy, and systematised by Samuel Hopkins, which reaffirmed the sovereignty of God while at the same time emphasising human freedom realised through justification by faith, a process which proved to be a tremendous force for improvement. From a religion of despair, Calvinism was transformed into a religion of hope.

The American Enlightenment of the eighteenth century was the secular version of the great awakening of the 1730s. The two were particularly synonymous. When Hopkins' *System of Doctrines* was published ten years after the Declaration of Independence Calvinism had marked out the happiness of man as a necessary precondition of the glorification of God.[63] As Sacvan Bercovitch wrote, what in Geneva, England and Holland led to an a priori antithesis between the saints and the state became in the United States the twin pillars of a unique federal eschatology. The fact that the colonisation of the United States followed the Reformation was considered to be a sign of God's special dispensation. As Ernest Tuverson concluded in his own study of *Redeemer Nation*, God was seen in the early United States as 'redeeming both individual souls and society in parallel courses'.[64]

Ever since in the country's many religious revivals the belief has been implicit that men's souls and society must be saved at the same time.[65] Evangelists, revivalists, reformed confessionalists, Baptist traditionalists, many of them movements bringing together in the loosest federation people of diverse opinions, have all seen the world outside the United States as a giant battleground for a Manichean struggle between good and evil. In religious fundamentalism there is little room for differing social perspectives or political systems; compromise is sinful.[66]

At different times since the Second World War these evangelical movements have tested their members and defined themselves by reference to specific foreign policy issues. For Christian Voice, founded in 1978, the test was Taiwan, a 'Christian' ally defending itself against a godless People's Republic of China. In 1979 the test was Zimbabwe-Rhodesia, 'a democratically elected racially integrated country' fighting the 'atheist' forces of Communism represented by the forces of the Patriotic Front. At the heart of much evangelical morality lies the fallacy identified by Niebuhr, 'we must never deify freedom. It is not God. It is not even 'an absolute virtue'.

Another way in which Puritanism was Americanised was the emphasis put on capitalism. Without entering into the still unresolved debate about the Protestant ethic and the spirit of capitalism, the American example – of all the case studies cited by Weber and Tawney – is the most difficult to refute. Weber's essay appeared in 1904-5, the work of a sociologist attempting to apply sociological methods to a historical problem. Inevitably, it incurred the enmity of historians because of his temerity in treading on their ground. Tawney's *Religion and the Rise of Capitalism* published in 1926 was a socialist tract. Whilst accepting the broad thrust of Weber's thesis Tawney preferred to focus less on Calvinism and more on Protestantism. For the critics of both writers the distortion was all the more dangerous because Tawney's thesis was more subtly accomplished. To quote one American critic, 'one might wonder whether Calvin was a Calvinist . . . for both John Wesley and Benjamin Franklin are quoted to show what Calvinism was'.[67]

For both men Protestantism was central to the development of capitalism in three crucial respects. First, it removed the sin of usury as well as the guilt of making a profit by suggesting that the Christian prospered for God's glory; that a man's commercial success was a manifestation of divine approval. In addition, the Protestants invested labour with a dignity it had never previously enjoyed. The labourer's life might be hard but he derived his sense of grace from the conscientiousness with which he worked; in short, from his productivity. Finally, because Protestants were as opposed as Catholics to the sin of idolatory, they insisted that the hoarding of possessions was anathema to God. Accumulated wealth should be reinvested or spent on wealth creation.

The idea of making money as an end in itself was an early American tradition. Benjamin Franklin quoted biblical authority: 'See thou a man diligent in business? He shall stand before Kings' (Proverbs 22:29). What Franklin was extolling was not love of money for its own sake, but the obligation to make money for the greater honour of God (or capital accumulation). In today's consumer society the United States is far removed from this Puritan ethos. Capitalism has removed 'the transcendental other worldliness motive' and transformed a calling into a job.[68] In Paul Theroux's nightmare novel *The Mosquito Coast*, Allie Fox, driven out of the United States by the descent of capitalism into consumerism, takes his family to Honduras to carve out a new society in the wilderness, a wilderness that had been left incomplete by the Creator so that man might still realise his full potential.

The historical debate, while absorbing, is not strictly of material interest to us. The important point about the fact that the United States was Protestant, was that its Protestant earnestness – the great awakening of the 1730s, a significant religious revival – gave birth to a spirit of restlessness and self-improvement that militated against the constraints of British imperialism. Take *The New Whole Duty of Man*, a tract which first appeared in the 1720s and retained its popularity for a century or more. What is so interesting about the publication is that its author was the first of the American moralists to consider worldly success of great importance:

as titular dignities entitle men to an outward respect and observance, so also doth wealth and large possessions....for which God bestows upon one man a larger fortune and possessions than on another, he doth thereby prefer and advance him into an higher sphere and condition.

The New Whole Duty does not contradict Weber or Tawney, but neither does it vindicate their critics. It suggests instead that the process was a symbiotic one; that one should seek in the social changes of the period the explanation for changes in religious outlook, and changes in religious outlook for influences on social movements.

For the United States the American dream – the creation of wealth – and its use to improve the republic's position in the world is not cause for guilt but congratulation. In accepting the Republican nomination Richard Nixon reiterated his belief in the dream because it had come true for him. With the exception of John Kennedy and George Bush every President since the war has worked his way to power. For men like Alexander Haig the work ethic (whether strictly Protestant in origin or not) is the base of the American dream and of the United States' success: 'The first generation will endure hard labour and practise frugality for the sake of the second. A nation is the sum of its families and ...families and nations are built by work, and above all by a well founded optimism about the future.'[69]

A third way in which Puritanism was Americanised was the challenge the United States itself offered the first settlers. New England was rugged enough for that challenge to take on a religious manifestation; to prove the early settlers were indeed graced by God. Even in the late nineteenth century New England was still a harsh place: 'in winter at least the saddest country', Charles Kingsley recorded, 'all brown grass, ice polished rocks sticking up through copses, cedar scrub, low swampy shores; an iron land which only an iron people could have settled in'.[70] Recalling the atmosphere in *Oldtown*

Folks (1869), a book written at about the same time, Harriet Beecher Stowe observed:

the underlying cycle of life...in New England was one ... which regarded human existence itself as a ghastly risk and in the case of the vast majority of human beings an inconceivable misfortune.[71]

Survival alone gave the Americans a vision of themselves as a providential people destined to expand, to redeem the land to the west, the frontier. Manifest destiny was an intensely religious concept first associated with John O'Sullivan, an Irish-American editor writing in 1845, later with the westward movement, the moving frontier inherited from the writings of Frederick Jackson Turner. As the contemporary poet Robert Pinsky expresses it:

> A boundary is a limit. How can I
> Describe for you the boundaries of this place
> Where we were born, where possibility spreads
> And multiplies and exhausts itself in growing
> And open yawning to swallow itself again?
> What pictures are there for that limitless grace
> Unrealized, those horizons for ever dissolving?[72]

For the United States manifest destiny did not come to an end when the frontier was finally reached in 1890. The Americans have been living in its shadow ever since, reinterpreting it with every generation. As early as 1945 Vannevar Bush, the Director of the Office of Scientific Research and Development, dubbed science 'the endless frontier', in the belief like Pinsky that the frontier was always one step beyond the next horizon.[73] For Lyndon Johnson the United States had a chance to extend its frontier to south-east Asia, a region where he hoped to leave America's 'footprints' by converting the Mekong Delta into another Tennessee Valley Project. Johnson was governed by a strong biblical compulsion, a belief in the religious sanction of the United States' destiny in south-east Asia, its *mission civilisatrice*.[74] As a Senate subcommittee report noted in 1965, 'the idea of manifest destiny still survives.' Officials often made sweeping declarations of the United States' world mission, and frequently committed the nation to policies and programmes far beyond its resources.[75]

Since the late 1960s, the Vietnam War notwithstanding, the Americans have remained convinced that they are responsible for what happens in the world at large; that their country 'has an inherent right – a sort of modern Manifest Destiny', wrote two of the CIA's most persistent critics, 'to intervene in other countries' internal affairs'.[76] Perhaps the real question is whether an epic development such as manifest destiny is still possible, and if so whether the United States is on the side of the Devil or God. 'Did God voyage out of NASA', Norman Mailer asked in *Of a Fire on the Moon*, or was the Devil 'our line of sight for the stars?' If the United States is to engage in another epic race for the frontier – in space or elsewhere – it must work with other nations, not against them. Any return to a purely national destiny, Mailer maintains, would be anachronistic – a nation cannot be young twice.

In so far as the expanding frontier, however, has been identified with 'empire' it has drawn criticism from the Left, criticism which is also Puritan in origin. It is one thing to have Wilsonianism, intervention to end all wars, to establish a US peace (a policy which George Ball quite correctly called Winthropism or Williamism after the United States' two great Calvinist preachers, John Winthrop and Rogers Williams);[77] it is quite another to use such rhetoric as a mask for naked ambition. There is in the American Puritanical tradition a strong distaste for power politics. Winthrop preached his sermon about 'the city on the hill' on board ship before the colonists landed in Massachusetts Bay. One of the reasons why Roger Williams was driven from the Massachusetts Bay Colony in 1637 was his intransigent insistence that the colonists were building their city on someone else's hill – in this case that of the American Indians.[78]

Throughout its history the Left has not hesitated to appeal to the language of religion to express its misgivings about the distortion of US redemptionism. As Thorstein Veblen wrote in 1923, 'born in iniquity and conceived in sin, the spirit of nationalism has never ceased to bend human institutions to the service of dissension and distress.[79] 'On the Left', argues Ole Holsti, 'there is a consistent call for a revolutionary transformation of capitalist America as a necessary and sufficient condition for solving mankind's most pressing moral and social problems.'[80] Against those preachers who claimed the United States not only had a national right to fight in Vietnam but also a moral obligation,[81] there was a long tradition dating back to Twain and Melville who questioned the 'pious hypocrisies' which justified the expansion of US power across the globe.

Twain's *A Connecticut Yankee at King Arthur's Court* destroys the society he is attempting to redeem. Melville's Ahab tries to redeem himself but plunges into the infernal regions. Both are pilgrims trying to redeem themselves, or other people 'from time'. Twain's American actually goes back in time to save Arthur's Camelot; all he leaves behind him, however, is a battlefield of electrocuted corpses. The United States has sought so often to obliterate time (or history) by cutting itself off from its roots that it has destroyed other cultures in the process, the American Indians for one.

In *Of a Fire on the Moon* Mailer writes that the Americans are 'the most Faustian, barbaric, draconian, progress-oriented and root destroying people on earth'.[82] Is it too fanciful, he asks, to suggest that the United States is unwilling to look history in the face? In a salutation speech from the nineteenth to the twentieth century Twain advised that America's soul was so full of meanness that she should be given a towel and soap, but spared the looking glass.[83] Redemptionism is not a creed for the faint-hearted.

EXEMPLARISM

'So we beat on, boats against the moment, borne back ceaselessly into the past'
Scott Fitzgerald, *The Great Gatsby*

In addition to the two versions of the past just discussed, there is a third, a secular form of redemptionism, a belief that by setting an example other nations may eventually follow, the United States can save mankind from its own follies. Like the other two this third version of 'parable history' with its roots in the late eighteenth century, draws its inspiration from the Founding Fathers. For Madison the United States was not 'the workshop of the world' but the 'workshop of liberty'.[84] In his 'Dissertation on Feudal Law' John Adams remarked that Providence has designed the United States to be not only the illumination of the ignorant, but also the hope of emancipation for the enslaved.[85]

Exemplarists are not born, they are created, forged through experience, fashioned often in war. For William Fulbright, who in 1943 had seen the United States as the only power able to 'turn tragedy into ... a tremendous opportunity', the passage of time brought wisdom of a kind. Writing two years after publishing *The Arrogance of Power* he insisted, 'inevitably our major impact on the world is not what we do but what we are: the way we govern outselves.'[86] The two Presidents he criticised most forcefully, Lyndon Johnson and Richard Nixon, were both to speak of a generation standing at the gate, a generation that was 'tempered in the fire [of war] for a great purpose; to make the kind of peace the next generation will be able to keep'.[87] At times, although waiting at the gate and spending ever more on defence, they seemed to be waiting for nothing in particular.

The hopes of the Founding Fathers were not, of course, realised immediately; nor have they been two hundred years on. As Acheson recognised when he came to write his memoirs, the United States had not been able to escape from the flotsam and jetsam which had been washed up from the Old World on the shores of the New by retreating into the rhetoric of the nineteenth century, or finding guidance in abstractions or general moral principles derived from America's constitution.[88] The world has too many non-democratic tyrannies, regimes which had paid the US constitution scant attention, for Americans to draw much hope that exemplarism, like virtue, would prove its own reward.

Back in the early days of the last century Americans were openly debating the morality of offering hope to those who were denied any if the republic had no intention of backing up its words with deeds. When President Polk tried to universalise US ideals throughout the Western Hemisphere, he was challenged by conservatives such as John Calhoun who argued that no wise man would pledge by declaration what it was beyond his power to execute. 'True dignity consists in making no declaration which we are not prepared to maintain.'[89] More recently Patrick Moynihan lambasted President Carter's human rights policy for bringing the United States' 'integrity' into question. How could the United States ask the rest of the world to follow its example when the Carter administration's own actions were so demonstrably qualified (or sullied) by commercial considerations such as the sale of soya beans or grain?[90]

As time has passed, those sympathetic to the Calhoun tradition have grown more voluble, not less. Speaking of human rights Morgenthau opined that 'ethics in the abstract judges action by its conformity with the moral law; political ethics judges action by its political consequences.'[91] In his memoirs Henry Kissinger echoed the same sentiment more forcefully because he spoke from the experience of political office. 'There are certain experiments that cannot be tried, not because the goals are undesirable but because the consequences of failure would be so severe.'[92]

The fear that association with dubious causes, and even more dubious regimes, might compromise the US experiment were voiced long before the twentieth century. John Quincy Adams was an exemplarist, not a redemptionist, a 'well wisher' of freedom, but 'a champion and vindicator' only of America's own. As Lincoln once remarked during the Civil War, if the United States were to become involved in helping other countries, it would no longer be 'ruler of its own spirit'; it would be corrupted by the exercise of power, however worthy the ends to which its power was used.[93] This intrinsic distrust of Messianic-Redemptionism haunted Morgenthau all his life, even to the point where he condemned Truman's mission to make the world safe for democracy.[94]

The great flaw in the exemplarist's case is not that of parochialism (the problem with exceptionalism), nor delusion about the extent of US power (the problem with redemptionism) but the illusion that non-intervention is itself a viable policy. Not to intervene is, of course, a form of intervention which is why the United States has often found it necessary to act even against its better judgement. More importantly perhaps, as Acheson pointed out a few years before he died, 'the mode by which the inevitable comes to pass is effort.'[95] Without effort can the United States achieve anything? Is setting an example enough?

As it happens the American Revolution was based on a negative conception of freedom which actually made it unnecessary to save the world by its exertions. The example set by the new republic was adjudged quite sufficient.

Isolationism, for example, was not a political policy, but a moral declaration which was political in form. The United States saw itself as a participant in a great moral experiment, the creation of a new type of political community.[96] As Hartz put it – the United States was able to dream of emancipating the world at the very moment it chose to withdraw from it. It was able to see itself as a political saviour at the same time that it withdrew into isolation.[97] That was one reason among many why Charles and Mary Beard identified only two schools of thought in the 1930s: 'collective internationalism' and 'imperial isolationism'.[98]

The negative conception of freedom also comes out clearly in the Atlantic Charter (1941), in which Churchill and Roosevelt endorsed four freedoms: freedom of speech, freedom of worship, freedom from fear and freedom from want. The British who were party to the Charter never took it especially seriously. As Malcolm Muggeridge records in his memoirs *Chronicles of Wasted Time*, when he cabled the Foreign Office from Mozambique in 1944, 'What is our policy on Freedom from Want?' he received the cynical reply, 'the same as Freedom from Fear – only more so'.[99]

For the United States however, the last two freedoms – from fear and want – specified two kinds of restraint which it would have liked to have removed. If freedom is the absence of restraint then the United States has no actual need to act. The Declaration of Independence itself separated the immediate from the future; the immediate attainment of liberty from the future pursuit of happiness. Even with respect to the two positive freedoms the United States has always been able to rely on the argument that freedom is not an absolute value, an end in itself, only a means to an end; an essential need, perhaps, but only a sufficient condition. As a means rather than an end the United States has no immediate need to advance it. The American dream shows what a free society has created on its own, without the assistance of others. As an example the United States is an inspiration to the world; a country, however, not a cause, a state that can survive and thrive without exporting its success at all.

In this situation the question of morality is more important than that of political power. The exemplarists must be more concerned with the struggle to ensure the United States remains faithful at home to the tradition of its own Founding Fathers, whom Dean Rusk once referred to as 'the distant stars of American foreign policy', if necessary by avoiding any political entanglements which might compromise this central objective. This does not mean they are indifferent spectators, mute bystanders, condemned to sit out the future in a mood of subdued passivity. On the contrary, exemplarism is based on the need for the United States to assert itself whenever an opportunity presents itself. If they have resisted the temptation to take a historical short cut by creating a political opening through a policy of self-assertion, the explanation is to be sought in a Panglossian self-confidence that all will come right at the end of the day

TWO PROMPTERS FROM THE WINGS[100]

'We are a nineteenth century people. Our minds are our great, great mothers' and fathers' minds. We aren't a twentieth century people. Our ideas are inherited ideas.'
Dean Acheson, This Vast Eternal Realm

It may be useful by way of drawing these different strands together to look at the ideas of two statesmen who have represented two very different traditions, who have escaped into the past to justify their present actions, or in the case of the first, George Kennan, to explain their past behaviour. The English poet Stephen Spender once accused the Americans of treating 'history as though it were geography, themselves as though they could step out of the present into the past of their own choice'.[101] With so many 'authentic' pasts from which to choose, each sanctioned by the Founding Fathers, each wearing Clio's clothes, the Americans are more flexible than most other 'imperial' people. Their flexibility, of course, explains much of their inconsistency. The lack of a firm or robust historical tradition, which would make administrations less unpredictable, and their policies more consistent, has long been lamented by allies and enemies alike.

GEORGE KENNAN AND THE RETURN TO EXEMPLARISM

At the end of the second volume of his memoirs Kennan raised an important question, only to volunteer a depressingly honest answer.

What use was there in attempting to protect in its relations to others a society that was clearly failing in its relations to itself? It was under the pressure of this relentless question that I...tended more and more...to seek in the interpretation of history a usefulness I could not find in an interpretation of my own time.[102]

Kennan's subsequent writings suggest that one cannot seek through a study of history a total understanding of one's own age. Unless one is prepared to come to terms with the present, one will be quite unable to understand the past.

It was not the first time he had raised this problem. At the end of his first volume of memoirs he recalls writing in August 1950, the year in which he finally left Washington (although not the public service) that the foreign policy establishment spent its time wandering around in a labyrinth of ignorance and error, in which truth was intermingled with fiction at a hundred points, in which unjustified assumptions attained the validity of premises, and in which there was no recognised and authoritative theory on which to hold. That is why he believed no one in his position could contribute very much unless he first turned historian, earning public confidence and respect through the study of an earlier day, so that he might gradually educate the public to an understanding of its own history.[103]

Kennan has remained true to the belief in the need for history to liberate the United States from its past ever since. He has continued to deplore the emphasis on political science in schools and universities as a surrogate of history; the lack of communication between historians and their readers; the failure to learn any lessons from the past. Truth in human affairs, he once remarked in the late 1970s, is brought out dialectically, by the process of comparison. People cannot make comparisons, however, if they do not possess historical depth.[104]

Yet Kennan is as much a victim of the past as the younger generation is today, or his colleagues were in the late 1940s. Turning historian has not liberated him from those national eighteenth-century myths which Acheson berated in his own memoirs, after confessing that he had succumbed to them too readily when in power. Kennan also remains a Calvinist in spirit. Indeed his criticism of China in 1979 for 'lacking in a capacity for pity and the sense of sin'[105] could have been treated derisively as a manifestation of complete lack of cultural understanding, were it not for the Puritan tradition which still limits the American imagination, and makes it difficult for many US historians to comprehend societies radically different from their own.

Kennan's memoirs, like all his writings since he left office, have essentially been a justification of his break with the Truman administration in 1948; a series of *pièces justicifatives* which have convinced few but his most ardent and unthinking admirers. What does a man do in the face of developments which reveal his ideas are running against the grain of events, not with them? In the face of such a predicament Kennan could have beaten a retreat, or dug in. In choosing to do the latter he been sustained by the 'past', not history.

His most recent memoir *The Cloud of Danger* (1979) reveals he is obsessively dependent on his own understanding of the United States' past in providing solutions to problems about which he knows little – the development of the Third World for one. Like a severe pedagogue he warns that the developing world 'will have to work its passage as did our own forefathers, or the passage will not be made.[106]

For years he refused to accept that history rendered his own views of containment redundant almost as soon as they were articulated, or that his suggestions, although useful in 1947, were overtaken by events which he could not possibly have foreseen or predicted. As a historian he is not content to write as an outsider who was once on the inside. The answers he has volunteered to his own questions about the United States' relations with the Soviet Union or the question of nuclear deterrence have little do with reality, but everything to do with a reaffirmation of the US past, with high rhetoric posing as conviction. Most Europeans would not have maintained such a large following for long. The fact that Kennan has done so speaks of the ease with which Americans can abandon one past for another. The retreat is not a retreat at all, but a long march into another historical world, one more congenial than that from which Kennan first emerged, and from which he derived his initial ideas. His progress from redemptionalism to exceptionalism explains his conversion from Cold War warrior to Cold War *ingénu*. The study of 'history' at Princeton to which he has devoted his remaining years, has, in that respect, contributed very little, other than to provide facts with which to illustrate the hypothesis he adopted as early as 1957, the year of his Reith Lectures in Britain.

In conversation with George Urban he appeared to break with the past, with the belief in the 'American experiment' when he claimed he no longer believed the United States had anything to offer the age in which he now lived. Yet at the next moment he confessed to being persuaded that the Founding Fathers had more convincing values, not least their dislike of urban civilisation, in particular Jefferson's belief that great cities were 'pestilential to the morals, the health and morality of mankind'.[107] He criticised the student Left during the Vietnam War not as a protest movement against the government or even the war itself, but as a product of urban existence, a product both metaphysical and tragic.[108] His criticism of the post-Vietnam generation was that it had no values, no religious faith, no appreciation of the element of tragedy that constitutes part of man's predicament (the human condition), and no understanding of the consequent limits to social and political achievement.

Kennan's failure to look the late twentieth century in the face, with its urban underclass, its purposeless youth, its rootless, historically ignorant, upwardly mobile rich, is particularly revealing for he is as much a product of the age as those he condemns. It is precisely in his act of turning away from that age that the importance of his criticism springs. Sometimes he sounds like neo-conservative writers, Norman Podhoretz for one, sometimes like writers on the Left, like Susan Sontag. What makes him very different from them is that his is the stance of a writer whose retreat into the past has made it impossible for him to understand his own age.

GEORGE BALL: THE EXEMPLARIST *MANQUÉ*

George Ball also spent most of his active political life convinced that it was the United States' duty to make history, to redeem the world from the mistakes of governments or institutions over which it had previously exercised little control. He wrote his memoirs in 1982 a wiser and more chastened man, the only one of our two prompters from the wings, whose message has been one of scepticism, not to mention disappointment, about a past which is still part of the American tradition.

In earlier days Ball was a typical exponent of what Ronald Steele once called 'welfare imperialism' – a man who was more than willing to intervene to make the world safe for democracy. Before the escalation of the Vietnam War he claimed that the United States was engaged in 'something new and unique' in world history, a willingness to assume responsibilities which were very different from the territorial ambitions and sectarian national interests for which the world powers of the past had been notorious.[109] Never before in history, Ball later claimed, had a nation undertaken to play such a role except in defence of empire.[110]

After inheriting the overall direction of the foreign aid programme, Ball later came to question whether the United States should cast its relations with the rest of the world in such universalist terms, or whether it might not be more sensible to draw up some tacitly or explicitly agreed allocation of responsibilities.[111] Even this understanding, however, assumed that the United States could still 'manage' the allocation of food, or resolve international famines. It was still a redemptionist perspective, held by a man who confessed himself to be shocked by how precarious the world system of power had become. 'With faith in our achievements and unquestioning devotion to the idea of progress', he was to write some years later, the United States could ensure that 'the rational, civilised, ideals of Jefferson' remained relevant in an ever-changing world.[112]

Unlike Kennan, Ball found no great difficulty balancing principles and practice. He was a practitioner first and foremost. His philosophy represented a diverse set of historical insights which were part of the pattern of the US past he had learned at school. Reflecting on his life at the age of 80 he came to recognise that the past had 'another pattern', one which revealed that the moral certainties of the United States were no more than those of a people who had turned in on itself, who no longer displayed the ebullience and *élan* of a nation confident of its destiny – or even its desired destination.[113] A dyed-in-the-wool Protestant, he found in a poem by Matthew Arnold a description of how the American people had lost their faith in God and their mission, why they appeared to be lost 'on a darkling plain...swept by confused alarms of struggle and flight'. Without an abiding faith in the past, life was too complex to deal with. Without faith he agreed with the Marxist historian William Appleman Williams that the American people would look for certainty in 'a furtive preoccupation with self for which psychoanalysis provides a confessional'.

Fifteen years earlier he had suffered no such doubts about his country's future or the ability of the young to confront it from a position of strength, from the entrenched foxholes of historical conviction. In those days he believed they were conscious of their country's history, and more important, its larger meaning. 'The Founding Fathers having studied the pattern of Old World history' with its dynastic intrigues and narrow room for manoeuvre, had gone on to reject it, to produce a very different pattern consistent with the values the New World had produced.[114] Jefferson, he recalled, had complained in a letter to Joseph Priestley in 1801 of the 'disorders' and 'contagions' of the monarchical world, of a world 'crowded with limits either small or overcharged'.[115] By the time he came to write his memoirs in 1982 the same description appeared to be not entirely inappropriate of the United States, a country which had become *terra incognita* for a generation brought up to believe that if the United States could not redeem the world it could at least redeem itself.

CONCLUSION

'Devotion to the past is one of the most disastrous forms of unrequited love'
Susan Sontag, *Unguided Tour* (1977)

In the last days of the Eisenhower administration one of the United States' leading political scientists argued that the national image was essentially historical – that it was 'an image which extends through time backwards into a supposedly recorded or perhaps mythological past, and forward into an imagined future. The more conscious a people is of its history, the stronger the national image is likely to be'.[116] In the case of the United States such national images, as we have seen, are linked to three very different pasts.

A nation, of course, is constantly renewing itself. It is not just a personality; as Michelet wrote of France, a country is a multitude of personalities which are in constant movement.[117] Put another way, the shifts in the United States' role since it became a nation are a good illustration of Sorokin's 'principle of permanent change'. Change is inherent in any dynamic society. Society itself produces it. It is endogenous, not exogenous; it is a response to an internal not external challenge.[118]

Rereading Henry Stimson's 1947 article in *Foreign Affairs* one can appreciate how a politician who had to manoeuvre in the narrow confines of the 1930s felt liberated after the war, liberated by history in the name of the past:

I have served as Secretary of State in a time of frightened isolation, and as Secretary of War in time of brave and generous action. I know the withering effect of limited commitments and I know the regenerative power of full action.[119]

The problem, as Sorokin notes, is that no single system (or past) 'comprises the whole of truth, nor on the other hand is it entirely false'.[120] If that is the case the oscillation between moods becomes comprehensible. 'Only when one system becomes monopolistic and drives out the other truths [does] its false part begin to grow at the expense of the valid part.'[121] Redemptionism met its nemesis in Vietnam; exemplarism in the Neutrality Acts of 1938, when political leadership appeared to have become a mere memory, a dream of a former era.

It is unlikely that the pattern will change fundamentally in the near future. As we have seen, politicians of all political hues have constantly referred back to the same past to find sanction for their own actions. Providence has found such unlikely bedfellows as John F. Kennedy and Ronald Reagan. 'Our nation', intoned Kennedy in 1962, 'was commissioned by history to be either an observer of freedom's failure or the cause of its success.'[122] 'We in this country, in this generation', Reagan declared on the campaign trail in 1980, 'are by destiny rather than choice the watchmen on the walls of world freedom', a line he lifted from one of Kennedy's speeches.[123]

By contrast, one of the main criticisms of Carter's Presidency was his lack of historical perspective, which denied him a voice and left the American people bewildered and adrift. Brzezinski recalls that he wanted the President to speak not only to the American people but 'on some occasions also to history'. Because he failed to respond to such advice he did not succeed in capturing the nation's imagination.[124] Schlessinger, Democrat though he was, was critical of the President in 1980 for spending too much time addressing policy questions, rather than the question of the United States' destiny, with the result that he communicated no sense of purpose and 'no central vision'.[125]

As the evening shadows lengthen, as US power sets on the horizon, the United States appears to be at a crossroads, not for the first time in its history, between two ages, trying to relocate itself in time, to renew itself through a different past from the redemptionist model which has been the dominant influence in US foreign policy since 1945.

Divided from the world by its past the United States has always striven to find an authentically American language, a language appropriate to what it escaped from in 1776, a language of self-discovery. The United States has been discovering itself for two centuries, most recently translating its anti-Communist crusade into another form of manifest destiny in an attempt to adjust to a world it has neither escaped from, nor made.

As one writer once put it, 'out of the arguments with ourselves we make poetry, out of the arguments with others rhetoric.' As the United States has progressed since 1949 it has begun to realise that in throwing itself so wholeheartedly into the conflict with the Soviet Union it has traded increasingly in used words, flimsy gestures and outdated clichés. The poetry of the past has not been transmuted into the effective rhetoric of international relations.

We probably delude ourselves however if we feel the United States is about to retreat into itself as George Ball fears, to find in self-discovery the certainties it has failed to find in discovering the outside world. The demands on its future are clear; its past offers not one role but three, which may keep it at the centre of world events for the foreseeable future. The danger is that the past is not the best point of departure for the United States in an age of transition. It is likely to serve it less well than it has hitherto. It has not served it especially well anyway. There was a time in the 1970s when historians hoped that in rediscovering its history the United States might be able to come to terms with itself, to cast off the past altogether. This no longer appears possible. Indeed, as history loses its hold in the schools, and is replaced by political science in the universities, the United States seems about to discover the truth of Susan Sontag's remark that of all forms of unrequited love devotion to the past is one of the most disastrous.

NOTES

1. The impact of national values on political culture has rarely been considered important in most works on US foreign policy. It merits a single chapter in the third edition of the much respected book by Charles Kegley/Eugene Wiltkopf, *American Foreign Policy: problems and processes* (London: Macmillan, 1987). Frequently, it merits no mention at all, or is relegated to a chapter on 'the historical background'. For an eccentric but interesting interpretation see Moria Harrington, *The Dream of Deliverance in America Politics* (New York: Knopf, 1986), in which she identifies three schools of thought which are becoming increasingly irrelevant in the modern world – majoritarians, localists and functionalists. See also Emily Rosenberg, *Spreading the American Dream* (New York: Hill & Wang, 1982), in which she discusses liberal-developmentalism at length.
2. John Steinbeck, *The Grapes of Wrath* (London: Heinemann, 1970), p. 79.
3. William Barrett, 'Introspective America', *Confluence* 1:1 (March 1952) p. 44.
4. The *New York Times* (8 March 1983).
5. See *Public Papers of the President of the United States: Ronald Reagan 1981* (27 May 1981) p. 464. See also for Reagan's other rhetorical flourishes, *A Time for Choosing: the speeches of Ronald Reagan 1961–82* (Chicago, 1983); and *Ronald Reagan Talks to America* (Connecticut: Grenada, 1983).
6. Henry Steele Commanger, 'Is the world safe for anything?', *Saturday Review* (9 November 1968) pp. 21–4.
7. J. P. Stern, 'Nietzsche and the idea of metaphor', in Malcolm Pasley (ed.), *Nietzsche: imagery and thought* (London: Methuen, 1978) p. 70.
8. W. H. Auden, *The Dyer's Hand* (London: Faber and Faber, 1963) pp. 278–9.

9. For a Marxist interpretation of how the government drums up support for its actions, see Michael Parenti, 'We hold these myths to be self-evident', *Nation* 232 (11 April 1981); and *Inventing Reality* (New York: St. Martin's Press, 1986).
10. Bruce Russert and Donald Deluca, 'Don't tread on me: public opinion and foreign policy in the '80's', *Political Science Quarterly* 96 (Fall 1981).
11. Richard Alstyne, *The American Empire: its historical pattern and evolution* (London: Historical Association, 1960) p. 83.
12. C. van Woodward, *American Attitudes Towards History* (Oxford: Clarendon Press, 1958) p. 15.
13. In times of crisis the Americans have gone back to their 'past' to reaffirm their central values. The Founding Fathers were seen for example in a more respectful light in the 1930s than they had been before the First World War. (A. H. Jones, 'The search for a viable past in the New Deal era', *American Quarterly* 23 (1971) pp. 715–20; J. Pocock, *Politics, Language and Time: essays on political thought and history* (New York: Atheneum, 1972) p. 248.)
14. J. H. Plumb, *The Death of the Past* (London: Penguin, 1973) p. 73.
15. See Peter Gay, *A Loss of Mastery: Puritan historians in colonial America* (Berkeley, Calif.: University of California Press, 1966); Samuel Klinger, 'Emerson and the usable Anglo-Saxon past', *Journal of the History of Ideas* 16 (1955) pp. 476–93.
16. Louis Hartz, *The Liberal Tradition in America: an interpretation of American political thought since the revolution* (New York: Harcourt Brace, 1955) p. 38.
17. Ada Bozeman, 'The Roots of the American commitment to the rights of man', in *Rights and Responsibilities: international, social and individual dimensions* (Los Angeles: University of Southern California Press, 1980) p. 76.
18. J. R. Pole, *The Pursuit of Equality in American History* (University of California Press, 1978) p. 56.
19. George Watson, 'How radical is revolution?', *History Today* (November 1988) pp. 45–7.
20. Rolf Gruner, *Philosophies of History: a critical history* (London: Gower, 1985) p. 96.
21. Sigmund Freud, *Civilisation and its Discontents,* trans. Jean Rivière (London: Hogarth, 1930) p. 135.
22. P. K. Javanagh (ed.) *The Essential Chesterton* (Oxford: Oxford University Press, 1987) pp. 94–9.
23. J. A. Pocock, *The Machiavellian Moment* (Princeton, NJ: Princeton University Press, 1975) p. 543.
24. Reinhold Niebuhr, *The Philosophy of History in Our Time* (New York: Charles Scribner, 1949) pp. 198–200.
25. *ibid.*, p. 201.
26. George Kennan, *Memoirs 1925–50* (Boston: Little, Brown, 1967) pp. 6–7.
27. Hubert Humphrey, 'National power and the creation of a workable community', *Department of State Bulletin (DSB)* 52:1357 (28 June 1965).
28. George Ball, *Diplomacy for a Crowded World* (London: The Bodley Head, 1976) p. 325.

29. Moorhouse Millar, *Unpopular Essays* (New York: Fordham University Press, 1928) p. 110.
30. Kenneth W.Thompson, 'Ethics and national power', in Kenneth Mail (ed.), *Moral Dimensions of American Foreign Policy* (New Brunswick: Transition Books, 1984) p. 7.
31. Dean Acheson, 'The Lawyer's path to peace', *Virginia Quarterly Review* 42:3 (Summer 1966); see also his Forward to Franco Nogueria, *The Third World* (London: Johnson Publications, 1967).
32. Vernon van Dyke, *Human Rights, the United States and the World Community* (Oxford: Oxford University Press, 1970).
33. William Bennett and Jeane Kirkpatrick, 'History, Geography and Citizenship', Washington DC: *Ethics and Public Policy Center Essay* 64 (April 1986) p. 5.
34. John Ruskin, *Praeterita* (London: Rupert Hart-Davis, 1949) p. xxii.
35. Cited in Samuel Hynes, *The Auden Generation: literature and politics in England in the 1930s* (London: The Bodley Head, 1976) p. 423, n. 26.
36. Zbigniew Brzezinski, 'The twin strands of American foreign policy', Address before the Baltimore Council for Foreign Relations (May 1980) p. 7.
37. Zbigniew Brzezinski, 'Remarks before the Women's National Democratic Club, Washington DC, 21 February 1980', *White House Press Release* (21 February 1980).
38. For a political science approach to redemptionism see Yehoshafat Harbarki, *The Bar Kochba Syndrome* (New York: Russell Books, 1983) pp. 150–1. See also Harold Laski, *Faith, Reason and Civilisation* (London: Victor Gollancz, 1944) pp. 28–34, 80–140.
39. Arthur Schlessinger, *The Washington Star* (2 May 1976).
40. Arthur Schlessinger, *The Cycles of American History* (London: André Deutsch, 1987) p. 14.
41. James Field, *America and the Mediterranean World 1776–1882* (Princeton, NJ: Princeton University Press, 1969) p. 7.
42. James Morris, *Pax Britannica: the climax of an empire* (London: Faber and Faber, 1968) p. 34.
43. *New York Times* (23 August 1982).
44. James Burns, *The American Idea of Mission* (New Brunswick: Rutgers University Press, 1957) p. 14.
45. Dean Acheson, *Morning and Noon* (Boston: Houghton Mifflin, 1965) p. 18.
46. Cited in William Herberg, *Protestant–Catholic–Jew* (New York: Doubleday, 1960) p. 258n.
47. John Foster Dulles, *War, Peace or Change* (New York: Harper & Row, 1939).
48. Cited in *Dulles on Diplomacy*, ed. Andrew Berding (Princeton, NJ: Princeton University Press, 1965). Eden called him 'a preacher in world politics', Anthony Eden, *Full Circle* (Boston: Houghton Mifflin, 1960) p. 71.
49. For a study of Dulles' religious beliefs see Dean and David Heller, *John Foster Dulles: soldier for peace* (New York: Holt, Reinhart, 1960).
50. Berding (ed.), *Dulles on Diplomacy, op. cit.*, p. 103.
51. Dulles, *War, Peace or Change, op. cit.*, p. 217.
52. Kurt Tweraser, *Changing Patterns of Political Beliefs: the foreign policy*

operational codes of John William Fulbright 1943-67 (London: Sage, 1969) p. 41.
53. *ibid.,* p. 32.
54. Richard Rubenstein, 'Reflections on religion and public policy', in Morton A. Kaplan, *Global Policy: challenge of the '80's* (Washington DC: Institute for Values in Public Policy, 1984) p. 262.
55. Gaddis Smith, *Morality, Reason and Power: American diplomacy in the Carter years* (New York: Hill & Wang, 1986) p. 32.
56. June Bingham, *Courage to Change* (New York: Charles Scribner, 1981).
57. For this Calvinist strain in American thinking, see Maxwell Taylor, *Responsibility and Response* (New York: Harper & Row, 1967); and Harland Cleveland, *The Obligations of Power* (New York: Harper & Row, 1960).
58. Perry Miller, *The Puritans*, vol. 1 (New York: Harper & Row, 1963) p. 11. See also George L. Hunt (ed.), *Calvinism and the Political Order* (Philadelphia: Westminster Press, 1965) pp. 23-45, pp. 108-29; Felix Gilbert, *To the Farewell Address* (Princeton, NJ: Princeton University Press, 1960).
59. William Haller, *The Rise of Puritanism* (New York: Columbia University Press, 1938) p. 162.
60. Cited in Christopher Hill, *God's Englishman: Oliver Cromwell and the English Revolution* (London: Weidenfeld and Nicolson, 1970) p. 227.
61. *ibid.,* pp. 230-1.
62. Perry G. E. Miller, *The New England Mind: Seventeenth Century* (New York: Macmillan, 1939).
63. Alan Heimert, *Religion and the American Mind* (Cambridge, Mass.: Harvard University Press, 1966).
64. E. Tuverson, *Redeemer Nation: the idea of America's millennial role* (Chicago: University of Chicago Press, 1974) p. 12.
65. Perry Miller, *The Life of the Mind in America: from the Revolution to the Civil War* (New York: Harcourt Brace Jovanovich 1965) p. 10.
66. Marsden, *Fundamentalism and American Culture: the shaping of American evangelism 1870-1925* (New York: Oxford University Press, 1980) p. 3. See also Gillian Peele, *Revival and Reaction: the Right in contemporary America* (Oxford: Clarendon Press, 1984) pp. 111-12.
67. Alan Hyman, *Renaissance to Reformation* (Grand Rapids, Michigan: Eerdmans, 1955).
68. Kempt Fullerton, 'Calvin and Calvinism: an explanation of Weber's thesis', in Robert Green, *Protestantism and Capitalism: the Weber thesis and its critics* (Boston: Heath, 1959) p. 20.
69. Alexander Haig, *Caveat: realism, Reagan and foreign policy* (London: Weidenfeld and Nicolson, 1984) p. 23.
70. Hugh and Pauline Massingham, *The Englishman Abroad* (Bromley: Sovereign, 1984) p. 176.
71. Harriet Beecher Stowe, *Oldtown Folks* (Boston, Mass.: 1869) p. 368.
72. Robert Pinsky, *An Explanation of America* (Princeton, NJ: Princeton University Press, 1979). p. 42.
73. Vannevar Bush, *Science: the endless frontier* (Washington DC: National

Science Foundation Office, Office of Scientific Research and Development, 1960).
74. Goldman, *The Tragedy of Lyndon Johnson* (New York: Knopf, 1969) p. 63.
75. 'Memorandum of the Subcommittee on National Security and international operations of the Committee on Government Operations', US Senate, 89th Congress (1st Session 1965) pp. 2–3.
76. Victor Marchetti and John D. Marks, *The CIA and the Cult of Intelligence* (New York: Knopf, 1974) p. 251.
77. George Ball, *The Discipline of Power: essentials of a modern world structure* (London: The Bodley Head, 1968) p. 296.
78. Robert Bellsch, 'Religious influences in US foreign policy', in Michael P. Hamilton, *The American Character and the Formation of US Foreign Policy* (Grand Rapids, Michigan: Eerdmans, 1986).
79. Thorstein Veblen, 'Absentee ownership and business enterprise in recent times' (1923); cited in Michael Hunt, *Ideology and US Foreign Policy* (New Haven: Yale University Press, 1987) p. 192.
80. Ole Holsti, 'The study of international politics makes strange bed fellows: theories of the radical Right and the radical Left', *American Political Science Review* (March 1974) p. 233.
81. George R. Davis, 'The Vietnam War: a Christian perspective', in Michael P. Hamilton (ed.), *The Vietnam War: Christian perspectives* (Grand Rapids, Michigan: Eerdmans, 1967) p. 48.
82. Norman Mailer, *Of a Fire on the Moon* (Boston: Little, Brown, 1970) p. 10.
83. Mark Twain, 'A Salutation speech taken down in short hand by MT December 31, 1900'. See Frederick Anderson, *Mark Twain: a pen warmed up in hell* (New York: Harper & Row, 1972) p. 13.
84. Gary Bryner, *In Search of the Republic: public virtue and the roots of American government* (New Jersey: Rowland and Littlefield, 1987) p. 67.
85. ibid.
86. Tweraser, *Changing Patterns of Life*, op. cit., pp. 44, 46.
87. 'Address at the Commencement Exercises at the Airforce Academy, Colorado, June 4, 1969'. Cited in Theodore Windt, *Presidential Rhetoric: the imperial age 1961–74* (Iowa: Hunt Publishing, 1978) p. 127.
88. Dean Acheson, *Present at the Creation: my years in the State Department* (New York: W. W. Norton, 1969) p. 118.
89. Cited in Norman Graebner, *Humanitarianism and Foreign Policy* (Charlottesville: University of Virginia Press, 1977) p. 2.
90. *The Washington Post* (24 July 1977).
91. Hans J. Morgenthau, *Politics among Nations* (New York: Alfred Knopf, 1973) p. 11.
92. Henry Kissinger, *The White House Years* (Boston: Little, Brown, 1979) p. 911.
93. Cited in Arthur Schlessinger, 'Human rights and the American tradition', *Foreign Affairs* 57:3 (1978) p. 502. n. 2.
94. Cited in J. Stoessinger, *Henry Kissinger: the anguish of power* (New York: W. W. Norton, 1976).

95. Dean Acheson, *This Vast Eternal Realm* (New York: W. W. Norton, 1973) p. 172.
96. E. Stillman and W. Pfaff, *Power and Impotence: the failure of American foreign policy* (New York: Random House, 1966) pp. 16–17.
97. Louis Hartz, *The Liberal Tradition in America: an interpretation of American political thought since the revolution* (New York: Harcourt Brace, 1955) p. 38.
98. Charles and Mary Beard, *America in Mid-passage* (New York: Macmillan, 1939) pp. 443–7.
99. Malcolm Muggeridge, *Chronicles of Wasted Time*, vol. 2: *The Infernal Grove* (London: Collins, 1972).
100. The title is taken from Anthony Hecht's poem, 'Three Prompters in the Wings', in *The Hard Hours* (New York: Atheneum, 1961).
101. Stephen Spender, 'Love-hate relations: a study of Anglo-American sensibilities' (London: Hamish Hamilton, 1974) p. 121.
102. George Kennan, *Memoirs*, vol. 2 (Little, Brown, 1972) pp. 88–9.
103. George Kennan, *Memoirs*, vol. 1 (Little, Brown, 1967) p. 500.
104. George Urban (ed.), *Encounters with George Kennan: the great debate* (London: Frank Cass, 1979) p. 47.
105. George Kennan, *The Cloud of Danger: some current problems of American foreign policy* (New York: Little, Brown, 1979) p. 106.
106. *ibid.*, p. 40.
107. *Encounters with Kennan*, *op. cit.*, p. 4.
108. George Kennan, *Democracy and the Student Left* (London: Hutchinson, 1968).
109. George Ball, 'The dangers of nostalgia', *DSB* 52:1346 (12 April, 1965) pp. 535–6.
110. Speech before the National Foreign Trade Convention, 12 November 1964. Cited in Richard Barnet, *The Roots of War* (London: Penguin, 1971).
111. William Atwood, *Reds and Blacks* (New York: Harper & Row, 1967) p. 226.
112. George Ball, *The Discipline of Power*, *op. cit.*, pp. 9–14.
113. George Ball, *The Past has Another Pattern* (London: W. W. Norton, 1982) p. 490.
114. Ball, *The Discipline of Power*, *op. cit.*, p. 293.
115. *ibid.*, p. 25.
116. Kenneth Boulding, 'National images and international systems', *Journal of Conflict Resolution*, 3:2 (June 1959) p. 122.
117. Fernand Braudel, *The Identity of France*, vol. 1: *History and Environment* (London: Collins, 1988) p. 18.
118. Pitirim A. Sorokin, *The Crisis of Our Age* (Sydney, London: Angus & Robertson, 1942) p. 104.
119. Henry L. Stimson, 'The challenge to Americans', *Foreign Affairs* 26:1 (October 1947) p. 7.
120. Sorokin, *Crisis of Our Age*, p. 109.
121. *ibid.*, p. 114.
122. Cited in Lloyd C. Gardner, *A Covenant with Power: America and the world order* (Oxford: Oxford University Press, 1984).

123. Ronald Steel, *Pax Americana* (London: Hamish Hamilton, 1967) p. 12.
124. Zbigniew Brzezinski, *Power and Principle: memoirs of the National Security Adviser 1977—81* (London: Weidenfeld and Nicolson, 1983) p. 525.
125. Hedley Donovan, *Roosevelt to Reagan: a reporter's encounters with nine Presidents* (New York: Harper & Row, 1985) pp. 233-5.

2. Not the end of the world news: the United States and the origins of the Cold War

'Our commitment to international affairs has been decided by history. It cannot be undone and the only remaining relevant question is what its forms and goals will be.'

Zbigniew Brzezinski, *Between Two Ages: America's role in the technocratic era*

'History is not a redeemer promising to solve all human problems in time; nor is it a man capable of transcending the limitations of his being. Man generally is entangled in insoluble problems; history is a constant tragedy in which we are all involved, whose keynote is anxiety and frustration, not progress and fulfillment.'

Arthur Schlessinger, *Partisan Review* (1949)

It is traditional to begin accounts of US policy in the post-war era in 1945. The explanation is self-evident, or so it would at first appear. The United States emerged from the war a superpower, a status unique in history, for which there was no precedent, or even intimation. One author was still able to write in 1988 that 'US military pre-eminence dates without question only from World War 2. Its military predominance in 1945 over all other states (even at this point the Soviet Union) was unprecedented for any power at least since the time of Napoleon.'[1]

It is a plausible picture, but a deceptive one. Of the three criteria we use to measure superpower status: military force, economic strength and the possession of nuclear weapons, the United States having attained a pre-eminent position, went on to surrender it abruptly, before regaining the commanding heights of the international community during the Korean War (1950–3).

At the Yalta conference (1945), the last but one of the three power summits held during the war, Stalin had defined a superpower as a country with an army of at least 5 million men. In the years which followed, the United States' industrial capacity (which was already 43 per cent of the world's industrial output) clearly outstripped that of every other nation, most notably that of Britain. Its national income doubled in three years alone between 1946 and 1949. Its trade surplus was so great that the world's current account deficit with the United States had reached almost $35 billion on the eve of the Korean War. Finally the possession of the atomic bomb – indeed its exclusive possession until 1949 – further contributed to the perception that the United States occupied a position unique in history.

The real situation was a little different during the crucial years which led to the outbreak of the Cold War. Between 1945 and 1947 the United States' armed forces declined from 12 million to 1.5 million men, as the majority of troops were demobilised and sent back into civilian life. In August 1946 the US Defense Secretary, James Forrestal, recorded in his diary that even the United States Navy had been stripped down to 'a dangerously low point of efficiency' and that a large number of vessels in the active fleet could not go to sea because of the lack of competent personnel.[2]

So concerned where the Joint Chiefs of Staff by the extent of the demobilisation that they advised President Truman in 1947 that only Britain could be defended in the event of war with the Soviet Union. If Western Europe were to be occupied by the Russians, the United States would have to launch another D Day invasion against a far more formidable adversary than the Third Reich, one which would also be fighting not on three fronts, but one. The Americans did not even have enough forces to honour their NATO commitment in 1949. As Dean Acheson informed Congress in testimony which was not made public until 1974, it would have taken the United States eighteen months to build up the beginnings of a major force, two years for 'something more', and four years for 'something really substantial'.[3] By the time the United States did have something substantial, the Soviet Union had something more substantial still, one reason why it has been forced to rely ever since on nuclear deterrence.

In fact the United States' military weakness was largely of its own making. It had been inherent from the beginning in the way the Americans had elected to fight the Second World War. Out of a population of 169 million in 1941 only 15 million were called up (of whom 1,850,000 had to be rejected on 'neuropsychiatric' grounds, a disturbingly large number).[4] If Saint Beuve is right that every age and every social group has its own special malady then neurosis may be validly branded as the illness of the twentieth century. Fear of society did not stem from an extraneous source (the fear of Germany) but was a particularly virulent endogenous neurosis, an example of an intense and debilitating anxiety complex.

Throughout the war Stalin berated the United States for not recruiting 'a continental army' as another island power had done – Japan. It is easy to forget that at the time of General MacArthur's island-hopping campaign, a million Japanese soldiers were fighting a successful, if inconclusive, war in China, while deploying 650,000 men in Manchuria to deter any possible

Soviet invasion. For that matter as late as June 1944 there were more British Empire troops in the Pacific theatre than there were American.

In 1918 the Western allies were able to defeat Germany without Russian support (aided to be sure by the large number of German cavalry policing the Brest-Litovsk Treaty). In 1945 the Western allies were only able to defeat Germany so quickly after the Normandy landings because for every German division in France there were four on the Eastern Front. On the ground, if not in the air or at sea, it was the Soviet Union which played the major role in winning the European war. In the Cold War that followed the United States proved equally reluctant to mobilise men in sufficient numbers to deter the Soviet Union from attacking Western Europe. That is why it had to rely after 1954 on nuclear deterrence, particularly massive retaliation.

In that regard the United States was the victim of its own history. The ever-perceptive de Tocqueville had written in the 1830s that standing armies were so disliked in the United States that a military career was little esteemed. Escaping conscription bore no social stigma. Every war including the First World War allowed those who could afford it to buy their way out of military service. The revolution after all had distinguished republics which produced peace from monarchies which, to quote Paine, 'throw mankind into confusion'. In time this distinction, although patently false, grew in the American consciousness until it acquired the stature of a national myth. In *The Federalist Papers* Madison argued that the United States might escape war altogether; even the cynical Hamilton believed it might become 'the most pacific of all nations'. In his last message to Congress Madison suggested that by the example it set and by its appeal to reason, the United States might be able to infuse into international law a spirit that might reduce the frequency of conflict,[5] a forlorn hope perhaps, but a much cherished one.

What of the United States nuclear monopoly, and nuclear weapons themselves? Just how powerful was the United States? It may have had 'exclusive' possession of the atomic bomb but the term meant very little. The Americans had only three bombs in 1945, two of which were dropped on Japan, and a third which went missing, a fact which can hardly be attributed to inefficient stock-taking, given the size of its nuclear inventory. One of the United States' first strategic plans, Operation Pincher, called for the destruction of the Soviet oil industry. During the Berlin crisis in 1948, however, the United States had only 47 bombs to carry out the mission, not enough to have achieved the objective.[6]

As late as 1956 according to one RAND report the United States Air Force (USAF) had no capacity to launch a nuclear attack on the Soviet Union, unless it was prepared to send its B47s on one-way suicide missions. Only Britain had the capability using Royal Air Force (RAF) bases in

Cyprus. But once it went nuclear in 1952 its Vulcan bombers were deployed in the United Kingdom, not the Mediterranean. The United States' operational stockpile of nuclear bombs, and later nuclear warheads, remained comparatively small as late as 1960.

As for the United States' much vaunted industrial power we should remember that although its economic performance far outstripped Britain's, Britain remained a more important military-industrial power than the United States until 1950. Surprisingly, it was the predominant technological power, spending more on Research and Development as well as on equipment than the rest of Western Europe put together. While the United States demobilised and the Soviet Union recovered, the United Kingdom by retaining rather than dismantling much of its war-time industrial base succeeded in exporting more aircraft and military equipment than either the United States or the Soviet Union. In the end, of course, it could not compete. The British were working at the outer frontiers of technology; the Americans were not. Their huge continental market gave them economies of scale which proved their worth during the Korean War, when it took only nine months, not three years, to reach 1944 levels of production.

Prior to the conflict the United States was still insisting that Europe's economic recovery should come before rearmament, a point drummed home by Paul Nitze, Kennan's successor as Director of Policy Planning, on a visit to London in January 1949. Neither the explosion of the first Soviet atomic bomb in the same year, nor the conclusion reached six months later that the Russians might be capable of launching a nuclear attack on Western Europe by 1954 significantly changed American thinking.

It was the Korean War which made the difference. From $17 billion in 1950 military spending rose to $50 billion in 1953. By February 1951 aircraft production was back to its 1944 peak, an increase that made possible the development of an entire series of military programmes which dominated the political landscape throughout the 1950s and beyond – the development of tactical nuclear missiles, the deployment of four extra divisions in Germany, the world-wide deployment of the Strategic Air Command (SAC), and the construction of a nuclear-powered carrier fleet.

Second, the Korean War convinced the United States of the need to deploy troops in Western Europe. At one of their many meetings Senator Vandenburg, one of the most eloquent voices of isolationism before the Second World War, had warned Truman that he would have 'to scare the hell out of the American people' if he expected to secure large defence appropriations from the Senate.[7] The Korean War turned the scales in Truman's favour. In 1951 Vandenburg was calling for an 'efficient nucleus' of troops to be sent to Europe – the 350,000 men who made up the Seventh Army, the first the United States had ever stationed overseas in time of peace.

Finally, the Korean War led to what Charles Bohlen was to call in his memoirs 'the militarisation of NATO' – the conversion of a non-reciprocal guarantee to the Brussels Pact (1948) into the Alliance we know today, with a Supreme Allied Commander, its own strategic and tactical doctrines, and parliamentary institutions such as the North Atlantic Assembly – in short, an Alliance without historical parallel.

The importance of these developments was twofold – the United States drifted into the Cold War between 1944 and 1948 not as a superpower with overwhelming military might, but as a deeply insecure power that had concluded by 1947 that it was in no position to take the Soviet Union to the brink of war and beyond; that it could not even initiate a crisis as the Russians were to do in Berlin in 1948 for fear that it might lead to war.

Second, the United States had to work by necessity, not choice, very closely with its war-time ally, the United Kingdom, a country which engaged in a cold war with the USSR much earlier than the United States, which actually called for the use of nuclear weapons during the Berlin crisis, and which was still parachuting military advisers into the heart of the Soviet Union to assist the Ukrainian national liberation army in the late 1940s. The Great Patriotic War did not end when Marshall Zukhov's armies entered Berlin. It was only brought to an end in 1952 when two Soviet armoured divisions finally crushed the resistance movement in the Ukraine.

Despite the faltering element of reciprocity on which the war-time alliance had been based, Anglo-American unity survived the War intact. Born of a common resolve to confront the type of aggression which both powers might have deterred in the 1930s had they worked more closely together, it was preserved in the climate of suspicion which tore the Grand Alliance assunder, in the petrified violence of the first Cold War. In that sense Churchill was quite right to interpret the arrival of the American era not so much a threat to British power as the conclusion of one phase in the history of the English- speaking peoples and the beginning of the next. If the British were forced to play a secondary role, they did not do so until after 1950.

At the time of the Berlin crisis the British and US armies were about the same strength. Deterrence as opposed to defence gave the services a renewed lease of life to which they clung tenaciously in the late 1940s. Even if in the 1950s the United States had more atomic weapons, only Britain had forward bases in Cyprus and Iraq, which would have enabled its own Vulcan bombers to penetrate far more deeply into the Soviet Union than the SAC. As it was, throughout the 1950s one-fifth of all U2 flights over the Soviet Union were carried out by the RAF from bases in the United Kingdom.

The Anglo-American relationship was important precisely because it renewed the self-confidence the British had lost with their self respect in 1938. Reviewing a march-past of the 8th Army in Tunis, the young Harold Macmillan wrote in his diaries that the British 'seemed to be masters of the world and heirs to the future'. The mandarins in Whitehall, of course, knew perfectly well that the position was upheld if not entirely sustained by the United States; that the special relationship was unique because it was the first time in history that one power had persuaded another to underwrite its position, to honour promissory notes which could never be cashed, to protract its decline, not hasten it, to allow it to carry on regardless of history. To remain a great power the United Kingdom had to define a threat which would permit it to remain a partner of the United States, not merely its principal ally, a relationship which a State Department paper actually described in the spring of 1950.[8]

The idea of partnership was not, of course, universally liked by the British. Only two weeks after the 1945 general election *The Economist* opined that Churchill's policy of deference towards the United States had hindered any effort to evolve a special 'British approach' to world affairs.[9] Whether Britain would ever have found a role to play other than the defence of its imperial position is still unclear. Whether it might have acted as an intermediary between the United States and the Soviet Union is more unclear still. If the two countries were at odds it was in their vision of the future. When the British talked of defending Greece and Turkey from Soviet aggression, they did so in terms of spheres of influence and the balance of power, concepts with which the Americans felt deeply uncomfortable. Even Nitze and Bohlen, not to mention John Foster Dulles, wanted to open up new horizons as crusaders in search of a democratic ideal.

As the British discovered too late in 1952 when Churchill tried to find in *détente* a formula for mitigating the worst aspects of the Cold War, in their conception of themselves and their awareness of their latent power to reshape the world, American sensibilities were very different. If the British helped bring on the Cold War to remain a great power, they did so as a country on the defensive, not as a power preparing new lines of advance.

DIALOGUE OF THE DEAF

Considering the magnitude of the political changes produced by the war it is not surprising that they were accompanied by an equally profound political change in the relationship between the two superpowers. Indeed perhaps in no other period of US history was change in the balance of power so rapid, and at no other time did the rapidly changing pattern of international politics raise so many acutely disturbing dilemmas. The United States doubted its role, never its mission. Its aspiration to defend the principle of self-determination was coloured by its view of the past.

The Soviet threat to that aspiration could not be ignored as the German threat had been prior to the United States' entry into the two World Wars. Every word, every policy, every image was an indictment of the Soviet Union, an indictment that the Truman administration framed with care to allow no loophole for acquittal or abdication of its responsibilities. So conscious was the United States of those responsibilities that conflict with the USSR seemed inevitable even before the War had been brought to an end.

The Cold War first began to take shape with the discussions for the post-war reconstruction of Europe. The die was cast at the Quebec Conference, not at Yalta or Potsdam, in August 1943 when the Soviet Union offered to surrender its seat on the Allied Control Commission for Italy if it were given a 'free hand' in Eastern Europe instead. The question which divided US policymakers was their interpretation of what a free hand might mean. Did it mean that Soviet influence in the East would be paramount, or did it mean something more – Soviet control? If the former the United States should not have been surprised; indeed it was largely responsible for the outcome.

At Versailles in 1919 President Wilson had insisted on an outdated nineteenth-century understanding of self-determination, which had condemned Hungary, Czechoslovakia and Poland to be economic satellites of either Germany or the Soviet Union. It was a fate clearly perceived by the historian E. H. Carr in his book *The Twenty Year Crisis*, published in 1939, when he was the first to coin the term 'neo-colonial' (a word now so much in vogue in the Third World) to describe a country which had been given the trappings of political sovereignty while denied its economic and political substance. In the 1930s the principal power had been Nazi Germany. Germany not only penetrated Eastern Europe economically, becoming the main trading partner of Hungary and Czechoslovakia, its trading partners had to adjust to the realities of political life as well.

In May 1939 the National Socialist Party emerged as the second largest party in the Hungarian Parliament. In 1947 the Communist Party also came second with 22 per cent of the popular vote (which though small was actually a higher percentage than the National Socialists had won on the eve of the Second World War). In Romania the National Socialist Iron Guard won 16 per cent of the popular vote in the 1937 election, despite the fact the election was rigged to prevent them from increasing their political influence. In each case the size of the vote was not important. Much more significant was the strength of their external patrons, Germany in the 1930s, the Soviet Union after the Second World War. On each occasion the vote for National Socialist or Communist Parties had an importance which was quite disproportionate to the number of votes cast. In short, Eastern Europe was forced to come to terms with whatever political dispensation was in the ascendant long before the onset of the Cold War.[10]

Conclusive proof of this proposition was given by the Soviet–Czechoslovak Treaty of December 1943 which was signed by the exiled Czech government in Cairo a year before the Soviet army marched into Prague. Benes, one of Eastern Europe's few pre-war democratic leaders made three concessions to the Soviet Union which he accepted would replace Germany after the War as the hegemonic power in the region, the minimum concessions he considered necessary to maintain the state's independence in the 1950s.

1. He agreed that the Communist Party would be a major force in Czechoslovak political life, although it would not be necessarily be represented in the government, a major concession, indeed, considering the fact that in the last free election of 1935 it had secured only 7 per cent of the popular vote.
2. He agreed that central economic planning, not the free market, would be the economic model Czechoslovakia would pursue.
3. He agreed that the Soviet Union, not Western Europe, would become the country's main trading partner – a goal that was not acutally achieved until 1957.

Benes may have given away more than he needed to, but as late as 1947 Thomas Masaryk, Czechoslovakia's second leading political figure, admitted, 'If I have to choose between East and West, I would have to go with the East.'

Unfortunately the version of history which the United States inherited ignored the fact that the allies had behaved in 1919 in the most arbitrary fashion in parcelling up Eastern Europe. According to Keynes (not always a reliable source), Woodrow Wilson had evinced only the vaguest notion of how a new European order might be built.[11] Harold Nicolson, one of the British delegates at the time, recalls entering a room during the Peace Conference guarded by US Marines to discover Lloyd George seated in an armchair, Clemenceau in another, and Wilson kneeling on the floor, peering at an enormous map spread upon the hearthrug. 'Outside the window . . . another marine paced up and down, with his bayonet fixed. This I thought to myself is what is called arriving at a covenant openly.'[12]

The second problem inherited from the Wilson years was the American belief that self-determination was an absolute right, when the matter was not so simple. The United States needed to define a new moral language to enable it to come to terms with the reality of politics in the East. Unfortuntely, it failed to do so. The Americans thought it was sufficient to stand by the principle of self-determination, because the principle was absolute. They failed to comprehend that the kind of compromise to which Benes had agreed voluntarily, suggested – in Peter Strawson's words – that 'the region of the ethical is the region where there are truths, but no truth', a region in which two conflicting attitudes may coexist. What Strawson is saying is not that we should find as a new truth 'a synthesis', but accept that a degree of cultural pluralism may be necessary in the world that exists, rather than the world we might prefer.[13] Whilst self-determination for a regime like Stalinist Russia could never mean what it meant for Woodrow Wilson, or for that matter the Czechs, it might have constituted something short of satellite status.

Finally, the United States remained blind to the consequences of its own actions. Buoyed up by the extent of its victory, Henry Luce captured the mood of the times when he wrote only a year after the United States had entered the Second World War: 'Because America alone among the nations of the Earth was founded on ideas and ideals which transcend class and caste and racial and occupational differences, America alone can provide the pattern of the future.'[14]

Such was the United States' self-confidence during the War that it even toyed with the idea of reconstituting Western Europe as well, bringing in the New World to redress the balance of the Old. In his book *The Foundations of Victory* (1941) Lord Davies proposed that the world should be entrusted after the peace to an Anglo-American Commission based on the principles of the Atlantic Charter, a document which had no standing in international law, and which was not even ratified by Parliament or Congress.[15] In the United States authors like Quincy Wright took it for granted that London and Washington would have direct responsibility for world affairs in the post-war era, that they need only provisionally recognise the governments of Western Europe (including the majority in exile in London) without being bound to reinstate them at the end of the War. In the light of such thinking it is somewhat surprising that the democracies should have expressed such indignation at the cavalier manner in which Stalin was later to treat the 'provisional' governments of Eastern Europe.

In retrospect, the United States cut the unfortunate figure of a country which had severed itself from the outside world in the inter-war years, and thus had cut itself off from reality. The United States was essentially a one-dimensional power which treated Eastern Europe, as it had under Wilson, as raw material for its mission. The tragedy of US foreign policy was that the United States found itself present at the creation ready to remake a world it had not experienced.

The Second World War of course produced many sterling speeches. After Yalta Roosevelt told Congress that the summit 'ought to spell the end of the system of unilateral action, exclusive alliances, the spheres of influence, the balance of power and all the other expedients that had been tried for centuries and have always failed'.[16] The United States was in a position to deny itself the expedients; unfortunately, neither Britain nor the Soviet Union found themseles in quite the same position. What was an expedient for the United States was a policy based on experience for the other two countries. As Churchill's percentage agreement illustrated, spheres of influence were as much part of Britain's agenda as Stalin's, whether the United States believed in them or not.

It was not always clear of course what the United States did believe in while the War was in progress. Evelyn Waugh recalls that when Macmillan heard the news that Roosevelt and Churchill had consented to the destruction of Lithuania, which had been an independent state before 1940, 'he showed obvious satisfaction, saying "Well, that's one problem the less".' Interestingly, in recalling this event in a letter to Ann Fleming in July 1963 when Macmillan was Prime Minister, Waugh added, 'You must remember that the PM like Sir Winston . . . is half American and cannot be judged by English standards.'[17]

Despite Wilsonian self-determination, however, the Truman administration did accept certain facts of political life in Eastern Europe quite early on. The President accepted, for example, that the agreement negotiated between Finland and the USSR, which was later described pejoratively as a process of Finlandisation, was the best the West could hope for, not least because Finland had fought on the German side. Benes' policy in Czechoslovakia was received favourably as well in the State Department in 1946. Despite the State Department's advice to the contrary, the President was also prepared to work closely with a pro-Soviet (though not yet Communist) government in Hungary.

In the end it was the form, rather than the substance of Soviet influence, which so upset the United States, first in Poland and then elsewhere. Indeed as early as 21 April 1945 Averill Harriman, the US ambassador in Moscow, had begun to speculate that the USSR seemed intent on establishing not a sphere of influence, but satellite states in Eastern Europe. And it was this which concentrated America's mind on the immediate issue of self-determination, on which the United States claimed to have fought the War, even though Germany had declared war on America, not vice versa.

The next question, therefore, we must ask is whether the Soviet Union was prevailed upon to move towards the satellisation of Eastern Europe by the actions of the United States, as many Cold War revisionist historians claim.

Stalin could be forgiven, perhaps, for supposing that the United States had written off Eastern Europe in a way that it had not written off the two other countries occupied by the Soviet army: northern Norway and northern Iran. Unlike the latter where the Soviet Union was forced out under US pressure, the United States' representatives on the 4-Power Allied Control Commission in Romania and Bulgaria made no attempt to establish contact with the Communist Parties of either country. Nor did they find themselves in conflict with the USSR as France frequently found itself in conflict with the United States and Britain on the Allied Control Commission in Germany. Although the Polish Communist leader, Gomulka, was known to be unacceptable to Stalin (as Tito was in Yugoslavia) the United States made no attempt to enter into negotiations with him before the Soviet take-over of Poland in 1947.

Second, the defeat of the Italian and French Communist Parties by 1948 (after their good showing in the 1946 elections) may have influenced Stalin to go for what he could get: Eastern Europe, even if this meant dividing Europe into two armed blocs and setting back the chances for Communism in the West for years to come. To the extent that the United States was influential in defeating the Italian Communist Party in 1948 Stalin's mind may have been made up for him. 'How many divisions has the Pope?' he once asked derisively. He received an answer in the Italian elections when the Pope reminded the electors that while God could see how they voted, Stalin could not.

Finally, the United States' decision to merge the allied economic zones in West Germany (which amounted to a partition in all but name) marked a severe setback for the Russians. The Soviet Union wished to disarm Germany permanently, not to divide it and thereby encourage West Germany's rearmament. It wished to establish a security council for Europe which would guarantee Germany's permanent neutrality (a proposal which was later vetoed by the US Secretary of State on French advice). The United States seems to have upset Stalin's timetable. The East German Communist Party (SED) was set up in 1946 for the anticipated all-German national elections two years later, in the expectation of winning complete power of a neutralised German state within fifteen years. By 1948 it was clear to Stalin that a separate East German state might be the second-best solution, or, at least, better than nothing.

Does this mean that in forcing the Soviet Union's hand, however inadvertently, the United States was responsible for the Cold War? The answer is that history is never that simple. The revisionist historians are too ready to hunt for guilty men, to reduce history to a costume drama of cardboard personalities. If a culprit does not exist it is necessary to invent him. In the end the culprits of history nearly always elude us. Lost in the mass of events and our own reflections, they were probably of little enough consequence anyway. They may not even have existed.

It is also misleading to identify catalysts, turning-points, or other historical events as a sufficient condition, rather than a necessary cause, for a crisis. It would be fairer to say that certain US initiatives, three to be precise, none of which were intended to be anti-Soviet, may have contributed to Stalin's paranoia.

(1) The Soviet Union may have concluded quite early that the United States was anxious to blackmail it into revising the Yalta and Potsdam agreements, having had second thoughts about their desirability once the War was over. Stalin's hope of US economic assistance in the aftermath of the War foundered on several decisions – the abrupt cancellation of Lend Lease, the refusal to provide further loans, and the decision not to allow the allied sectors in Germany to provide the reparations agreed upon at Yalta. It is significant that these decisions met with little public support. Belief in the Soviet Union's good intentions was so strong in October 1945 that more Americans were prepared to provide loans to the USSR than they were to the United Kingdom.[18]

Certainly, the United States was carried away by its economic power. It soon came to the conclusion that the grand alliance had never been an alliance of equals. In November 1945 the House Special Committee on Post-War Economic Policy and Planning made it clear what the United States wanted in return for aid was a pledge that it would not be spent on arms; that the Soviet Union would make a 'full and frank' disclosure of its production statistics; that it would promise to withdraw its forces back to the Soviet Union; that it would disclose its terms of trade with Eastern Europe; and that it would open up Russia itself to Western travel and inspection.[19]

Confronted with such demands, the Soviet Union may well have felt genuinely aggrieved. The allies had opened their Second Front against Germany eighteen months later than promised, when Russia's fate was still in the balance. The Russians had pledged to enter the Far East war on 8 August 1945, which they proceeded to do exactly three months to the day of their pledge at the Potsdam Conference. They had also engaged two-thirds of the German army from 1942, yet had gained only one-third of its territory, and only 30 per cent of German industrial production. While the Russians had lost 7 million citizens and soldiers in the Great Patriotic War, the United States had created 17 million new jobs safe from enemy bombing. By 1944 the total goods and services available to the US citizens outside the armed services had exceeded the previous record of 1936.

Yet despite all this the allies seemed unwilling either to allow the Soviet Union to exploit the Western zone of Germany, to receive the reparations they had been promised, or to support the Soviet recovery programme. Of course, we must also ask if Stalin would really have accepted Western aid. The revisionists frequently argue that continued dependence on US loans and Lend Lease provisions would have denied the Soviet Union a 'free hand' in its dealings with the United States. This may, indeed, have been Stalin's view, but if that was his conclusion the revisionists can hardly argue that

Washington's refusal to extend Lend Lease or advance unconditional loans made the Cold War inevitable. Both propositions cannot be true at the same time.[20]

The fact that Stalin refused Marshall Aid suggests the price of US cooperation would have been considered exorbitantly high. He was not even prepared to allow the East Europeans to accept US assistance, clearly recognising the political implications such a relationship would have involved. Benes' decision to accept Marshall Aid forced his hand, and resulted in the Prague coup (1948). The Czechoslovak decision had been doubly threatening because it followed the refusal of aid from the Soviet Union, an offer which had been made at the Cominform meeting the same year. Clearly, the Russians were not prepared to see their client states suborned or bribed into the Western camp.

The real dilemma for Stalin was that with Western aid would come Western ideas; that economic aid would be used as a means of socialising the Soviet Union, rendering it a more responsible power, or one more responsive to US wishes. The real threat was American ideas, from liberal democracy to consumerism. Containment was not a US policy; Lenin invented the term in the 1920s. Stalin gave it wider currency in his book *The Problems of Leninism* (1947) in which he wrote that the Soviet Union would have to contain the United States by erecting a barrier against 'every manner of invasion'.

American ideology was a threat to Stalin and the Communist Party in a way that Nazi ideology had not been. Hitler's New Order offered the Russian people no other role than that of labourers building autobahns in the Ukraine, down which German tourists would drive to their holiday homes in the Crimea. It offered Russian women no other role than that of chalet maids cleaning the new homes or dachas. Not for them a life as 'market gardeners and museum curators', which Hitler envisaged for the French. His one concession was that the Russians would have to be taught how to read the road signs, and so not be run over by the super Volkswagens crossing the Ukraine on their journey south. Truman's 'New Deal' would have offered them a standard of living, indeed a quality of life, that the Communist Party of the Soviet Union (CPSU) had not been able to deliver for 30 years. That is why the Nazi–Soviet Pact (the first example of *détente* between two opposing socio-economic systems) could not be replaced by a Soviet–American Pact in 1945. *Détente* between the superpowers had to wait another 30 years.

The ultimate reason was that fear made the United States hasty to judge and overtly threatening without realising it. That is the major difference between fear and aggression. The United States was not aggressive to the Soviet Union but its obsessive fear of Stalin blinded it to the effects of its own provocation. Macbeth tells himself he is protected by the witches' prophecy (which he is) but then murders Macduff's family to 'make assurance doubly sure' - an act which in the end destroys him. Obsessive fear, not aggression, began the Cold War. Obsessive fear made the United States indifferent to the economic consequences the Soviet Union would have faced had it left Eastern Europe without any security guarantees in return. Countries rarely think of consequences for others when they have a mission (to socialise the Soviet Union), particularly when their view of their own past makes it especially difficult for them to distinguish fear from aggression.[21]

(2) There are two other reasons, to which historians do not usually refer, which make the very idea of *détente* in the late 1940s entirely academic. Both are cultural. On the Soviet side the Russians refused to behave 'reasonably'. Molotov was rude, contemptuous and blustering; the British were not. 'What the Russians most fear about us', wrote a British official in 1946, 'is not our power, but our ability to make friends.'[22] It was an ability which amounted in Britain's case to naked appeasement, the appeasement of a stronger power by a much weaker one, a policy which had worked since it was first applied in the 1890s. Appeasement is the usual policy for a lesser power to apply to a stronger one. It only failed in the case of Germany because Hitler, unlike the Japanese or Mussolini, could not be 'bought off'.

The Soviet Union was unwilling to acknowledge what its relationship with the United States actually was for fear of the consequences. Russian history had taught one lesson more clearly than most: countries that admit their weakness, usually suffer the consequences; nations that question their power soon find themselves exploited or abused by more powerful and self-confident neighbours. During the Marshall talks in Paris in 1947, Molotov displayed the same truculence and boorishness which had so surprised his German hosts after the fall of Paris, which was a catastrophic event for the Soviet Union since it had left it entirely beholden to Hitler's goodwill.

In 1940 the Ribbentrop-Molotov talks had broken down because instead of appeasing Germany as Hitler expected, the Russians insisted on rewriting certain clauses of the Nazi-Soviet Pact, giving themselves considerably greater freedom of action in Eastern Europe than the Germans, who were still the 'neo-colonial power'. Anxious that Hitler might interpret any sign of conciliation as an admission of weakness that he might be tempted to exploit, Molotov offended his German hosts in a manner which no one had ever done before. Events repeated themselves exactly, in Paris seven years later when Molotov came over with an 89-man delegation to discuss whether or not the Soviet Union would accept Marshall Aid. The talks broke down because the Soviet Union demanded more than the United States could or would concede. It was Stalin's greatest blunder.

(3) At the end of the day, however, the United States could never have made peace with the Soviet Union because its war aims had not been achieved. When probing American millennial thought, Ernest Tuveson saw war as 'the ultimate problem solver'. The United States regarded all great wars in which it had fought as the 'last', a victory for a permanent era of peace or democracy.[23] Any other reason for going to war is quite unacceptable in the redemptionist tradition. 'Can there be in our age any peace that is not honourable, any war that is not dishonourable?' Charles Sumner had asked in 1845.[24] One peace the United States had learned was dishonourable was that based on the naked appeasement of an aggressor, a Munich-style pact bought at the expense of other nations. One war it knew to be honourable was a crusade for freedom, 'a rite of passage to a new era of international government' as Cordell Hull promised the American people after returning from Moscow in 1943.

As Samuel Huntington once observed, 'for the American a war is not a war unless it is a crusade.' From the beginning there was confusion between those who supported the idea of redemption through war and those who did not. Hamilton changed his mind, initially justifying the American Revolution by referring to the laws of nature, before reverting to the limited war tradition of the eighteenth century, 'to a specific cause not a universal one'.[25] For the most part, the crusading imperative, however, prevailed. Thomas Mason believed that the United States could only draw swords in a just cause; that a just war was essential to the American character, a view which can even be found in Jefferson's *Summary View of the Rights of the Colonies*.[26]

In more recent times belief in redemptionism reached its logical end when one writer congratulated the United States in the 1950s on never having fought a war for a 'specific, political or economic purpose', but for such legitimate ends as 'a war to end all wars'.[27] If the First World War had been fought 'to end all wars', the Second had been fought to destroy totalitarianism. Unfortunately, Germany's unconditional surrender left the Soviet Union a stronger totalitarian power than ever.

Even during the War the misunderstanding between the two sides had begun to show. The Russians were amazed to learn that the US Army preferred to clear a path through minefields by setting off the mines by an artillery barrage – to them this method was an 'irresponsible' waste of shells. The Americans had been equally shocked to learn that their allies usually cleared minefields by marching troops through them, often convicts or political prisoners at the point of a gun.

Once the War had ended the Americans also had to confront other factors of Soviet life they had preferred to ignore. Concentration camps, for example, did not disappear. During the Berlin crisis in 1948 they learned that special liquidation complexes had been set up in the Kolyma peninsular to which 3 million Russians were sent for execution if the crisis had developed into war.²⁸ By 1948 the Americans had lost any illusions they had harboured about Stalinist Russia.

When and why the Cold War broke out is difficult to say. Certainly it was not during the Second World War, in which the United States deferred to Stalin (much to Britain's dismay). The years 1943–5 saw a certain friendliness develop, fuelled by hopes of a new post-war era. The impulse to compete did not exist; it came some years later. Perhaps it will never be possible to say exactly when the crusading zeal started, as opposed to festering suspicion, or when the confrontation began although the Berlin crisis is a good enough date. The Cold War crept up upon a world which had been prepared for it. It took the Truman Declaration and the Marshall Plan to turn a crusading impulse into action. Truman's words would have achieved nothing, however, if the impulse had not been there.

In the end, the struggle against the Soviet Union was a patchy affair, a case of chipping away at the edges. It was no crusade. The Russians were contained and deterred, but there were no grand-scale designs like 'rollback'. The idea of using military force never drew much support, despite the urging of Ernest Bevin that the US use its atomic monopoly to shape the post-war world as he argued at the height of the Berlin crisis.

In the event, the United States was prepared to go to war as the French and British had done between September 1939 and April 1940 – not to drop bombs but leaflets, to engage in a phoney war, a war of propaganda and subversion, not military offensives. When Truman's approval for NSC-4A was finally approved in December 1947 it was for propaganda activities only. These did not contribute to the Czechoslovak coup or the Berlin crisis as his critics maintain. That was the price the Americans paid for recalling the past. The price Eastern Europe paid was somewhat higher. The War, far from being phoney, was appallingly real for its victims, the people of Eastern Europe, on whose behalf the United States found itself engaged in a long and debilitating contest which was to last for the next 40 years.

NOTES

1. Bruce Russert, 'US hegemony gone or merely diminished, and how does it matter?', in Takasi Inoguchi and Daniel Okimoto (eds), *The Political Economy of Japan*, vol. 2: *The Changing International Context* (Stanford, California: Stanford University Press, 1988) p. 89.
2. Walter Millis (ed.), *The Forrestal Diaries* (New York: Viking Press, 1951) p. 107.
3. Theodore Draper, *Present History* (New York: Random House, 1983) p. 53.
4. The United States was not unique. During the First World War one military

psychiatric centre in France discovered that no less than 46 per cent of its patients were 'constitutional psychopaths', while another 23 per cent were suffering from neurasthenia or hysteria. The centre succeeded in curing a quarter of the patients, discharged another quarter from the army and sent the rest to convalesce. See Theodore Zeldin, *France 1848–1945*, vol. 2 (Oxford: Oxford University Press, 1977) p. 836.

5. Reginald Stuart, *War and American Thought: from the revolution to the Monroe Doctrine* (Kent, Ohio: Kent State University Press, 1982) p. 151.
6. Michael Mandelbaum, *The Nuclear Question: the United States and nuclear weapons 1946–76* (Cambridge: Cambridge University Press, 1978) p. 54.
7. Stephen Ambrose, *The Rise to Globalism: American foreign policy 1938–70* (London: Pelican, 1971) p. 151.
8. Robin Edmonds, *Setting the Mould: the United States and Britain 1945–50* (Oxford: Clarendon Press, 1986) p. 210.
9. *ibid.*, p. 26.
10. J. Lukacs, *The Last European War September 1939–December 1941* (London: Routledge & Kegan Paul, 1976) pp. 5–7.
11. E. Stillman and W. Pfaff, *Power and Impotence* (New York: Random House, 1966) p. 38.
12. Cited in Ernest Lefever, *Ethics and US foreign policy* (New York: University Press of America, 1986) p. 3.
13. Peter Strawson, *Freedom and Resentment and other Essays* (London: Methuen, 1974) pp. 28–9.
14. Cited in Ralph Levering, *The Public and American Foreign Policy 1918–78* (New York: William Morrow, 1978) p. 91.
15. Lord Davis Davies, *The Foundations of Victory* (London: Collins, 1941).
16. John Gaddis, *The United States and the Origins of the Cold War 1941–7* (New York: Columbia University Press, 1972) pp. 282–315.
17. Mark Amory (ed.), *The Letters of Evelyn Waugh* (London: Penguin, 1982) p. 610.
18. Michael O'Leary, *The Politics of American Foreign Aid* (New York: Atherton Press, 1967) p. 16.
19. Ambrose, *The Rise to Globalism, op. cit.*, pp. 12–13.
20. Eugene Rostow, *Peace in the Balance: the Future of American Foreign Policy* (New York: Simon & Schuster, 1972) p. 5.
21. Mary Midgley, *Wickedness: a Philosophical Essay* (London: Ark, 1984) pp. 85–6.
22. Thomas Brimelow writing in March 1946: 'The one quality which most disquiets the Soviet government is the ability which they attribute to us to get others to do our fighting for us . . . They respect not us, but our ability to collect friends.' Cited in *The Guardian* (12 February 1986).
23. Ernest L. Tuveson, *Redeemer Nation: the idea of America's millenial role* (Chicago: University of Chicago Press, 1968) pp. 124–50.
24. Arthur A. Ekirch, *The Civilian and the Military* (New York: Longmans, Green, 1956).
25. Stuart, *War and American thought, op. cit.*, p. 23.

26. See Thomas Jefferson, *Summary View of the Rights of the Colonies, ibid.*, p. 20.
27. T. B. Kitteridge, 'National peace objectives and war aims', *Marine Corps Gazette* 40 (1956) pp. 8–9.
28. Nicolai Tolstoy, *Stalin's Secret War* (London: Jonathan Cape, 1981) p. 354.
29. John Prados, *Presidents' Secret Wars: CIA and Pentagon covert operations since World War 2* (New York: William Morrow, 1986). Paramilitary activities were not authorised by Truman until 18 June 1948 in NSC 10/12.

3. Rite of passage: containment and the legacy of George Kennan

'Deus ex machina. God has waited patiently and now sets forth from the atom.'

Elias Canetti, *The Human Province*

'When it looked as if a nuclear war might break out between America and the USSR over Cuba, Melanie was of an age to read the papers and to follow the news on radio and television. It seemed to her that a breath of fresh air was sweeping through the world and her lungs swelled with hope. For, to deliver her from her prostration, it would take nothing less than the immediate destruction and appalling hetacomb of a modern war. The threat was dispelled and the lid of existence, which for a moment had been half lifted, closed on her again and Melanie realised that there was nothing to be expected from History.'

Michel Tournier, *The Fetishist and Other Stories*

US policy has been remarkably consistent for the last 40 years. Its overwhelming preoccupation has been to realise the promise of history, not bring it to a close. Its principal and overriding obsession has been to manage the nuclear relationship with the Soviet Union, while containing the threat by non-nuclear means. Containment has gone under many names: the Eisenhower Doctrine in the 1950s, the Nixon Doctrine in the 1970s, the Carter Doctrine in 1979. Secretaries of State such as George Marshall may have given their name to economic initiatives; Secretaries of Defence to nuclear strategies, of which the Schlessinger Doctrine (1974) was one. Only Presidents, however, have attached their authority to the broad strategic objective of containing the Soviet Union.

It may be useful at the outset to identify six phases of US policy since 1947, to adopt an approach which if necessarily simplistic, may help to explain the goals which different administrations have set, as well as the reasons why they have rarely been realised.

(1) Containment as a doctrine was first enunciated by George Kennan, who has spent his life dissociating himself from its implementation almost from the day of its inception. It was a period which began with the Truman Doctrine, and culminated in the decision to fight the Korean War, a period

which imposed a set of basic premises which have rarely been challenged. In determining US thinking ever since, they have encapsulated the sense of Chesterton's epigram: tradition is the democracy of the dead.

(2) Following the limited success of the Korean War, the Eisenhower administration, drawing from its lessons nothing but despair, tried to escape the logic of containment, to avoid the open-ended commitment of defending a divided Germany, a divided China, even a divided Korea. Ironically, having failed to prevent the division of yet another country in Asia, Vietnam, the period ended with the decision to send military advisers to Saigon, to support yet another society which appeared to be ripe for insurgency and revolution.

(3) The return to containment *à outrance* found a persuasive, even eloquent exponent in John F. Kennedy. It also found its nemesis in the killing fields of Cambodia and the collapse of Saigon. If Kennedy called on the American people to pay any cost for defending the freedom of others, they began to show a marked reluctance to sign blank cheques for corrupt, decidely non-democratic societies which seemed to make up a large part of the Free World.

In his inaugural address in January 1965 Johnson had told the American people:

The American convenant called on us to help show the way for the liberation of man, and that is our goal. Thus, if as a nation there is much outside our control, as a people no stranger is outside our hope.

It was a noble concept, but an increasingly expensive one. The eternal quest for freedom seemed unending, and in the end, unrewarding. In his memoirs Acheson had quoted William the Silent: 'It is not necessary to hope in order to act, or to succeed in order to persevere.'[1] He chose to ignore the fact that William had been a rebel fighting the superpower of the day, the Spain of Philip II. As a philosophy it was a counsel of despair for the United States because it offered a goal without an end, a vista of unending struggle. As *The New York Times* commented on the day that Saigon eventually fell to the North Vietnamese army, the end of the United States' 'misguided adventure' in south-east Asia had made it easier to return to another version of the past – to 'Lincoln's vision of the American destiny'.[2]

(4) As the costs increased, as the rise in nuclear warheads made the prospect of war between the superpowers even more unthinkable, as the Cuban missile crisis injected a sense of urgency into arms control negotiations, the United States sought to contain the Soviet Union by other means. *Détente* may soon have lost general support, but in its heyday (1972–4) it offered the brief promise of release from an endless series of proxy wars in which the United States sometimes found itself directly or indirectly

engaged. Unlike Michel Tournier's heroine the American people did not seek release from life through history, but hoped to realise its promise through co-operation. They were soon to be disappointed.

(5) Unrealistic expectations in turn gave rise to yet another attempt at containment in the last years of the Carter administration, although it had to await the inauguration of Ronald Reagan to find its voice or authentic expression. Reagan offered the American people containment on the cheap, not at any cost. In the end they were not even taxed for the massive defence expenditure of the 1980s. The money was simply borrowed from abroad.

(6) It was the cost, of course, which eventually turned even Reagan round to a more accommodating view of Soviet aims and ambitions. Where US commentators like Kissinger had once written with confidence of an innate sense of the United States' superiority, they now wrote burdened with a sense of despair. At the time of writing it remains to be seen whether their preoccupation with decline and imperial 'overreach', which has stimulated them to ask historical questions, has merely encouraged them to reply with unhistorical answers. It is not at all clear whether the second experiment in *détente*, like the first, will prove to be a historical dead end. In its unqualified hopes the second period defies any final analysis. A glimpse into one opportunity reveals a whole range of dilemmas which many Americans have not even begun to confront, or even acknowledge.

INTO THE NEW WORLD: GEORGE KENNAN AND CONTAINMENT

The United States adopted containment as its fundamental policy three years after the end of the Second World War, a period in which it had hoped that the grand alliance might be saved. Was the policy either desirable or possible, as originally envisaged by its author George Kennan? Kennan has since derided its execution, absolving himself from much of the blame. Ironically, more than anyone else, he himself must bear much of the responsibility for the mistakes that were made.

Kennan introduced the policy in an article he wrote for the journal *Foreign Affairs* in 1947, under the pseudonynm of 'X', since at the time he was still Director of Policy Planning in the State Department. As one of the few experts in the United States who had a knowledge of the Soviet Union and an understanding of Marxism-Leninism, its governing creed, the article had an immediate impact, even though only three pages were devoted to actual policy recommendations. The article was short on prescriptions, long on analysis. As always in Kennan's charmed career this telling limitation has not been held against him. Indeed, his flawed recommendations, far from diminishing his intellectual stature, seem only to have enhanced it with the passage of time.

Kennan's essential premise was that while Marxist ideology might be important, it was so ambiguous that its interpretation relied on the role of an intermediary; in this case the Soviet government. 'Truth is not constant, it is actually created.'[3] The Soviet regime used ideological maxims to justify policy decisions which had already been taken. In short, unlike Nazi Germany the Soviet Union was a country which could be contained. Because Soviet national interests were important in themselves, it was likely to prove a pragmatic, even cautious power.

Kennan's second premise was that unlike Hitler, Stalin had no fixed timetable. He was not in a hurry; he could wait, confident that history would determine the future in a direction most favourable to international Communism. The longer Russia waited, of course, the more likely it was to be frustrated as it saw events cutting against the grain of its ideological beliefs, instead of running with the grain of history as Marx had predicted. In time frustration might give way to self-questioning about the nature and future of Communism itself. True to his own convictions Kennan was highly critical of those who were in such a hurry to face the Soviet Union down in a crisis. 'It is not our lack of knowledge which causes us to be puzzled by Russia', he had written in a despatch from Moscow in September 1944, 'it is that we are incapable of understanding the truth about Russia when we see it.'[4]

Even at the time, however, Kennan had critics who were far from naïve, or even confrontational. Walter Lippmann, for one, was critical of the whole concept on three grounds. First, if the United States was expected to confront the Soviet Union at every point in the world, it would be able to choose the time, place and even nature of the confrontation. The USSR would have the initiative; the United States would merely be called upon to respond, possibly in support of allies of dubious moral character.

As it happened Kennan recognised this problem quite early one. As Director of Policy Planning he opposed the Truman Doctrine because it offered the Free World a blank cheque. He himself would have preferred the United States to have identified very precisely which countries would be defended and which would not, namely the United Kingdom and those of Western Europe. In 1948 he advocated that the United States should withdraw from China and South Korea, demilitarise Japan and the Phillipines (which had gained its independence from the United States in 1946) and withdraw to the island fortresses of Guam and Okinawa. What he seemed to ignore was that this policy too would have been tantamount to offering a blank cheque – this time, however, not to the United States' allies, but the Soviet Union. Having marked out such a restrictive sphere of influence the USSR would have been given a free hand to intervene anywhere outside that sphere as and when it wished. Indeed, a week after Dean Acheson announced to the world that South Korea was not covered by the Truman Doctrine the Korean War broke out. It was not an auspicious beginning.

Lippmann's second criticism was that Kennan had failed to make clear what were the roots of Soviet behaviour; whether they were strictly ideological or national in nature. In so doing he had obscured the distinction between Soviet expansionism and the spread of international Communism. Lippmann wished to draw a clear distinction between the Red Army and the Red International, to ensure that one was not confused with the other, that countries beyond the actual reach of the Red Army might be considered non-aligned or even friends of the West, not client states of the Soviet Union.

Kennan was not unaware of this dilemma either. In a speech he made at the University of Virginia in 1947 he argued that Communist regimes beyond Stalin's immediate reach did not necessarily constitute a threat to the United States; that China, in particular, by virtue of its very size and history was unlikely to become a Soviet satellite like Poland. Kennan supported the offer of Marshall Aid to Eastern Europe precisely because he wished to divide the Communist world. Ironically, by offering aid to Czechoslovakia in 1948 the United States precipitated the Prague coup, and thus the Cold War itself.

In retrospect, both Lippmann and Kennan were somewhat disingenuous. The only time we know that the Soviet Union ever contemplated attacking a 'neutral' state in the immediate aftermath of the war was in 1948, when Stalin ordered the invasion of Yugoslavia (only to cancel the order at the eleventh hour).[5] Stalin could accept independent capitalist states, but not independent Communist ones. Let Eritrea return to Italian rule, he told Djilas; the colonies would fall like rotten fruit in good time. 'In the old days', Stalin observed, 'kings who could not agree over the booty used to give disputed territories to their weakest vassal so that they could snatch them from him later at some opportune moment.'[6] Playing off Stalin against his own allies, however, was a dangerous business, for which the Western world might well have had to pay a price disproportionate to its immediate returns.

Lippmann's third criticism was that Kennan's article had actually contributed to Stalin's paranoia. The Russians read *Foreign Affairs* too, even if they were not members of the Council for Foreign Relations. At the height of the Cold War David Lawrence, a noted political columnist, struck a particularly redemptionist (or crusading) note: 'We must stop deluding ourselves with the idea of "negotiating" with criminals. We must instead exalt morality. We cannot end tension by making a deal with the immoral and the unscrupulous.'[7] I have taken the quotation from a book published by the Council for Foreign Relations seven years after Kennan's article appeared in *Foreign Affairs*. It was a book which bore the revealing title *Diplomacy and the Communist Challenge*. Unfortunately, it did not need Kennan's critics to contribute to the redemptionist message, which ruled any deal with the Soviet Union out of court from the beginning.

Kennan himself argued that containment was a moral goal, not a narrowly pragmatic one, that the Soviet threat represented an opportunity as well as a challenge. The 'thoughtful observer', he argued, would find no 'cause for complaint in the Soviet threat'. Instead he would thank Providence which in providing the American people with such a significant challenge, had made their security dependent on the assumption of responsibilities which history had plainly intended them to assume.

Even in his memoirs he pointed out the important impact on world opinion if it could receive 'the news that America had shed the shackles of disunity, confusion and doubt, had taken a new lease of hope and determination and was setting about her tasks with enthusiasm and clarity of purpose'.[8] It was a mood which was captured most vividly of all, perhaps, by Joseph Jones who wrote the original draft of the Truman Doctrine. Writing of the fifteen weeks which elapsed between Britain's announcement that it could no longer support Greece and Turkey against Communism and the Truman Declaration, Jones recalled that he had been present at one of those rare moments of history when the shackles fall away from the mind, allowing a nation to discover new standards of what is promising and what is possible, a time when men think not what could be done, but what should be done, a time of bold decisions and generous responses, 'a good time to be alive'.[9]

In the end, of course, Kennan came to the conclusion that containment had cast the United States in the role of a *poète maudit* – a historical outcast, not a historical actor, a role that was less than heroic even though it might have appeared heroic at the time. By the mid-1950s he recognised that containment promised only an endless series of conflicts, a campaign without end, a war without purpose or meaning. Kennan the redemptionist became an exemplarist, wedded to Washington's Farewell Address which had cautioned that permanent enemies like permanent friends would confound the United States' quest to be free from foreign entanglements.

In a curious metamorphosis which marked him out from his contemporaries Kennan chose not to abandon the allies, but conjure away the threat. Perseus had worn a magic cap so that monsters might not see him. Kennan chose to pull the cap over his eyes and ears to make believe there were no monsters at all. In the Reith lectures he delivered in 1957 he referred to a moment of revelation, much like Gibbon's in the ruins of the Palatine at dusk. Standing amid the ruins of Hamburg in 1949 he suddenly realised that they represented an unanswerable symbolism which we in the West could not afford to ignore. If the Western world was really going to make valid the pretence of a higher moral departure point . . . then it had to fight its wars morally as well as militarily, or not fight them at all.[10]

By 1957 much of his redemptionist fervour had abated. By the time he penned his memoirs he had been made aware how complex, indeed problematic a programme containment had become. Its purpose, he wrote, had been to buy time, to persuade the Soviet Union to negotiate, to recognise the need for compromise which might have involved the reunification of Germany, even the end of the division of Europe. 'It was not containment which failed', he wrote, 'it was the intended follow up which never took place.'[11] In particular, three errors had been made by his successors which he had not forseen in 1947.

(1) He had not forseen the Europeans' reluctance to accept Marshall Aid without a military guarantee; a guarantee that had only drawn the lines of engagement in Western Europe at Eastern Europe's expense. If Germany had not been rearmed, if NATO had not been created, the Soviet Union would soon have recognised the full extent to which it too was overcommitted. Its disengagement from part of Eastern Europe would have done more than anything else to challenge the 'imposing and forbidding facade' which the Soviet Union presented to the outside world in the 1950s, a façade which did more than anything else to convince the United States that it faced a monolithic Communist threat.[12]

(2) He had never intended containment to be a strategy to meet a military threat, but a means of defusing a political challenge. Certain language for which he had been responsible, for example 'the adroit and vigilant application of counterforce at a series of constantly shifting geographical and political points', had lent itself to misinterpretation. As a result the United States had found itself overcommitted militarily, fighting proxy wars, or even direct engagements when diplomatic or other means of defence might have been applied more successfully and at lesser cost.

(3) By demarcating Western Europe as the United States' principal security interest the United States had been forced to reassure the Europeans that its security guarantee was not worthless, that it would indeed be honoured if the situation ever demanded decisive action. As General MacArthur testified to Congress, the Korean War was fought to reassure the Europeans that the United States could be trusted, not because of any intrinsic strategic importance which the United States attached to the Korean peninsular.[13]

Although all these factors had a grain of truth, Kennan was curiously remiss in ignoring three other developments in the late 1940s which led to the 'militarisation' of containment. Even if he could not have predicted them in 1947, he should at least have acknowledged their existence, if only to state the case against containment in terms which were historically consistent.

(1) Truman would never have persuaded Congress to vote for Marshall Aid unless he had deliberately blurred Lippmann's distinction between Soviet expansionism and international Communism. McCarthyism at home may have been the price Truman paid; but the forces which supported the junior Senator from Arkansas were also most critical of containment in 1947. The Truman administration had to exaggerate the Soviet threat to get its defence allocations and economic aid programmes through Congress. It had to do so using the same redemptionist language which Kennan himself had used while at the State Department.

(2) The remarkable growth of the US economy in the 1950s, assisted in part by the post-Korean War boom, enabled the Eisenhower administration and its successors to ignore the distinction Kennan had been forced to draw between commitments and costs. The 'X' article had been written at a time when the United States had demobilised because it did not believe it was possible for the US economy to sustain a huge defence establishment in peacetime. On the same understanding isolationists like Senator Taft had been opposed to another European war in the 1930s, but not necessarily to a war with Japan, convinced that the latter would require neither the mobilisation of the economy nor the introduction of conscription, that it would give rise to a conflict that could be fought at sea with regular forces, not conscripted troops.[14]

What changed American thinking so dramatically was the conclusion reached by the National Security Council in 1950 in a document entitled NSC 68. Believing it possible to sustain huge defence spending without a commensurate increase in population Truman was able to go beyond what Kennan had imagined possible: to ask in the words of NSC 68 not how much security the United States could afford but how much it actually needed.[15] The doubling of national income (1946–9) made possible a policy short of war, the expenditure of $475 billion in 1962 (at 1954 dollars) compared with a war-time expenditure of $296 billion in 1943. In the NSC's own words the United States was able

1. to block the further expansion of Soviet power;
2. expose the falsities of Soviet pretensions;
3. induce a retraction of the Kremlin's control and influence; and
4. in general, so foster the seeds of destruction within the Soviet system that the Kremlin is brought, at least, to the point of modifying its behaviour to generally accepted international standards of behaviour.[16]

(3) Finally Kennan did not foresee the emergence of the imperial Presidency. Truman, for whom he had worked, had not been an imperial President. He had even thought twice about dismissing General MacArthur, and even then had to stomach his valedictory address to Congress, and a

ticker-tape reception in New York. It was the almost universal criticism of Acheson and Truman for losing China, for fighting the war in Korea half-heartedly (i.e. without nuclear weapons), and of the State Department for harbouring crypto-Communists in its ranks which forced Eisenhower to extend Presidential authority by appealing to the nation in terms which evoked the United States' historical destiny. As one historian wrote at the time:

Suddenly we are called to take the status of a world power. We cannot evade it any more. It has become our manifest destiny; it is indeed the inevitable consequence of what we are, what we have achieved, what we possess.[17]

One way of doing so was to exaggerate the Soviet threat (a device Kennan justly deplored), creating a Manichaean world in which the forces of evil and justice had to contend. With the exception of Kennedy the imperial Presidents knew perfectly well that the contest between the superpowers resembled a struggle between impotent rivals, a Hindu Dashera duel between two hollow statues locked in motionless and simulated combat. They chose to talk, however, in the language of redemptionism to outwit their opponents at home, their critics on the Left who wanted to pare down the defence budget, but even more their critics on the Right who spent most of the 1950s increasing budget allocations on defence, not reducing them as Congress was to do in the 1970s.

The period of history in which Kennan lived remains in many ways a puzzle for many historians. Kennan's obligatory insistence that his conception of containment was grossly misunderstood is no substitute for original thought. Indeed, the mere recounting of what went 'wrong' unintentionally helps to mythologise it, to think of it as inevitable, to see it as the United States' destiny. Kennan simply cannot distinguish between examples of American incompetence and history's ambiguities.

Leo Labedtz is surely right to argue that the author of containment cannot renounce his creation, yet insist he was misinterpreted by his colleagues.[18] Only by reinterpreting containment after 1949 could the United States apply the policy to the world as it was, not as Kennan imagined it to be. The revisionist historians, of course, have since challenged the United States interpretation of Soviet actions as grossly unfair, if not disingenuous. Their arguments have a certain appeal, now that we know as much as we do. Unfortunately, their appeal has been minimised by the fact that within years Kennan had joined their ranks, or rather anticipated them, for he became his own revisionist.

Kennan's arguments during the last 25 years have been marked by a high degree of intellectual coherence, but an equally large element of historical legerdemain. He has arrogated for himself the right to determine what should be studied and what should be counted as admissible evidence. In so doing he has blatantly disregarded the first rule of the historian: that although he must be allowed a point of view, he must also consciously recognise it and not regard it as absolute.'[19]

Consequently his own doubts have been cast not as new interpretations of history, but of Kennan himself; how he was deceived or misunderstood; how his advice was ignored or went unacknowledged in a peculiarly self-absorbed age. He has made no attempt to analyse what changes took place in society itself – such as the development of the imperial Presidency which made redemptionism possible, and even probable given the United States' system of values at the time. Instead, Kennan asked of the United States what it had never before conceded, and what it could not possibly concede in the 1950s: that it should break with the past, that like Simon Stylites it should sit above the common struggle – that it should become, in short, a 'receptive' nation. Thirty years after writing the 'X' article Kennan urged his countrymen to change from 'an exclusive to a receptive nation in psychology and in practice . . . there is no salvation for America in a frame of mind that tries to shut out its world environment.'[20] Brave words indeed, even wise ones, but they were wholly out of tune with the times. In that sense it can be argued that Kennan's main fault was that he had no understanding of his age. His version of history was not contemporary history as Croce understood the term. His account of events cannot even be fitted into Kühn's scientific paradigms, by which the latter explain the slow evolution of (scientific) thought.

As Kühn observes, 'when (scientific) paradigms change, the world itself changes with them.' In Croce's explanation of the evolution of historical thinking, when the world changes the paradigms change too. When society discovered that the earth revolved around the sun, it could never again regard itself in the same light.[21] In that sense, Kennan was a pre-Copernican living after Copernicus, a man who remained adamantly attached to the world in which he had lived and written in 1947, a world in which the United States was not the superpower it became in 1951. Kennan simply ignored the historical changes that occurred at the time and has continued to do so ever since. His version of containment was absolute. He deserved it. The United States did not deserve George Kennan.

THE NEW FRONTIER: DULLES AND LIBERATION

'The state of equilibrium is attractive only when one is on a tight rope; seated on the ground, there is nothing wonderful about it.'

André Gide, *Journals*

Max Weber was doubtless correct in his belief that in politics the ethic of responsibility is preferable to the ethic of conviction, but US Presidents were not given the room for manoeuvre to demonstrate the 'responsibility' Kennan demanded.

Most knew containment was a liability; few had any other policy to put in its place. In the words of Karl Popper all they could do was try, err and try again, and in that sense give history meaning. The only alternative was to argue against containment in the highly redemptionist language of 'rollback' and 'liberation', a policy which appealed only to Eisenhower and John Foster Dulles.

But for the Korean War, of course, it is possible that containment might have been abandoned anyway, that the United States might have felt strong enough not to roll back Communism but come to terms with it, by dividing the Communist world against itself, the Soviet Union against China, and after 1956 China against North Vietnam. As Acheson reported to Congress China had not been 'lost' to Communism in 1949. The Nationalist armies had not even been defeated; they had simply disintegrated because of the corruption of the Kuomintang. History had proved time and time again that a regime that lost faith in itself, and an army which had lost its morale could not survive the test of battle.[22]

In May 1950, a month before the Korean War, Acheson's closest confidants Dean Rusk and Paul Nitze proposed United Nations Trusteeship for the island of Formosa, as a preliminary step to recognising Mao's regime.[23] Only when the People's Republic entered the war on P'yonyang's side was it seen in Rusk's graphic phrase as 'a Slavic Manchuko on a large scale', a Communist regime that had 'not passed the test' which the United States had applied.[24]

The Korean War itself confirmed Lippmann's worst fears, and disproved many of Kennan's naïve hopes. To begin with the United States found itself supporting an ally who, in many respects, was even worse than the Communist alternative. Between October and December 1950, the only time that US forces have ever occupied a Communist country (if we exclude Grenada in 1983), the North lost a higher proportion of its population than the Soviet Union had lost in four years of war on the Eastern Front. Most of the casualties were inflicted not by UN forces, but by the South Korean army on instructions from Seoul.

Conversely, when Synghman Rhee had reoccupied South Korea three months earlier he had executed 100,000 of his own citizens for 'collaborating' with the enemy. Against their better judgement the US military authorities made no attempt to stop him. What the generals, however, preferred to ignore by turning their backs, the ordinary enlisted soldier witnessed with his own eyes.[25]

Second, as Lippmann had also warned, the Soviet Union chose the 'moment' to attack on 25 June 1950, almost a week after Dean Acheson had informed the world in a speech at the National Press Club that the United States intended withdrawing its protection from the South Korean leader Synghman Rhee.

As it happened, the question of who fired first was academic. As the head of the US Military Advisory Group General Roberts reported in August 1949 the South Koreans had invaded the North to a depth of four miles or more several times before. Between 1948 and 1950 cross-border fighting claimed over 100,000 lives. The only difference was the scale of the fighting in June 1950, and the fact that the Soviet Union encouraged North Korea to launch a full-scale and, as it hoped, final attack, confident that the United States would not respond. In this it miscalculated badly.

Finally, the Korean War forced the United States to conscript soldiers to fight a war in which few believed, in defence of a country of which most had not even heard. To conserve as many lives as possible, and thus disarm criticism of the War at home, the US Army was encouraged to use long-range weapons, of which the bomber was the most effective. During the three years of the conflict the USAF dropped more bombs on North Korea than it had during the entire strategic bombing campaign against Germany. Inevitably, this too reduced support in the field for the objectives the United States had set. It also angered the European allies, the British especially, who for the last time agreed to serve in an army, made up mostly of American troops, under US military command.

In the event, the Korean War might have been won by the end of 1950 had the United States chosen to stop at the 38th parallel, the frontier between the two Koreas. It chose to press on to the Yalu river instead, a decision which brought the Chinese into the War, and extended the fighting by another two years until an armistice, not a peace treaty, was finally negotiated. The reason the Americans decided to eliminate the regime in Pyonyang owed much to the legacy Kennan had left; a quite natural wish to escape an open-ended commitment to South Korea's defence, which has lasted ever since. As Acheson wrote to Paul Nitze, Kennan's successor, the War had, at least, provided a unique opportunity the United States had been denied in Germany or China: the chance to reunite a divided country under a pro-Western government that would not require a permanent US guarantee once the fighting had ended, still less the permanent deployment of US troops.

Even after the Korean War the Americans hoped that reunification might still be possible. Eisenhower's Vice-President elect Richard Nixon assured Rhee in 1952 that if the peace treaty the Republicans had promised the American people were signed, the South could begin the war again in twelve months. His Secretary of State John Foster Dulles told the United Kingdom a month after the armistice that he still hoped for reunification within five to ten years, even if this meant Korea becoming a neutral (i.e. non-aligned) state.[26]

In a word, looking back on the whole sorry episode, a draw, not a defeat; if a victory, a Pyrrhic one, Walter Lippmann's pessimism about containment had been proved right. In language that was to become all too familiar ten years later in Vietnam, General Bradley said that it had been 'the wrong war, at the wrong place, at the wrong time, and with the wrong enemy'.[27] Dulles was equally aghast that the United States had become engaged in 'treadmill policies' that would not advance its interests and which might well exhaust it over time.[28]

Redemptionism came into its own in the election campaign of 1952. Eisenhower denounced containment not on the grounds of its expense and intractability, but its fundamental amorality: 'The American conscience can never know peace', he told an audience in New York on 25 August, 'until [the East Europeans] were restored again to being masters of their own fate.' In his book *Peace and War* Dulles talked of the need to 'wage peace', a phrase with particular resonance for roll-back and the liberation of Eastern Europe.[29]

Dulles believed the United States had to keep faith with a natural law which the Soviet Union had challenged: 'We should be dynamic, we should use ideas as weapons and these ideas should conform to moral principles.'[30] He also found the threat of nuclear war challenging, in much the same way that Kennan believed that the Cold War had provided the United States with the unique opportunity to take upon itself the leadership of the free world. Indeed, Dulles actively disliked any talk of disarmament for fear that it would offer a 'relief from harassment', and thus relieve the United States of a historic role.[31]

He disliked the concept of containment most of all. As he wrote in the notes he drew up in 1952, the policy had not contained the Soviet Union; it had contained the dynamic spirit of the United States, and its 'contagious love of freedom' which up to then had made the republic the despair of tyrants and the hope of the oppressed.[32]

The United States, he argued, wanted no more Koreas, but it did want the liberation of Eastern Europe from Communism by propaganda and subversion, a policy which 30 years later the strategist Colin Gray was to call 'dynamic containment', now that roll-back had lost all credibility.[33] It remained for the ever-perceptive Lippmann to find in roll-back a policy as dishonest and bankrupt as containment itself. If he had to choose he disliked the latter even more, noting that the incitement to revolt was matched in Dulles's thinking only by reliance on words, on propaganda, a policy 'short of war, and not carrying . . . a commitment to go to war if the revolutionists which are incited and financed were to rebel'.[34] His opposition to encouraging actions the United States could never possibly support, and if it said it would, it could not possibly mean recalled Calhoun's criticism of Polk's missionary zeal in Latin America a hundred years earlier.

As the United States' passive response to the rising in East Germany (1953), and the invasion of Hungary (1956) were to show, the Eisenhower administration lacked the will to force the issue when it came to the test. 'It is of the utmost importance', Dulles had told the American Society of Newspaper Editors in 1952, 'that we should make clear to the captive peoples that we do not accept their captivity as a permanent fact of history.' Yet when they rose up against Soviet tanks he was soon to be found cautioning against the use of force by the United States, though not by the subject peoples whose right 'to shed blood for freedom' was treated as a moral absolute.[35] 'We can never rest until communism is defeated, Ike had promised, but rest they did in their speeches.'[36]

Dulles through his speeches seems to have been speaking to us for so long that we have forgotten another aspect of his character. The popular caricature is of a man who felt everything but knew very little, whose heart overcame his mind. His speeches seemed to be buttresses in search of something to support once roll-back was exposed as a fraudulent promise.

In one respect, the portrait is not totally unfair. For ten years Dulles accompanied his proposals for containing the Soviet Union with insistent demands that Eastern Europe be liberated and Communism rolled back. He repeatedly stated that the United States could not stand on the defensive for ever, aware that Washington had warned in the Farewell Address that 'a nation which indulges towards another an habitual hatred . . . is in some degree a slave'.[37] 'Our forebears', he told an audience in 1955:

believed in a Divine Creator who had endowed all men with inalienable rights. They believed in moral law and its concepts – they had a sense of mission in the world believing it their duty to help men anywhere to be able to do what God designed.[38]

Others, apart from Dulles, voiced similar sentiments. If Henry Luce had called the post-war world the American century, Max Lerner looked forward to an era of 'militant democracy', or 'democratic dynamism'. Esther Brunauer, the head of the American Association of University Women, a league to be reckoned with, called for an era of 'democratic power politics',[39] a concept which would have appealed to Kissinger whose sense of irony was far more developed than Dulles's.

Dulles repeatedly stated that he would be prepared to take the United States to the brink of nuclear war to realise the nation's aspirations. Indeed, brinkmanship was intended to be one of the cardinal principles of his policy. It was of course, nothing of the kind. The more closely we look at his actions, the more melancholy he appears as a political figure. In his career as Secretary of State, in his dealings with allies, even with the Soviet Union he was often generous and imaginative. His pragmatism in fact was privately renowned.

In 1945 he had written of the need for flexibility towards the Soviet Union, in the form of some acceptance of expanding 'zones of national influence'.[40] As late as 1948 he had made the startling suggestion to Marshall that the United States should propose a four-power administration of the Ruhr, so that Stalin would not feel entirely cheated of the spoils of victory.[41] In 1958 at the very beginning of the Berlin crisis he proposed that the West should surrender two of its four air corridors to Berlin, much to Adenauer's horror. In January 1959, the last year of his life, he summed up his foreign policy by maintaining that the United States only intended to hold the line until such time as it could co-operate with the Soviet Union, until such time as their interests began to coincide.[42]

What he might have achieved had Stalin died before he came to office, and Khruschev established himself before 1957 can only be left to speculation. Little of this conciliatory attitude comes out in his speeches, in which he chose to convey the image of an implacable opponent, first and foremost of Communism but also of non-alignment, those countries who preferred not to choose sides, who were condemned in his cosmos to the same fate as those poor creatures in the Divine Comedy whom heaven would not admit and hell would not receive. The image he left of himself was of a hater of allies who were 'soft' on Communism, of enemies and friends alike, a hater, in short, of the world in which he lived.

The pessimism to which Dulles yielded with more than a little self-indulgence originated, one suspects, in his clear understanding of the dilemmas of containment. It eventually grew to the point where it distorted his vision and frequently rendered him unable to trace new lines of advance in place of the old political landscape. In the end, he seemed to recognise that the United States' past offered no answers, only stock political formulas which were beginning to sound increasingly hollow.

It was only in his last year when he spoke of the need for *détente* that he analysed those sentiments of scepticism and distrust which had already convinced Kennan that the United States should become a receptive nation. Like Kennan he came to realise that the American people had lived out politics as a perpetual drama, taking heroes to heart like Rhee and Diem who were entirely unheroic, flawed characters of modest interest in themselves, cardboard cut-outs of Third World dictators who soon faded from memory because they were so unmemorable.

On some occasions Dulles still considered the Cold War to be a heroic confrontation; on others he was terribly disappointed, even as he expounded its virtues. The Berlin crisis of 1948 may have been a moment of glory, but what followed in the streets of Budapest in 1956 was far from glorious, even for the participants.

In time the heroic impulse waned. Forbidding the CIA even to parachute supplies to the Hungarian rebels, as the USAF had done to the Polish Home Army in 1944, Dulles became disenchanted with the Cold War, with his countrymen and in the end with himself. The inability to liberate, to mount an offensive, to redeem the world from Communism forced him to place his faith in the most depressing policy of all: massive retaliation, or nuclear terror, a form of containment on the cheap.

By 1956 the US deterrent became a reality for the first time. The B52s could now fly to Moscow and back. It was the United States' Year Zero, or as Eugene Rabinovich put it, 'ADI: the first year of deterrence', which saw the advent of peace through mutual terror.[44] More accurately, perhaps, it was as Bernanos had predicted, 'the ultimate triumph of technique over reason', a triumph in which the United States' past hardly figured at all.

THE WEARYING TITAN: KISSINGER AND *DÉTENTE*

Détente was made necessary by a clear acceptance by Nixon that there could be no more 'Vietnam's', that the United States and the Soviet Union both needed to work out a 'code of conduct' which would make such conflicts otiose in the future. The code he conceived went under the name of *détente*, a policy which derived from three concepts especially dear to its principal architect, Henry Kissinger.

First, Kissinger believed that rational calculation revealed the limitations of power as well as its possibilities. He was on the side of reason; he was also the victim of it – he allowed the system of ratiocination a position of primacy in his approach to the world. Second, he maintained that in any era of history it was possible to discern historical trends. Finally, he argued that having turned its back on a geo-political tradition the United States had spent much of its history predicating a foreign policy on such questionable principles as human rights, international law, and self-determination, instead of accepting that equilibrium, or the balance of power, was the only rational objective a superpower should pursue in the nuclear age.

From the first principle Kissinger derived the belief that the utility of force in the modern world was not only highly suspect, but that its opportunity costs outweighed its advantages.

No nation or bloc of nations can impose its narrow interests without tearing the fabric of international co-operation. Whatever our ideological belief or social structure we are part of a single international system on which our national objectives depend. Our common destiny is not a slogan, it is an unmistakable reality.[45]

Unfortunately, it was to be another twelve years before the Soviet Union was to use the same language, the language of interdependence and military sufficiency. Even then it used the words in a way that suggested to many that they were slogans in a different conflict, not a cold war this time, but a war of words to disarm the enemy not by fashioning swords into ploughshares but an endless stream of policy statements.

From his second premise Kissinger came to the conclusion that the two superpowers were already entering a transitional period in their history: the Soviet Union a period of decline, the United States a period of adjustment to a pentagonal world in which power would be shared with countries such as Japan, and organisations such as the European Community. In a sense, Kissinger's belief that the Soviet Union was an empire on the defensive enabled him to escape Kafka's Castle, which had been a potent symbol of the Soviet Union in the 1950s, a confined, forbidding world for those who had lived in its shadow, a persistent motif of the Cold War.[46] Like Kafka's hero, Kissinger was much less impressed as he grew older, as the Castle showed no signs of life. The longer he looked at it the more its contours began to dissolve.

From his final premise Kissinger believed that the balance of power revolved around the United States' relationship with China, that an understanding with the Soviet Union was only possible if the United States established a much closer link with the People's Republic and the Soviet Union, than either shared with each other. *Détente*, in a word, represented a triangular relationship with China at the apex of the triangle and the superpowers at the bottom.

Kissinger's strategy was just another way of following Dulles's approach to China, forcing a Soviet client to make unreasonable demands on its patron, rather than trying to suborn or bribe the client to defect. Both Dulles and Eisenhower had believed that the best way of provoking a Sino-Soviet rift was to increase China's dependence on the Soviet Union, an approach which Gaddis characterised as an attempt to split the alliance through fusion rather than fission.[47] Eisenhower's support for Taiwan in the Quemoy and Matsu crises (1954–5, 1958) was not a response to the China lobby, but a calculated attempt to drive a wedge into the relationship between China and the Soviet Union by forcing the Chinese to turn to Moscow for help, in the knowledge that they would be disappointed.

Why then did *détente* fail? Why did its promise prove so short-lived (1972–6)? Why did it survive for less than five years?

There are two main explanations with which Kissinger himself would probably agree. First, American public opinion expected more of *détente* than either superpower could, or would deliver; they expected it would bring superpower conflict to an end, or dilute it to the point where neither power had to exert itself as the United States had done in the 1960s. Second, like his two nineteenth-century heroes Bismarck and Castlereagh, Kissinger failed to create a popular consensus for *détente* which would survive his passing. He forgot, in the words of Walter Lippmann, that 'the final test of a leader is that he leaves behind him the conviction and the will to carry on'.[48]

Détente produced only one policy document, the Washington communiqúe of 1973, which promised that neither superpower would try to take unilateral advantage at the other's expense. Unlike the process of Ostpolitik in Europe, which produced the Berlin Treaty (1972) and the Helsinki Agreement (1975), the process was not 'irreversible' as Nixon claimed precisely because it committed the two powers to so little. It did not guarantee a 'new structure of peace' as Nixon told Congress in 1973, any more than it produced 'a code of conduct' as Brzezinski was to maintain in 1978. All it promised in Kissinger's own words was 'an environment in which competition [could] regulate and restrain [superpower] differences, and ultimately move them from competition to co-operation'.[49]

In a word, it was never intended to remove the issues which divided the two superpowers, only to ameliorate them. It was, to quote Coral Bell, 'a mode of [managing] adversial power', a way not of ending conflict but defusing it.[50] In contrast to the nineteenth-century European Concert of Powers Nixon's structure of peace relied almost exclusively upon a common interest: the avoidance of nuclear war, not a common duty to work together. The avoidance of war meant arms control agreements, such as the Anti-Ballistic Missile (ABM) Treaty and the Strategic Arms Limitation Talks (SALT) I Treaty of 1972. At one stage Nixon declared, 'We must either live together or die together.' In the end the architects of *détente*, and its apologists, sought to prop it up by reducing it to a hard-core avoidance of nuclear war. In so doing they implicitly suggested it was only another form of containment by other means – an alternative to war itself. In giving *détente* undeserved credit for an impasse brought about by the mutual destructiveness of nuclear weapons, they betrayed a misunderstanding of both.[51]

Second, Kissinger's open disdain for Congress, and Congress's hostility towards Richard Nixon (which long predated the Watergate crisis) ensured that neither the President nor his principal adviser on security bothered to mobilise public opinion in support of *détente* until it was far too late. As Stanley Hoffmann once observed, *détente* was far too complex for the public to understand and much too simplistic for the successful management of the world's problems, given Kissinger's notorious tendency to reduce everything including the North–South debate to an East–West equation.[52] The United States was slow to respond to the changes in the Third World in this period. Political 'turning points' passed before any notice was taken of them. Kissinger's world had already changed by the time he came to office, but he failed to acknowledge the changes. So did the Soviet Union, trusting as it did to Marx. At least Marx, unlike Kissinger, however, had the excuse of being born in the age of the camera obscura.

Unfortunately, the public expected more than either superpower could deliver: rules of behaviour, or the moderation of means, before any agreement had been reached on the ends of their respective foreign policies. Since neither side could agree on the kind of world they wanted to emerge in the 1980s, such rules proved elusive. The search for a code of conduct inevitably led to disappointment, mutual recrimination, and, in the end, deep suspicion that one power was attempting to undercut the other as quietly as it could. Ironically, Kissinger was so distrusted by his own side for selling out to the Russians that he dared not appear at Gerald Ford's side at the Republican Party Convention (1976) for fear of being booed off the platform.

The two crises which undermined *détente* were the Middle East War of 1973 and Cuban intervention in Angola. Both exposed a basic flaw: the fundamental unwillingness of the United States to concede the fact that the Soviet Union was its equal as a superpower, or, to quote Gromyko in 1971, that there was no area of the world, not even the Western Hemisphere, from which the Soviet Union could be excluded in the management of regional security. In reality, the United States could exclude the Soviet Union if it wished to, to deny it the ticket of admission to the first rank of powers which *détente* had apparently offered. As Vernon Aspurturian put it some years later the Soviet Union recognised that its equality with the United States was still ascriptive. Although its leaders expressed confidence that history would render it real, they were quite aware that that time had not yet arrived.[53]

Before the 1973 Washington summit which preceded the last Arab-Israeli war by a few months the United States had actually co-operated with the Soviet Union in the Middle East. On two separate occasions William Rogers had tried to launch the two-power and four-power initiatives (1970/72). The two sides had also delayed selling arms to their respective clients, in the case of the United States Phantoms to Israel in 1971, in the case of the Soviet Union SSMs to Egypt between 1970 and 1972. As late as December 1973 Egypt's President Sadat accused the superpowers of conniving at a 'no peace, no win' situation for their own advantage.

After 1974, however, Kissinger discovered that Egypt was prepared to enter into a close relationship with the United States in order to get the Israelis out of the Sinai peninsular. Later still after the Sinai Disengagement Agreements of 1974 and 1975 in which the Soviet Union played no part, the Americans were able to grasp the opportunity of a separate peace treaty between Egypt and Israel, a treaty which the Carter administration was able to persuade both powers to sign in 1979.

It was partly in response to these series of initiatives that the Soviet Union intervened in Angola in 1975. As *Isvestia* said at the time – not entirely disingenuously – Soviet intervention at the expense of the United States, without prior consultation, should have been seen as an 'investment in *détente*' (a quid pro quo for Kissinger's unilateralist policies in the Middle East the previous year), an initiative which might keep *détente* alive a little longer. Unfortunately, true to form Kissinger refused to concede that the Soviet Union had any legitimate interests in an area of the world that had been regarded for so long as a Western sphere of influence. Long before the arrival of 40,000 Cuban troops after October 1975 and his criticism of 'Soviet intervention', Kissinger had condemned the Soviet Union's 'involvement' in the developing struggle, despite the fact that it had armed the most powerful of the national liberation movements for the past thirteen years. Later still he chose to use the United States' opposition to Soviet policy as a 'lecturing point' to teach the Russians 'the meaning of *détente*, a phrase which recalled Kennan's argument that 'we must train the Russians to make their whole machine ... respond sensibly to our approaches.'[54]

Unfortunately, the argument's point of departure was also its destination. Neither went further with this pedagogic advice; each initiative was an old terminus. Is not the main criticism of Kissinger, at least, that he was unable to fuse a critique of his age with his very real insight into Soviet policy? He could hardly expect on the one hand grain sales and the promise of more favourable terms for technology transfer to create a 'stake' for the Soviet Union in the existing political order,[55] while on the other, excluding it from regions of the world which the United States considered strategically vital. The misunderstanding between the two sides could not have been greater. Throughout his years in office Henry Kissinger, who began life as a professional historian turned political scientist, spoke of the need for the United States to remain true to its historical heritage as though the republic was condemned for ever to be 'weighed down by the nightmare of tradition'.[56]

He was accused at the time of being a determinist, heavily influenced by his understanding that the United States and the Soviet Union were already in decline. Determinism in this sense has no place in the US historical tradition, certainly not in terms of the fatalism and despair one usually associates with its Spenglerian gloss. If Kissinger was a determinist, however, he was a determinist in quite another sense of the word – a man who believed that history, in revealing the limits of power, enables man to realise ambitions he may never have thought possible to begin with. Far from being a fatalist Kissinger was a supreme optimist, as accessible to the revealed 'truths' of the Founding Fathers as any of his more orthodox colleagues. As Peter Dickson makes clear, although not heir to the Calvinist tradition, he was Protestant enough in his outlook to be a man whose 'standards clash[ed] frequently with the viciousness of history', the limits which the past imposes on individual or collective action.[57]

Dickson is by far the most trenchant and persuasive of the many scholars who have analysed Kissinger's understanding of history. Two of his assertions, however, seem questionable to say the least: the first that Kissinger subordinated the pursuit of values to achieve a very pragmatic understanding with the Soviet Union;[58] the second, that Kissinger's willingness to work with the Soviet Union represented 'a radical transformation of America's mission'.[59]

In fact, if not a redemptionist in the true sense of the term, Kissinger was a true Providentialist. He never questioned the belief that the United States had a unique role to play in history. As an avid reader of Niebuhr when an undergraduate at Harvard he had looked to history for lessons, not the theological lessons Niebuhr had sought, but those which would enable America to move with history, as well as enabling it in certain circumstances to move history itself. In his first book *A World Restored* he wrote that the statesman, like many of the heroes in Greek tragedy, was a Cassandra who had a vision of the future which he could not transmit directly to his fellow men, or validate its truth.[60] Fortunately, the United States was not bound by the conventions of an earlier era. Where truth could not be validated, it could be created instead.

Like Charles Beard he thought it was quite possible to discover 'the structure of the past', on which it would be possible to build what Nixon was to refer to as a 'structure of peace': *détente*. Indeed, Beard had challenged his colleagues in arguing that it might be possible through 'a great act of faith' to see the whole of human history as a movement towards a 'collectivist democracy'.[61] Beard's act of faith, of course, conflicted with his life's message that history could not be told 'as it was'; that all history is relative to the age in which it is interpreted and recorded by historians. In the end, however, he allowed himself to succumb to a very American faith in progress.

So did Kissinger. Because he had identified the challenges facing the United States, he believed implicitly that they could be met, that the United States' decline could be arrested, if not reversed, provided its statesmen acted in time: 'no nation can choose the timing of its fate. The tides of history take no account of the fatigue of the helmsman. Posterity will reward not the difficulty of the challenge, only the adequacy of the response.'[62]

Far from abandoning the two traditions of US history that Dickson identified, Kissinger was victim to two of its illusions: that nations can shape events, and that the United States, being in some senses outside history, could shape history itself. Although a scholar of Bismarck he did not share Bismarck's highly European view that 'the best a statesman can do is to listen for the rustle of God's mantle through history and try to catch the hem of it for a few steps.' For Kissinger, the statesman created his own reality, unlike the politician who responded to events. As he once claimed in office,

'We are in a pivotal moment in history. If the world is in flux we have the capacity and hence the obligation to help shape it.'[63]

The word 'obligation' would never have passed Bismarck's lips. Yet it holds the key to understanding Kissinger's statecraft, and his view of *détente*. He differed from Dulles and Kennan only in recognising that the United States was no longer powerful enough to act on its own account. It needed the support of its allies. 'America's challenge today', he wrote, 'is to demonstrate a new kind of leadership – guiding by our vision, our example and our energy, not by our predominance.'[64] If the means of containment were more limited, the ends remained the same.

THE LAST RALLY? REAGAN AND THE SOVIET UNION

Even before President Carter left office the United States had returned to the containment of the 1960s, although this time on the cheap. Carter himself never believed in *détente* as such, only accommodation with the Soviet Union. In his first two years in office he was ambivalent and inconsistent. He clearly had difficulty identifying any coherent or discernible conception of US interests in the world or even potential threats to them.[65] The Soviet decision to send Cuban troops to reinforce the Marxist regime in Ethiopia posed the question of cost for the United States, long before the invasion of Afghanistan brought the experiment to an abrupt end. As Brzezinski noted at the time, the Ethiopian crisis forced the administration to ask whether *détente* could ever be an end in itself.[66]

The decision to suspend the naval arms control talks in the Indian Ocean was taken before Soviet troops entered Kabul. The decision to increase defence spending, which followed swiftly upon it, marked a return to power politics, a return, however, which found neither its true voice nor successful execution, until the coming of Ronald Reagan in 1981.

Reagan carried with him the hopes of a generation that wished the United States to keep faith with its past. In the run-up to his election in 1980 he dwelt on the theme of the United States as a country in decline, that had lost the number one position in a 'world out of control', that had even lost the self-confidence to impose its own agenda.[67] In a speech to a group of Italian businessmen Jeane Kirkpatrick, Reagan's ambassador at the United Nations, claimed that the administration had returned to Eisenhower's wish to go beyond containment; that it had restored its military power so that liberal democracy might be promoted, not merely defended against enemies internal and external alike.[68] It was a sentiment Reagan himself clearly echoed when he claimed that the United States would not merely contain Communism but 'transcend it'.[69] In March 1986 he was able to tell the

American people that he had given them an effective foreign policy which had shaped events in accordance with their values, rather than one which had merely responded to the initiatives and actions of others.[70]

If Carter had returned to human rights policy to create a consensus at home for the application of US power, a consensus based on a positive support for liberty, compared with the traditional negative containment of Communism, Reagan made his support for liberty unequivocal from the beginning. Although he referred to human rights very little in his Presidency it would be wrong to imagine that his administration was indifferent to them altogether. As the State Department's Human Rights Report made clear in 1982, 'Other peoples express their yearnings for justice as a demand for rights.'[71] As George Schultz made clear, human rights were at the core of US foreign policy because they were central to the United States conception of itself.[72]

It was a demand to which the administration later responded in Haiti and the Philippines where it helped ease out the young Duvalier and Ferdinand Marcos. It even attempted to intervene in Paraguay by trying to destabilise Stroessner's regime. The Reagan Doctrine enunciated in 1986 explicitly maintained that the United States would redeem countries struggling to be free even from regimes which, although avowedly anti-Communist, were clearly beyond the pale of civilised conduct.

Despite this positive affirmation of democracy, however, the Reagan administration spent most of its energies containing the Soviet Union. A dramatic shift in the geo-strategic balance of power, as well as an equally disturbing change in the geo-political structure of the international system, both put the United States on guard.

The Soviet decision to intervene in the war between Ethiopia and Somalia saw a projection of Soviet military power beyond its own borders and that of its immediate satellites, on a scale that the West had never before had to confront. The 225 transport planes which at the height of the crisis took off from airfields in Transcaucasia every twenty minutes shocked the military planners. As West Germany's Defence Minister observed, the Soviet transport fleet had become 'a new strategic element' in the East–West balance.[73]

The Vietnamese occupation of Kampuchea, and the use by the Soviet Pacific fleet of Cam Rahn Bay also posed unprecedented problems for US naval planners in the Pacific for the first time since the Second World War. The invasion of Afghanistan was also seen by many as the first major threat to the West's access to the oil fields of the Gulf since the appearance of Field Marshal Kleist's First Panzer Group in the Caucasus in 1942.

In addition, a series of geo-political developments, of which the growth in international terrorism was perhaps the most dramatic, shattered the confidence of many officials in the non-military instruments of foreign policy in which they had been encouraged to believe for so long. US citizens or interests were the target of a third of all terrorist attacks between 1979 and 1985. In what William Casey, the head of the CIA called 'an undeclared war', 26 different federal agencies were authorised to 'go to source' and hold states accountable for the terrorism they sponsored.[75]

Apart from the raid on Libya (1986), which was a punishment for Qaddafi's indirect promotion of terrorism against US forces in Europe, perhaps the most symbolic response to the threat of terrorism came in October 1983 when an old Second World War battleship, the USS *Jersey* bombarded the Chouf mountains with its 16-inch guns in a vain attempt to dislodge the Druze militia. As the Long Commissioin reported the following year, the only explanation it could volunteer for the bizarre decision to send a US peacekeeping force to the Lebanon in the first place, was that Washington had wanted to prove to itself, it not the outside world, that it was possible to meet terrorism with force.[76]

For good or ill, Reagan came to power determined to reassert US military power, to re-engage the Soviet Union by returning to containment. Some saw the reassertion as an affirmation of strength, of self-confidence, of a deep-seated wish to return to the verities of the past. Others saw it as a confession of weakness, a loss of confidence in the non-military instruments of influence, the mark of an imperialist not imperial power that needed to intervene because it could no longer adjust to changing events and fluctuating historical patterns as readily as it had in the past. One contemporary observer believed the United States had chosen to 'lock itself into a strategically unfavourable position' by treating radical change in the Third World as a central test of US credibility.[77]

Whatever interpretation one wishes to apply, it is possible to argue that Reagan stumbled upon the secret of successful containment, an effective means of using force without cost to the body politic, or even the national treasury. His preferred method was not to intervene himself, but to force the Soviet Union onto the defensive. He also found it cheaper to use proxies such as South Africa and Israel to destabilise the Soviet Union's clients in Southern Africa and the Middle East.

Forcing the Soviet Union onto the defensive was a strategy that would probably have commended itself to any administration in 1981, if only because it was critically overextended. It cost the United States only $250 million a year in military aid to the Afghan rebels to tie down 100,000 Soviet troops in Afghanistan. It cost only $27 million a year to support UNITA to tie down 30–50,000 Cuban troops in Angola who might have found employment elsewhere. In Central America its policy was less rewarding, but not entirely unfruitful. Between 1981 and 1987 the United States spent only $200 million on the Contras, a sum insufficient to topple the Sandanista regime, but significant enough to cripple the economy and undermine popular support for the Sandanista cause. From $150 million, manufacturing exports fell to $20 million. The country's economy had to sustain an army of 70,000 men (compared with Somoza's National Guard of only 15,000). In the end the Contras were abandoned by Congress when aid was finally terminated in February 1987. By then, however, the Sandanistas had lost the key to political control: economic coercion. They remained putschists, not the true Marxist revolutionaries they had aspired to become.

To the extent that the Soviet Union did not intervene anywhere else in the world after 1979, the United States can be said to have successfully contained its opponent; although to what extent the Russians were deterred from intervening by Reagan's actions or their own assessment of their predicament will remain a matter of historical debate.

The use of proxies was more controversial, as well as more questionable. In the Middle East Reagan initially wanted a strategic partnership with Israel in September 1981, an offer that the Israelis refused, as they did again in November 1983. They had no wish to become too entangled in the United States' embrace. They also found the very idea of a US rapid deployment force based in Israel, or an Israeli force subsidised by the United States as implausible as the Arabs found it threatening. The Americans did, however, double military aid to Israel immediately before the invasion of the southern Lebanon in 1982, and then tacitly support the drive across the Litani river into the heart of Beirut in the hope of 'taking out' the Palestine Liberation Organisation (PLO) as well as Syria, the Soviet Union's two principal clients in the region.[78]

In southern Africa the United States also offered a strategic partnership with Pretoria in 1981, an offer which was also declined.[79] It was significant, however, that in the same year the South Africans began to attack the Angolan army for the first time, instead of SWAPO training camps in the south of the country, as a way of destabilising the Soviet Union's major ally in the region. The methods used by the two countries were much the same, whether it was the United States destabilisation of Nicaragua, or South Africa's destabilisation of Angola. Only their objectives differed. For South Africa destabilisation became an end in itself; for the United States it was intended to be a means to an end, to bring the Sandanistas to the conference table.

Only the near collapse of the government at home in the Irangate scandal (1986), and the rising budget deficit, which required a major retrenchment in defence spending, forced the Reagan administration in its second term in office to look again at the possibility of *détente* with the Soviet Union. The most successful promoter of the United States' past appeared to offer something new, this time not only arms control, but arms reduction in the form of the Washington Treaty on intermediate nuclear forces in December 1987.

THE LAST RETREAT?: THE RETURN TO *DÉTENTE*

The decision to engage in a dialogue with the Soviet Union was not, in fact, forced on the United States as much as the last comment may suggest. On arriving in the Pentagon in 1981 Caspar Weinberger had said, 'if the move from Cold war to *détente* was progress we can't afford more progress.'[80] By 1986 the United States had a greater understanding of the limitations of Soviet power, and less fear of it realising its own ambitions. Like *Détente* 1, *Détente* 2 was founded on a more realistic understanding that the USSR was not behind every crisis or revolution that occurred in the world. Like Kissinger, Schultz came to the conclusion that even its opportunities to exploit them were fast disappearing.

Brzezinski's own change of mind was symbolically captured when his institute at Columbia changed its name from the Research Institute on International Communism to the Research Institute for International Change. Reagan felt happier in entering into a dialogue with the USSR after 1986, in part because he recognised how little the world had changed since coming to power, in part because he recognised that the Soviet Union was not well placed to derive any immediate advantage from the changes that had taken place.

The neo-conservatives had been unhappy with Reagan anyway for failing to live up to the promise he had held out in 1981.[81] Not only had there been no roll-back, no sanctions of note against the Soviet Union, no attempt to challenge Soviet control of Eastern Europe, as his climb-down over the gas pipeline dispute with the Europeans had shown, the United States had even abandoned the propaganda war which, at least, had been endorsed by John Foster Dulles. The deputy programme director of the Voice of America who had wanted to 'destabilise' the Soviet Union and its satellites by promoting 'disaffection between people and rulers' was soon forced to resign. The administration even failed to produce any evidence for its claim that the Soviet Union had sponsored international terrorism. By default the charge had to be withdrawn.[82]

It came as no surprise, therefore, that early in 1985 Reagan went far beyond Dulles, even Kissinger, offering joint management of regional security, excluding the Middle East, in a speech to the UN General Assembly. But then he could afford to. Unlike Kissinger, Reagan was operating from a position of strength, not weakness. Despite the popular appeal of Gorbachev, the United States held most of the cards.

Far from offering the Soviet Union a veto over US actions in the Third World, the United States offered to ease the pain of disengagement from Afghanistan and Angola. In 1969 the United States had been deeply engaged in Vietnam, while tacitly supporting a string of Third World dictatorships against left-wing forces. In the 1970s fourteen countries produced coups or revolutions which brought left-of-centre governments to power. In the 1980s the Soviet Union found itself defending Marxist regimes from national liberation movements funded or supported by the United States. As Fred Halliday noted at the time the United States had learned to finesse upheavals in the Philippines, to contain them in El Salvador, to defeat them in Grenada. The Soviet Union, by comparison, was saddled with a string of weak, precarious allies, ridden by factional disputes and economic distress. It may not have abandoned military support for its allies, but it certainly evinced little interest in helping other regimes come to power.

In addition, the Reagan administration remained totally committed to military superiority over the USSR. The Strategic Defense Initiative (SDI) was not negotiated away, as some neo-conservatives feared. From Reykjavik to Washington the Americans refused to bargain it away for an arms control treaty, even an agreement on strategic nuclear weapons (START). The INF Treaty, while disastrous for the Europeans, was a triumph for the hardliners in Washington who wished to dilute extended deterrence, while concentrating on a qualitative conventional arms race which would enable the United States to confine a war to Europe, and prevail on the battlefield without recourse to nuclear weapons. At $350 million a day the NATO commitment might be expensive; but for the Soviet Union the Warsaw Pact commitment was more expensive still.

Even Gorbachev's acceptance of an interdependent world threatened Soviet interests, not those of the United States, since the only country which could determine whether the Soviet Union would be allowed to play an active role in the world economy was America. Washington held the key to the transfer of technology on which the success of *perestroika* depended. It also held the majority of votes in organisations such as the International Monetary Fund which Gorbachev hinted the Soviet Union might wish to join. For the Russians interdependence was based on regular agreements between states; for the Americans the concept played down the role of states, and played up the role of market and other transnational factors, factors which while not entirely under US control, were still determined by the decisions taken by US governments in the commodity and currency markets of the world.

In his book *Rethinking US-Soviet Relations* George Liska concluded, 'The time has come for the United States as it faces the advent of the Twenty- first century to develop an authentically American outlook on US-Soviet relations.'[83] Perhaps, for the moment, the most it can aspire to is 'self-containment' on the part of the Soviet Union in which it will be bribed or suborned into acting as the West wishes, a policy which George Schultz, borrowing a phrase of Brzezinski's, termed 'contestation' (a contest in which the rules of play are fairly narrowly defined).[84]

It is clear, however, why Liska wishes to pursue a US course, why he shares a sense of implicit guilt with Dulles and even Kissinger that more has not been achieved despite 40 years of endeavour, that the United States has still failed in its main purpose. It is the guilt felt by an elite that can neither oppose containment, nor surrender to it completely. In periods of crisis or change, the moral dilemmas facing an elite that has always prided itself on its moral leadership must indeed be acute.

CONTAINMENT IN RETROSPECT

In the final instance there cannot be an 'authentic' US approach to relations with the Soviet Union, if by authentic one means a relationship based on the past. The history of the United States until recently was a demonstration in historical terms of the validity of the hopeful legend, the legend of the second chance. Where the Old World had failed, the New would succeed. As Dean Acheson wrote in his memoirs: 'In a sense the post-war years were a period of creation for the ordering of which I shared with others some responsibility.' 'The American Adam' has had his chance, and failed. The creation is over. Both superpowers are now experiencing the Fall, exhausted by their labours, their energies spent, their enthusiasm no longer able to sustain them.

It is not difficult to understand, when one phrases the problem of containment in this way, why so many Americans fear they will have no policy at all if the Cold War were to break out again, if Gorbachev were to fail, or fall. In part, the problem is an old one, in part it is quite new. It is old because the United States has spent 40 years or longer in an agonising self-appraisal. Has it defined the Soviet challenge correctly? Has it done what it should to reassure the Soviet Union of its peaceful intentions? Have the Europeans done enough in terms of burden-sharing to justify the continued presence of the Seventh Army in Europe, whose presence ten years after its original deployment Eisenhower insisted would mark NATO's failure, not its success? This persistent self-questioning is both debilitating and self-defeating. As Nietzsche once remarked, if you look into the abyss long enough it will swallow you up.

The problem has been further compounded by a reluctance to explain to the American people what is being defended, except in terms of the society the Soviet Union used to be. Today as Soviet society changes it seems hard for US politicians to transcend the thought world of Flaubert's two troglodytes, Bouvard and Pécuchet. Flaubert's novel may not offer much of a guide to political behaviour but it does convey one simple and indispensable message: that the nicer one's intentions are, the more essential it is to avoid being intensely silly.

There is another problem, however, which is far more serious because it is also new, a problem of political identity. The United States has begun to falter in its sense of purpose in its negotiations with the Soviet Union and its relations with its European allies because it no longer knows what it stands for. It has no real sense of purpose or direction. If the United States no longer believes it can redeem the world, if the world is no longer in need of redemption, then what is its mission, what is its historical role? What does the United States stand for if not for the 'second chance'? If the Americans do not know the answer, how can their allies be expected to?

It is an ironic fate for a country locked in an ideological struggle with an adversary. In the fundamental question of the age, the US–Soviet relationship, the American belief system has previously not been so very different in its intensity from the Soviet. As Louis Hartz once argued, American pragmatism has been deceptive because it has rested 'on miles of submerged conviction'. The United States may not have subscribed to an ideology as such, but the past represented a value system which was ideologically pragmatic, or 'dogmatically undogmatic' as Brzezinski preferred to call it. The past was central to the United States' belief in itself. For all the doubts Dulles and others expressed about containment, it gave them at least a sense of purpose, it signalled a direction, even if it was not liberation but something which fell well short of it. Today the United States is no longer sustained by the past. The country has renounced its mission, and yet failed to don new clothes. The historical nemesis which Reagan's return to *détente* signified may be good news for the world if the Cold War really is at an end, but bad news indeed if it is far from over.

The United States' neo-conservatives, the last upholders of the past, have meanwhile found themselves out in the cold, dismissed as crude neophytes, reduced to writing of the Soviet threat in journals such as *Commentary* and *The National Review*, names which are unlikely to cause excitement in Middle America. Their articles, however plausible on first reading, are even more unlikely to be discussed in the offices of Wall Street, or the embassies of Massachusetts Avenue. In continuing to invoke the past they are largely addressing themselves. In forgetting how to engage in a real debate with the American people, they have finally made the past what it was never before, 'a foreign country', a land in which they find themselves prophets without honour, whose 'writing on the wall' is now considered not even a cruel forgery, but mere graffiti.

NOTES

1. Dean Acheson, *Present at the Creation* (New York: W. W. Norton, 1969) p. 728.

2. *New York Times* (23 April 1975).
3. George Kennan (X), 'The sources of Soviet conduct', *Foreign Affairs* (July 1947).
4. Despatch from Moscow September 1944, *Foreign Relations of the United States*, vol. 5 (1945) (Washington DC: Department of State, 1967).
5. Nicolai Tolstoy, *Stalin's Secret War* (London: Jonathan Cape, 1981) p. 357.
6. Milovan Djilas, *Conversations with Stalin* (London: Rupert Hart-Davis, 1962) pp. 165-6.
7. Cited in Joseph Barber, *Diplomacy and the Communist Challenge* (New York: Council for Foreign Relations, 1954) p. 39.
8. George Kennan, *American Diplomacy 1900-50* (Chicago: University of Chicago Press, 1951) p. 95.
9. Joseph Jones, *The Fifteen Weeks 21 February-5 June 1947* (New York: Harcourt Brace, 1955) p. 259.
10. George Kennan, *Russia, the Atom and the West (Reith Lectures, 1957)* (Oxford: Oxford University Press, 1958).
11. George Kennan, *Memoirs op. cit.*, p. 365.
12. *ibid.*, pp. 358-63.
13. Cf. MacArthur in 1944, 'We made the same old mistake of intervening in European quarrels which we couldn't hope to solve because they are insoluble – Europe is a dying system. It is worn out and run down.' Koen Rossay, *The China Lobby in American Politics* (New York: Macmillan, 1960) p. 12 with his testimony to Congress during the Korean War, 'If we lose the war to communism in Asia, the fall of Europe is inevitable.' Cited in William Reitzel, *US Foreign Policy 1945-55* (Washington DC: Brookings Institution, 1956) p. 279.
14. Roger Dingman, 'American policy and strategy in East Asia 1898-1950's: the creation of a commitment', in Joe Dixon (ed.), *The American Military and the Far East* (Washington DC: USGPO, 1980) p. 32.
15. Stephen Ambrose, *Rise to Globalism: American foreign policy 1938-70* (London: Pelican, 1971) pp. 190-1.
16. NSC 68, 'US objectives and Programmes for National Security', 14 April 1950, *Foreign Relations of the United States 1950*, vol. 1 (Washington DC: US Department of State) p. 240.
17. Ralph Gabriel, *The Rampart we Guard* (New York: 1950) pp. 107-8.
18. Leo Labedtz, 'The two minds of George Kennan; how to unlearn from Empire', in Leo Labedtz, *The Use and Abuse of Sovietology: essays critical and polemical*, ed. Melvin Lasky Survey 30:1/2 (March 1988) p. 224.
19. W. K. Fergusson, *The Renaissance in Historical Thought: five centuries of interpretation* (Boston: 1948) p. 388.
20. George Kennan, *The Cloud of Danger: some current problems of American foreign policy* (New York: Little, Brown, 1979) p. 112.
21. T. S. Kuhn, *The Structure of Scientific Revolutions* (London: Collins, 1970) p. 111.
22. John Girling, *America and the Third World: revolution and intervention* (London: Routledge & Kegan Paul, 1980) p. 232, n. 17.

23. Nancy Tucker, *Patterns in the Dust: Chinese-American relations and the recognition controversy 1949-50* (New York: Columbia University Press, 1983).
24. Cited in Steel, *Pax Americana* (New York: Viking Press, 1967) p. 129.
25. I have relied heavily in this section on Bruce Cummings, *Origins of the Korean War* (Princeton, NJ: Princeton University Press, 1981); see also Cummings (ed.), *Child of Conflict: the Korea-America relationship 1943-53* (Seattle: University of Washington Press, 1983).
26. Peter Lowe, *The Origins of the Korean War* (London: Longman, 1986) p. 213.
27. Cited in Christopher Bartlett, *The Rise and Fall of the Pax Americana:US foreign policy in the twentieth century* (London: Paul Elek, 1974) p. 124.
28. *ibid.,* p. 127.
29. Andrew Berding, *Dulles on Diplomacy* (Princeton, NJ: Princeton University Press, 1965) p. 103.
30. Edwin Rozwenc and Kenneth Lindfors, *Containment and the Origins of the Cold War* (Boston: Heath, 1967) p. 67.
31. Richard Goold-Adams, *The Time of Power: a re-appraisal of John Foster Dulles* (London: Weidenfeld and Nicolson, 1962) p. 80.
32. Bennet Korvig, *The Myth of Liberation: East-Central European US diplomacy and politics since 1941* (Baltimore: Johns Hopkins University Press, 1973) p. 114.
33. Colin Gray, *The Geo-politics of Superpower* (Lexington: University of Kentucky Press, 1988). Dynamic containment involves 'the organisation and where necessary the arming of actual and potential resistance around the Rimlands of Eurasia', 'aiding and abetting local elements among Soviet clients who wish to reverse the course of their incorporation into the socialist commonwealth'.
34. Cited in Korvig, *The Myth of Liberation, op. cit.,* p. 118.
35. John R. Beal, *John Foster Dulles* (New York: Harper & Row, 1959) p. 314.
36. Ambrose, *The Rise to Globalism, op. cit.,* p. 164.
37. Daniel Boorstein (ed.), *An American Primer* (New York: American Library, 1966) p. 223.
38. John Foster Dulles, 'The new policy of the struggle with international Communism', *DSB* 33:860 (19 December 1955) p. 1006.
39. Frank A. Ninkovich, *Diplomacy of Ideas: US foreign policy and cultural relations 1938-50* (Cambridge: Cambridge University Press, 1981) p. 72.
40. John Foster Dulles, 'The United Nations: a Prospectus', *Foreign Affairs* 24:1 (1945), p. 3.
41. Ole Holst, 'Cognitive dynamics and images of the enemy: Dulles and Russia', in D. J. Finlay and O. Holsti (eds), *Enemies in Politics* (Chicago: Rand McNally, 1967) p. 47.
42. *ibid.,* p. 83.
43. Ambrose, *Rise to American Globalism,* p. 158.
44. *Bulletin of Atomic Scientists* (January 1957) pp. 2-7.
45. Henry Kissinger, 'Address before the Sixth Special Session of the UN General Assembly', *Department of State News Release* (15 April 1974) p. 1.

46. R. E. Walters, *The Nuclear Trap: an escape route* (London: Penguin, 1974) p. 43.
47. John Lewis Gaddis, *The Long Peace: inquiries into the history of the Cold War* (Oxford: Oxford University Press, 1988).
48. Cited in Donald L. Hafner, 'Ronald Reagan's European policy', in Morton Kaplan (ed.), *Global Policy: challenges of the '80's* (Washington DC: Institute of Values in Public Policy, 1984) p. 93.
49. Henry Kissinger, 'Statement of US–Soviet relations', News Release of the Bureau of Public Affairs, Department of State, *Office of Media Services Special Report* (19 September 1973).
50. Coral Bell, *The Diplomacy of Détente* (London: Martin Robertson, 1976) p. 5.
51. Theodore Draper, 'Appeasement or *Détente*?' *Commentary* 61:3 (February 1976) p. 33.
52. Stanley Hoffman, *Primacy or World Order: American foreign policy since the Cold War* (New York: McGraw Hill, 1978) p. 87.
53. Vernon Aspurturian, 'Soviet global power and the correlation of forces', *Problems of Communism* 29 (May–June 1980) p. 9.
54. George Kennan, *Memoirs*, vol. 2, op. cit., pp. 561–3.
55. Henry Kissinger, *American Foreign Policy: three essays* (London: Weidenfeld and Nicolson, 1969) p. 74.
56. See for example Henry Kissinger, 'Speech 22 July 1976', *Department of State Bulletin* 75 (August 1976) p. 217.
57. Peter Dickson, *Kissinger and the Meaning of History* (Cambridge: Cambridge University Press, 1974) p. 186.
58. ibid., p. 152.
59. ibid., p. 154.
60. Henry Kissinger, *A World Restored* (New York: Grosset and Dunlop, 1964) p. 329.
61. Charles Beard, 'Written History as an act of faith', *American Historical Review* 39:2 (1934); reprinted in H. Meyerhoff (ed.), *The Philosophy of History in Our Time* (New York: Doubleday, 1959) p. 151.
62. Dickson, *Kissinger and the Meaning of History*, op. cit., p. 23.
63. ibid., p. 86.
64. ibid., p. 84.
65. John Lewis Gaddis, *Strategies of Containment: a critical appraisal of post-war American national security* (Oxford: Oxford University Press, 1982) p. 146.
66. Cited in Jerel Rosati, *The Carter Administration's Quest for Global Community: beliefs and their impact on behaviour* (Columbia: University of South Carolina Press, 1987) p. 64.
67. Ronald Reagan, 'Address before the Annual Convention of American Society of Newspaper Editors' (Washington DC: 10 April 1980).
68. Jeane Kirkpatrick, *The Reagan Phenomenon and Other Speeches on Foreign Policy* (Washington DC: American Enterprise Institute, 1983) p. 14.
69. Cited in Ivan Volgyes, 'The Soviet Union and Eastern Europe: old truths, new myths and permanent realities', in David P. Forsythe (ed.), *American Foreign*

Policy in an Uncertain World (Lincoln: University of Nebraska Press, 1984) p. 292.
70. *New York Times* (15 March 1986).
71. *Country Reports on Human Rights Practises for 1982*, Report submitted to Congress February 1983 (Washington DC: USGPO, 1983).
72. George Schultz, 'Address before the 86th annual Washington Banquet of the Crowe Club, Illinois', *Peoria* 27 (February 1984) p. 222, in David Newsom (ed.), *The Diplomacy of Human Rights* (New York: University Press of America, 1986).
73. See Christopher Coker, *NATO, the Warsaw Pact and Africa* (London: Macmillan, 1985) p. 110.
74. Robert Oakley, 'International Terrorism: current trends and US responses', *Department of State Current Policy* 706 (15 May 1985) (Washington DC: Department of State, 1985).
75. Michael Stohl and George Lopez (eds), *The State as Terrorist: the dynamics of governmental violence and repression* (Westport: Greenwood Press, 1984).
76. Fred Halliday, 'The Reagan administration and the Middle East', *Atlantic Quarterly*, 2:3 (Autumn 1984) p. 231.
77. Kenneth Oye, 'International systems structure and American foreign policy', in Oye and Lieber, *Eagle Defiant: US foreign policy in the 1980's* (Boston: Little, Brown, 1983).
78. Halliday, *Reagan Administration and the Middle East, op. cit.,* p. 229.
79. See Christopher Coker, *The United States and South Africa 1968–85: constructive engagement and its critics* (Durham, NC: Duke University Press, 1986) p. 225.
80. *The Observer* (12 April 1981).
81. See Norman Podhoretz, 'The neo-conservative anguish over Reagan', *New York Times Magazine* (2 May 1982); George Will, *Newsweek* (21 June 1982). Both were mindful of Brzezinski's caveat that 'a stand is not a policy'.
82. *New York Times* (9 February 1981).
83. George Liska, *Rethinking US–Soviet Relations* (Oxford: Basil Blackwell, 1987) p. 211.
84. *New York Times* (31 October 1985).

4. Squaring the error: the lessons of the Vietnam War[1]

'We are the Romans of the modern world – the great assimilating people. Conflicts and conquests are, of course, necessary accidents with us . . . Our army sword is the short, stiff, pointed *gladius* of the Romans; and the American bowie knife is the same too, modified to meet the daily wants of civil society. I announce at this table an axiom not to be found in Montesquieu or the journals of Congress – the race that shortens its weapons lengthens its boundaries. Corollary – it was the Polish lance that left Poland at last with nothing of her own to bound.'

Oliver Wendell Holmes, *The Autocrat of the Breakfast Table*

'In the course of the evening the conversation turned to the war in the United States. "There they are," said Carlyle, "cutting each other's throats because one half prefer hiring their servants for life and the other half by the hour."'

Thomas Carlyle, in Grant draft *Notes*, volume 1

During the 1950s, the United States looked with horror upon the thought of fighting another Korean-style war. Never again, Eisenhower promised the American people, would the nation be asked 'to fight a white man's war in Asia'. That the United States chose to fight another such engagement after 1965 was largely due to Kennedy's almost messianic redemptionism, his vision of the new frontier, his call on the American people to 'pay any cost' for the price of freedom. In his inspiring inauguration address Kennedy struck a redemptionist note that alas came to realisation. The less inspirational Lyndon Johnson also found his vocation as Vice-President on a visit to Saigon in 1961. 'In the faces of the crowds that massed' to see him 'he thought he saw the love and admiration of the common man.' 'Here in Asia', wrote Anthony Austin, 'he personified the United States of America in the fateful act of turning its eyes from the Atlantic to the Pacific.'[2] It was an image which was never to leave him.

Kennedy went into Vietnam arguing that the United States had no other motive than the defence of freedom. Later he insisted that no nation raised in freedom could be oblivious to the freedom of others. After Kennedy's death Johnson re-emphasised America's commitment in precisely the same terms. Adding that the failure of the United States in the 1930s had been a failure of the spirit, not the sword, he declared that he would not permit such a failure during his tenure in the White House.[3]

At the height of the Vietnam War Dean Rusk reminded the American people that while other states had interests, they had responsibilities. Rather forlornly one writer at the time entitled the chapter of a book 'The revolt against obligation'.[4] The United States found its mission in south-east Asia. It also discovered, like St Teresa of Avila, that more tears are shed over answered prayers than unanswered ones.

FANFARE FOR THE COMMON MAN

Bewildered, the Americans returned to containment in 1961 with the past very much in mind. They could only judge between competing claims on resources, or choose between divergent roles in terms of historical constructs of their own making. History, of course, was more influential when allied with political expediency; expediency was more acceptable when sanctioned by history. So prolific had these material considerations become that the United States had difficulty balancing commitments and costs. For once it found the sum of expediency beyond calculation.

In his inauguration address Kennedy spoke of the United States as a 'watchman on the wall of world freedom'. It was a vivid if disturbing metaphor suggesting an empire that was for ever keeping an enemy at bay. It was more disturbing still because it suggested that without an enemy the United States would lack a sense of mission, a conclusion which brings to mind Cavafy's poem 'Waiting for the Barbarians' (1904):

> . . . night has fallen and the barbarians haven't come
> And some of our men just in from the border say
> There are no barbarians any longer.
>
> Now what's going to happen to us without barbarians?
> They were, those people, a kind of solution.[5]

Kennedy knew who the enemy was; he wasn't sure of its most likely form of attack. He found the answer in a speech given by Nkita Khruschev on 6 January 1961, in which counter-insurgency and anti-Communism became inextricably interlinked. Khruschev's unequivocal support of national liberation movements so impressed him that he sent a copy of his speech to every government department and every US embassy in the world. Inevitably, this created the impression that every guerrilla organisation was

Soviet run and funded, a party, wittingly or not, to a global conspiracy to challenge the West. The obvious response was an open-ended commitment to 'pay any price' to prevail, to struggle through and win. As General Maxwell Taylor informed the Senate Foreign Relations Committee in 1966, the Johnson administration, like its predecessor, intended to 'show that the war of liberation . . . is costly, dangerous and doomed to fail'.[6] It was on that understanding that the United States chose to fight another 'white man's war' in Asia.

The decision met with criticism both before the event, as well as after it. Just as he had criticised the Truman doctrine, Walter Lippmann attacked Lyndon Johnson for allowing himself to be 'chivied into making public declarations about our willingness and readiness to fight a great war in hypothetical and undefined circumstances'.[7] Like many critics once the war had begun in earnest Lippmann believed the United States would never have committed itself to the struggle if it had known the price of its eventual involvement. As Kissinger later chided President Thieu the United States had chosen to expend $300 billion (in 1982 prices) in defence of a country that was not even a member of the Free World.

In Vietnam the Americans also found themselves defending yet another suspect regime, a 'government authoritarian enough to be unpopular, democratic enough to be inefficient',[8] a fact which had been known to the Eisenhower administration long before Vietnam became more than a distant shadow on the horizon of America's consciousness. Instead of holding elections in 1956 as agreed at the Geneva Conference Diem had called instead for a vote between himself and the French appointed emperor Bao Dai, a decision which was endorsed by a rising young Senator, Jack Kennedy. Diem won 98.8 per cent of the vote, winning more votes in Saigon than there were registered voters. It was a tactic which seems to have caught Kennedy's eye and that of Richard Daley for it was employed in Chicago to put Kennedy ahead in the 1960 Presidential race.

The question was whether reform was necessary to defeat the Vietcong, or perhaps more to the point, whether the Americans had any real understanding of what reform involved. As Henry Cabot Lodge, the US ambassador to Saigon, wrote to Kennedy in September 1963, finding a way to reform a Third World regime 'would be one of the greatest discoveries since the enactment of the Marshall Plan . . . because as far as I know the United States has as yet to control any of the very unsatisfactory governments through which we have to work'.[9]

Unfortunately, there were no social scientists who could realise Kennedy's new frontier, or help Johnson to export the Tennessee River Project to the Mekong Delta. The Americans found a society that was singularly impervious to their own aspirations. When the US Army discovered that political accommodations were being made in the Mekong Delta between the local population, the government and the Communists, which suited the interests of all because it helped to contain violence at an acceptable level, they brought such agreements to an abrupt end. The very idea of accommodation with the enemy lay outside the United States' imagination. Accommodation militated against the very idea of winning which was the sole reason the US Army was there.[10]

In the early days the Americans found even the reform programme they urged on Saigon was disingenuous if not counter-productive, because it gave rise to expectations neither party could meet. The degree of government control over the countryside was related to four indicators of land-tenure inequality: the percentage of owner-operated land, the distribution of landholdings, the proportion of land subject to transfer under Diem's land reform programme and the percentage of land formerly owned by the French. To their surprise they found that from the point of view of government control the ideal province was one in which few peasants farmed their own land, in which land distribution was unequal, in which no land distribution had taken place, and in which large French landholdings had existed in the past.[11]

In his book *The Economics of Insurgency in the Mekong Delta* (1970) Robert Sanson found many US officials were unwilling to admit that land reform programmes had aroused support not for the government, but for the Vietcong, with their promises of greater land redistribution to come.[12] As early as 1952 Graham Greene had written of Pyle, a disingenuous agent of the American dream, the 'Quiet American' who had come to Vietnam to channel aid to a mythical Third Force, to save south-east Asia from the insidious threat of Communism. As Greene's hero reminds Pyle the problem with militant individualism was that it offered no defence against Communism. The only man who was prepared to treat the peasant in the paddy field as an individual was the political commissar, a man who in promising sound justice, not freedom, accepted that the peasant had value as a person: 'it's they who stand for the individual, and we just stand for Private 23987, a unit in the global strategy.'[13]

The social scientists who flooded to Vietnam in the 1960s, were in Greene's eyes comedians, who had no faith but enthusiasm, whose agents, if they lost their lives, did so by accident like Pyle. In his description of another American client state, Duvalier's Haiti, Greene expressed himself more forcefully still:

The rootless have experienced, like all the others the temptation of sharing the security of a religious creed or a political faith, and for some reason we have turned the temptation down. We are the faithless, we admire the dedicated ... for their courage and their integrity, for their fidelity to a cause, but through timidity, or through lack of sufficient zeal, we find ourselves the only ones truly committed –

committed to the whole world of evil and good, to the wise and the foolish, to the indifferent and the mistaken.

As it happened where the social scientists failed in their attempts at social engineering, the US Army succeeded by default. By 1982 90 per cent of the countryside compared with 33 per cent in 1965 had been pacified, officially cleared of Vietcong insurgents, a crude but significant index of the United States' success.

What won the villagers over to the government in the end was not land reform but the sheer extent of military spending, which boosted rural income to a level it had never reached before. As Popkin discovered in the eighteen villages he studied, the income earned from rural pacification programmes: the building of bridges, roads and railways had enabled the peasant to reinvest his surplus crop for the first time in Vietnamese history. In addition the mechanisation of irrigation also enabled him to grow two crops a year instead of one, giving rise to a standard of living which was threatened only by the operations of the Vietcong.[14] The campaign to win the hearts and minds of the peasants had been won. In 1975 when the North Vietnamese launched their final offensive the army, instead of deserting to the other side, melted away into the countryside. No cheering crowds greeted the victorious North Vietnamese forces as they made their way south to Saigon.

Why then did the United States lose the war? Why on the military front did it fail while on the political front it succeeded? The reasons are many, and tell us a great deal about the extent to which the Americans as a nation were largely influenced by their past.

THE MILITARY PHILOSOPHERS

One of the reasons why Kennedy believed it possible to fight another Asian war, despite the experience of Korea, was the extent to which US military thinking was influenced by a new strategic doctrine in the late 1950s, that of limited war. It was a doctrine which emerged from the think-tanks and universities, the breeding-ground of what Arthur Waskow told the American Historical Association in 1967 was a new political class 'defined more by its relation to the means of total destruction than by its relation to the means of production'.[15] To Adam Yarmolinsky, MacNamara's principal Assistant Secretary of Defense, the theory of limited war 'made military solutions to our foreign policy problems more available and even more attractive' than had been the case hitherto.

At the same time the United States created a military infrastructure – a mobile fighting force with the ability to project military power at very short notice. Logistically, Vietnam was a much easier theatre of operations for the military than Korea. In 1950 it had taken US troops two weeks to reach Korea. It was a further month before the US Central Reserve arrived. In 1961 Robert MacNamara, Kennedy's new Defense Secretary, pushed through a series of rapid deployment programmes which included the procurement of the C5 transport plane, the construction of 1,400 new airstrips around the world, and the purchase of the F4, a combat aircraft which could be flown to Vietnam in 72 hours.

Unfortunately as a military philosophy, limited war had three grave flaws, which bedevilled its application from the very beginning. To begin with it was not limited for the people who were its principal victims: the non-belligerents on both sides. The United States had been spared bombing in the Second World War; as a result it was largely oblivious to its consequences for the civilian population. In that sense it was not racism which made it indifferent to civilian losses but historical misperception. The Americans were not victims of groupthink, but group thoughtlessness. Explaining why US soldiers had obliterated the municipality of Bentres with great loss of civilian life, an army major replied, 'It became necessary to destroy the town in order to save it.'[16] In the end the Americans were simply insensitive to the havoc they created.

In the late 1950s the distinguished political scientist Robert Osgood had even talked of using tactical nuclear weapons in underdeveloped societies such as south-east Asia where there were few major urban areas and a comparatively unsophisticated local economy.[17] During the Vietnam War the United States did not use tactical nuclear weapons, but it did use a weapon which had appalling effects: napalm. In the course of a single military operation in the Mekong Delta in 1968 US forces killed 5,000 civilians. America's pacification programmes also created 3 million refugees who, unlike Popkin's 'rational peasants', were soon won over to the Communist side. Where Communist propaganda had failed, the US military succeeded.

Second, limited wars were intended to limit the number of American casualties, an important political consideration given the fact that drafted soldiers, not regulars, were involved in much of the fighting. When the number of US troops rose to 625,000, the generals tried to limit their own casualties by maximising the number of casualties on the other side – by the use of technology – the new weapons about which American strategists had written so enthusiastically in the late 1950s. General Westmoreland created 'free fire zones' in which 7 million tons of bombs were dropped as the War progressed, or three times the tonnage of bombs the USAF had dropped during the Second World War. Clearly 'limited' war was a relative concept. In the end, Westmoreland talked not of 'battlefields' but 'integrated area control zones', which were as dehumanising for the US Army as they were for the people unfortunate enough to be trapped in them.

In the Second World War the USAF had dropped only 30 per cent of its bombs on the civilian population, preferring instead to come to grips with the enemy force – tactics which Wendell Holmes had recommended as a *sine qua non* of military success. During the Korean War the Air Force dropped 70 per cent of its bombs on civilians. In Vietnam it dropped 90 per cent – largely to conserve American lives. The only result was that it lost the war in the living-rooms of American television viewers.

The reluctance to send troops into battle was one of the most notable features of the Vietnam War. Although no fewer than seven divisions were deployed in 1968, as well as 63 artillery battalions, very few men actually saw combat, less than 80,000 in all. At the peak of the war the Air Force flew 300 sorties a day, the Marine Corps another 220, yet to reduce losses from gunfire pilots were forbidden to bomb at altitudes of less than 3,500 feet. Inevitably the innocent were killed in far greater numbers than the belligerents in the field.[18]

Finally, limited war was the option of an 'absolute' war society, a nuclear power denied an opportunity to use nuclear weapons. Unfortunately, Saigon was not fighting a limited war any more than was Hanoi. 220,357 South Vietnamese soldiers were killed and a further 570,000 wounded in defence of their country. North Vietnam went further still. It fought a total war in which it lost 600,000 of its citizens or 3 per cent of its pre-war population. As it happens this was a higher percentage than the Japanese lost in the Second World War (1.4 per cent), a nation that was considered so fanatical that rather than risk invading the island the United States chose to drop the bomb.

The Americans failed to recognise that the home front in Hanoi was even more crucial to a successful outcome than the home front in Washington. From the first they failed to recognise that the North Vietnamese leadership, or the war party led by the party's First Secretary Le Duan could not afford to 'lose' South Vietnam and retire to the country, as Acheson had 'lost' China in 1949 only to write his own account of the event twenty years later. If they had lost Le Duan and his supporters would not have survived.

Every negotiation by the North, in other words, was merely a tactic used to wittle away the United States' resolve. There were 2,000 such initiatives on the US side between 1965 and 1968 before Hanoi finally agreed to attend the Paris Peace Talks under pressure from Moscow. Even then the talks were never taken very seriously by the North Vietnamese. Under the terms of the eventual 1973 Treaty the United States agreed to pull out all troops from the South without insisting on a reciprocal promise that the North Vietnamese would follow their example. Until the documents are published we shall never know whether Nixon and Kissinger really believed the Peace

Treaty would buy time for Saigon to build up its defences, or whether they saw it as providing the United States with a 'decent interval' in which to disengage.

Clearly, however, the United States lost the battle of wills from the outset. A day after sending ground troops to Vietnam, in a speech at Johns Hopkins University, Johnson offered to buy off the North Vietnamese if they desisted from their aggression. This US form of Danegeld was hardly likely to influence the outcome except to convince the North that all it had to do was hold on. As Harry Summers observed, MacNamara, who as Secretary of Defense was the equivalent of the General-in-Chief and Admiral-in-Chief of the Armed Forces in earlier conflicts, never understood the critical importance of will, 'perhaps, because it could not be programmed into a computer'. When he later admitted that as early as 1965 he thought the war was militarily unwinnable, it was obvious his will had been broken before the massive US involvement in Vietnam even began.[19]

THROUGH A GLASS DARKLY

The questions raised by the concept of limited war threw into relief three fundamental problems about 'the American way of warfare'. The first, and probably most crucial, was that it flouted the very US tradition of war as a crusade. In the Civil War so confident had General Sheridan been in the justice of his cause, that he had seen nothing illegitimate in taking the war to the heartland of the Confederacy, to those who had cheered the soldiers on as they marched north but had not joined up themselves. As he confessed at the time, he wished to leave the enemy 'nothing but their eyes to weep with over the war', a war they would force to a conclusion because it would appear much graver than it had at the outset.[20] Fighting limited wars as Niebuhr predicted would arouse only the ire of the world, and the dismay of the American people. It would never have occurred to the North Vietnamese to have played at war, to have dropped toys over Hanoi on Christmas Day 1972 for the children who had been bombed and killed in B52 raids the day before.[21]

Moreover, to tell the American people that military success on the battlefield 'could not be translated into a permanent political advantage', as Henry Kissinger informed the readers of *Foreign Affairs* in 1961,[22] was a confession of defeat even before the war had begun in earnest. As Irving Kristol remarked in an article written in the same year, June 1950 was the first time that the American people had been called upon to support a war rather than a crusade. They should not have been asked to do so again.[23]

Once the American people were drafted the ends had to be unlimited, the objective unconditional victory, peace, not an armistice. 'The American people', wrote Kristol, could not provide 'the kind of mercenary professional soldiers' limited wars required.[24] Democracies may fight limited wars; democratic armies cannot. A hero must have a heroic task. Providence can be served only by heroes.

It was equally foolish to allow the enemy to define what he meant by victory. The European view as expressed by the French strategist André Beaufre was very different. Limited wars, he argued, were more akin to tough political negotiations than military conflicts. 'Limited wars are intended not to be won, but not to be defeated. The essential is still to be there' when the fighting ends.[25] Unfortunately, as Charles Ackley maintains, such scepticism clashed with the US ethical tradition which forbids the use of force except for a total (i.e. moral or ideological) end.[26] Since war is sinful, only a just war is permissible, a war fought by volunteers, not conscripted troops. Even in the Civil War drafted soldiers were held in far less esteem than volunteers.[27] The United States fought the Vietnam War not to destroy the enemy, but to undermine the enemy's will to fight, a principle the British call 'the selection and maintenance of sin'.[28] It was a tactic, alas, that was hardly likely to commend itself to America's *conscience historique*.

Unfortunately, the American people had to know what the end was; what they were fighting for. In his book on the Kennedy administration Roger Hillsman entitled one of his chapters 'How do you know if you are winning?'. If the administration could not communicate what it meant by victory to a democratic army in the field, it could not hope to keep it in the field indefinitely.[29] As Bernard Brodie perceptively remarked countries should seek limited objectives in order to keep wars limited, not the other way round.[30]

A second dilemma of the Vietnam War was the invidious position in which it put drafted troops. The United States had to democratise its wars if it wished to draw upon its citizens to fight as well as pay for them.[31] It had to create heroes as well, whose real heroism was directed not at the enemy but against secret doubts about the motives of the state that they volunteer to serve, a state whose power might be 'based on wilfulness that does not find justification enough in reason'.[32]

Quoting a writer in 1826 Andrew Goodpaster claimed that instead of being an appendage of the state, the US Army relied upon the people participating in its life, imbibing its sentiments and regarding itself as part of the community.[33] Because as Daniel Berringer argued in 1966, the Army existed to serve the good of the community, it was acutely vulnerable to changes in social moods and attitudes at home.[34]

The tragedy of Vietnam was that the War failed to produce any heroes. Many of those who fought felt they had been betrayed, or short-changed by their political leaders. The literature and, even more, the many films about the conflict may invoke the heroic tradition in American life, but the war itself brought into question many of the traditional heroic virtues.[35]

Coming Home (1978), with its evocative title, was one of the most vivid of the anti-war films, in part because it portrayed a Vietnam War veteran returning to the past to rediscover his virtue. The tragedy for the heroes of such films is that they have lost their virtue by acting in the service of an impersonal bureaucracy, a state which produced not only the tragedy of Vietnam, but the corruption of Watergate as well. What saves them in the end is not the honour won in battle, but rediscovery of the past through war, a past which does not sanction small ones against 'exploited' people.

Such films, of course, are frequently self-indulgent rather than profound, often revealing more about the emptiness of modern American life than the depths of human suffering. The importance of the anti-war movement was not its size, but its evocation of the past which helped to plant seeds of doubt about the morality of the war even in the minds of those who consented to be drafted, the 'silent majority' who supported the United States' involvement in the conflict to the very end.

Among the soldiers who fought in south-east Asia the war was no more unpopular than Korea until the casualty rates in 1968 began to outstrip those of the Korean War. Desertion among soldiers until 1971 was no higher than in 1944. At home the tactics of the protesters, the *jeunesse enragée* of the campuses, the flag-burnings and anti-US slogans ensured that support for the war actually increased after 1970. Those who did turn against the war did so not because they believed it to be immoral, but because they questioned the depth of commitment by their political leaders.[36] In retrospect, all that the Peace Movement achieved was to ensure by its attacks on Hubert Humphrey that Richard Nixon won by 400,000 votes in the election of 1968, and that by its support of Senator McGovern that Nixon won by a landslide in 1972.

The problem about the draft dodgers and flag burners was that they were victims too, casualties of the age in which they lived, envious of an older generation which had lived to serve something which they had believed worthy of their service. Vietnam robbed the young of their future; all that they had to identify with was not destiny, but decline, demoralisation and the general decadence of the body politic. On the Left Americans saw the war as a punishment or expiation, later as a journey of self-discovery – a punishment for betraying America's ideals, expiation for a mission which had become a nightmare, the discovery that the war was – in Susan Sontag's words 'an existential struggle' – about whether any life but that of an American's was worth preserving. McGovern's message 'Come home, America' was a call for salvation to save the soul of the nation. Frances Fitzgerald, whose Pulitzer Prize work *Fire in the Lake* (1971) was perhaps *the* text of the anti-war generation withdrew into herself. Her next book was called *America Revisited*.[37]

The third problem with the American 'way of warfare' was that those who fought in Vietnam became demoralised when they saw themselves as mere cogs in a technological war, which was as soulless as it was destructive. In the end Westmoreland's battlefield of the future traumatised the American draftee more than it did the Vietcong. Nathaniel Hawthorne had foreseen the result a century before, when he predicted that human strife would be transferred from the personality of man into 'the cunning contrivances of machinery'. The soldier who was emotionally distant from the battle might displace his aggression, ignore his pain, even lose his capacity for guilt.[38] The soldier who was conscious of the situation, however, might rapidly crumble under pressure.

Even the academics made their own unique contribution to the traumatising of the military mind. Popular sociologists like Morris Janowitz who thrived in the 1950s added an impenetrable and meaningless jargon to military science, or what they preferred to call 'sociometric analysis'. The language rapidly gained currency in the Army. A British officer was astounded during a military operation in 1966 to discover among US officers a 'futile preoccupation with the academic meaning of words' when they should have been going into action. 'I heard one American officer arguing about whether his company had been overrun or infiltrated. He was trying to persuade some helicopters it was safe to land.'[39] It is by such trivial pursuits that battles are lost and kingdoms won. In semantic confusion, rather than the ebb and tide of battle, the United States went on to lose the first war in its history.

THE DISYNCHRONIC WAR

Had the Americans chosen to fight a different war entirely, to draft only half the troops they did, to take the battle directly to North Vietnam, to close off the Vietcong sanctuaries in Cambodia and Laos, above all to define the war they were fighting, the result might have turned out very differently. Even today, however, American writers with a few notable exceptions are unwilling to recognise that the conflict was what General Westmoreland called 'disynchronic' – that the wars against the Vietcong and against the regular forces of North Vietnam took place simultaneously, that the Vietnam War was not what it appeared to be: a counter-insurgency campaign in the classical tradition.[40]

Thanks to the *Official Vietnamese History of the War* which was published in 1981, we now know that Hanoi was only restrained from attacking the South in 1956 by the Chinese who threatened to cut off arms supplies altogether if an invasion went ahead. Zhou Enlai expected the division of the country to be longstanding. He even turned down a request by Ho Chi Minh for financial assistance to organise the countrywide elections which had been scheduled for 1956 at the Geneva Conference the previous year. If this does not exonerate Diem, or the United States which supported his decision to ignore the Conference's ruling, it does at least apportion the blame between the two sides.

Thanks again to the Vietnamese version of events we also know that as early as 1957 the Vietcong were in receipt of arms from the North. More to the point, infiltration routes through Laos were set up as early as 1959 so that the Vietcong could move from political agitation to armed struggle. The Vietcong only officially proclaimed themselves the government of the South when permitted to do so by North Vietnam.

Finally, we know what the Johnson and Nixon administrations always claimed: that North Vietnamese units began to take an active part in the war as early as the autumn of 1964, a development which prompted Johnson to despatch ground troops to Saigon a few months later. The Vietcong's ambitions for a separate southern Marxist state were not shared by Ho Chi Minh, even if the Vietcong's leader Nguyen Van Tien envisaged a federation of the two countries once the War had been brought to an end. In 1968 Hanoi made doubly sure of the Vietcong's subservience by holding back its own troops during the Tet Offensive in which Van Tien's irregular forces were decisively defeated. It was a move reminiscent of Stalin's decision to halt the advance of the Red Army before the gates of Warsaw in 1944 during the Polish uprising to ensure that the Polish Home Army would be destroyed by the Germans. When Saigon was finally 'liberated' the few remaining Vietcong units were demobilised and their members sent off to labour camps to be 're-educated', or forgotten.[41]

Unfortunately, Johnson never drew the logical conclusion from the evidence before him: that the United States was engaged not in a counter-insurgency struggle but a war against North Vietnam. Instead of mobilising the economy, introducing conscription and declaring war on Hanoi, he chose to pay for the war by printing money, and to recruit soldiers to fight it by introducing the draft, a desperately unfair system which ensnared only one out of every three Americans who were eligible to be called up. In July 1965 he even refrained from calling up the Army Ready Reserve Force because of the unpopularity Kennedy had incurred when he had done so during the Berlin crisis of 1961.

He also delayed extending the draft to students until 1967. Up to that year the war was largely fought by the poor, the black underclass in the inner cities, who were still at the bottom of the social totem pole, looking up from what Nietzsche called 'the frog perspective'. An indication of the heavy black presence in the US forces was Senator Fulbright's question that if the administration was correct in its opinion that only by bombing North Vietnam would the Communists be brought to reason, why had black rioting in the cities, a development which so disfigured the social landscape in the late 1960s, not brought about recognition by the white community of the plight of the urban blacks.[42]

Instead of engaging in search-and-destroy missions in the countryside, in which the South Vietnamese army often performed better than the Americans, the United States might have pursued a quite different strategy altogether. True to its Indian war tradition the US Army performed as badly as it had under such Indian war generals as Wingfield Scott who refused to face up to the realities of frontier fighting, preferring instead to allow 'heavy columns of infantry and cavalry, locked to slow moving supply trains, [to crawl] about the vast western distances in search of an enemy who could scatter and vanish almost instantly'.[43]

The strategy the Joint Chiefs of Staff would have preferred was one which would have taken the war to the enemy directly. Westmoreland's request for an additional 200,000 men after the Tet Offensive was not a confession of failure but a plea made at the instigation of the Joint Chiefs to follow up the success of 1968 by eliminating the Vietcong's forward bases in Cambodia and Laos. The idea of placing troops astride the North Vietnamese supply lines in Laos had first been floated in 1965 – in the so-called Tchepone Plan.

The initial US military strategy was sound enough: to drive across the Demilitarised Zone and astride the North Vietnamese supply lines before going on the defensive. It was a strategy which would have allowed the US Army to have made maximum use of its greatest advantage: firepower, while allowing it to reduce the number of men under arms.[44] It would also have made the bombing of North Vietnam entirely unnecessary, and thus done something to disarm the United States' critics at home and abroad, for whom the bombing of civilians (in default of a declaration of war) was a clear violation of international law. Most of the effective fighting was on the ground, where by 1972 over 50 per cent of engagements were with North Vietnamese regular forces.

The bombing of the North achieved nothing. The rationale for killing civilians according to one of America's leading strategists Thomas Schelling is strictly limited: 'To inflict suffering gains nothing ... the only purpose must be to influence somebody; ... the power to hurt is bargaining power. To exploit it is diplomacy.'[45] Clearly the United States could not influence Hanoi by imposing suffering on its people. In a word, there was no clear military rationale for bombing the North at all, given the demands which the North Vietnamese leadership could make on its own population.

The only time the United States came close to adopting the tactics just outlined, it actually exceeded its own expectations. Alas, by then it was too late. When the North Vietnamese army sought to cut South Vietnam in half in Easter 1972 the Americans finally assumed complete control of the fighting. Using B52 strikes, and helicopters armed with armour-piercing missiles to destroy North Vietnamese tanks, General John Paul Vann, the director of the Second Regional Assistance Group, was able to drive the enemy back. In winning, however, he failed to see the fallacy of his own victory; that having to assume total command at the moment of crisis showed, if proof were needed, that Saigon no longer had the political will to survive.[46] Less than three years later, after the Americans had left, the North tried again, this time using 22 divisions. It was the Easter offensive revisited; only this time the US Army was not there to stem the tide.

There was also no military assistance to speak of either. In one of the most perfidious acts in US foreign policy Congress, ignoring the request of the executive, refused to vote major defence allocations to Saigon. From $2.5 billion in 1973 US military aid to Laos and South Vietnam fell to $700 million in 1975, or $350 million if freight costs are deducted from the total. When Hanoi resumed the War the South Vietnamese forces were in receipt of only 2 per cent of the funds that US forces had received in 1968. It took only six weeks for the South to collapse. It was not surprising that it took another ten years for the Vietnam War veterans who lost their lives to get their own memorial in Washington. Those who returned had to remake their broken lives without help or solace from a nation which preferred to forget them entirely. Since the war, 60,000 US veterans have committed suicide, more than those who died in it. Moving gingerly through a twilight of left-over lifetime, perhaps they were its principal victims.

NOTES

1. In an article in *Foreign Affairs* 46:3 (April 1968) p. 442, the British strategist Robert Thompson wrote that the trouble with the United States was that whenever it doubled its effort, it somehow managed to square the error.
2. Anthony Austin, *The President's War* (New York: Lippincott, 1971) p. 44.
3. Cited in Stephen D. Young, 'Ethnicity and the Indo-China war: reasons for conflict', in Winston van Horne and Thomas V. Tonnesen (eds), *Ethnicity and War* (Madison: University of Wisconsin, 1984).
4. Paul Seabury, 'The revolt against obligation', in Aaron Wildavasky, *US Foreign Policy: prospects and proposals in the 1970s* (New York: McGraw Hill, 1969).
5. C. P. Cavafy, *Collected Poems* (London: Hogarth Press, 1984) p. 14.
6. John Girling, *America and the Third World: revolution and intervention* (London: Routledge & Kegan Paul, 1980).
7. Cited in John Luskin, *Liberty and the Press* (University, Ala.: University of Alabama Press, 1972) p. 221.
8. Arnold Isaacs, *Without Honour: defeat in Vietnam and Cambodia* (Baltimore: Johns Hopkins University Press, 1983) p. 119.

9. Cable 19 September 1963. See *The Pentagon Papers* (Senator Gravel edition, 1971) p. 209.
10. Seymour J. Deitchman, *The Best Laid Schemes: a tale of social research and bureaucracy* (Cambridge, Mass.: MIT Press, 1976) p. 385.
11. Edward Michell, 'Inequality and insurgency: a statistical study of South Vietnam', *World Politics* 20:3 (April 1968) pp. 437-8.
12. Robert L. Sansom, *The Economics of Insurgency in the Mekong Delta of Vietnam* (Cambridge, Mass.: MIT Press, 1970). Much the same findings are to be found in Jeffrey Race, *War comes to Long An: revolutionary conflict in a Vietnamese village* (Berkeley, Calif.: University of California Press, 1972).
13. In *Our Man in Havana* (1958) Greene expressed the same philosophy in the words of Wormold, the novel's chief protagonist:

    I wouldn't kill for my country, I wouldn't kill for capitalism or Communism, or social democracy or the welfare state – whose welfare? . . . If I love or if I hate let me love or hate as an individual. I will not be 59200/5 in anyone's global war.

14. Samuel L. Popkin, *The Rational Peasant: the political economy of rural society in Vietnam* (Berkeley, Calif.: University of California Press, 1979).
15. For a classic study of the academics 'selling out' see Noam Chomsky, *American Power and the New Mandarins* (Harmondsworth: Penguin, 1969); for a critique see Christopher Coker, 'The Mandarin or the Commissar: the political thought of Noam Chomsky', in Sohan and Celia Modgil (eds), *Noam Chomsky: consensus and controversy* (New York: Falmer Press, 1987).
16. *New York Times* (8 February 1968).
17. Robert Osgood, *Limited War: the challenge to American strategy* (Chicago: University of Chicago Press, 1957). For some revised views see Osgood, *Limited War Revisited* (Boulder, Colorado: Westview Press, 1979).
18. Edward Luttwak, *The Pentagon and the Art of War* (New York: Simon & Schuster, 1985) p. 370.
19. Harry G. Summers, 'Conservatives, containment and Vietnam', *American Spectator* (June 1988) p. 30.
20. Thomas Leonard, *Above the battle: war making from Appomattax to Versailles* (Oxford: Oxford University Press, 1978) pp. 18-19.
21. See Erich Fried's poem 'Toys on Target' about the day of the Vietnamese Festival of Children when B52s dropped toys even on North Vietnamese villages in which children had been killed by their bombs the day before:

'Dropping
toys
instead of bombs
for the Festival of the Children

that, the market researchers said,
will doubtless make
an impression

It has made
a great
impression
on the whole world.

If the aeroplane
had dropped the toys
a fortnight ago
and only now the bombs

my two children
thanks to your kindness
would have had something to play with
for those two weeks.'

22. Henry Kissinger, 'The Vietnam negotiations', *Foreign Affairs*, 47:1 (January 1966) p. 212.
23. Samuel Huntington, *The Soldier and the State: the theory and politics of civil-military relations* (Cambridge, Mass.: Harvard University Press, 1957) p. 152.
24. Irving Kristol, 'A matter of fundamentals', *Commentary* (April 1961) pp. 55-6.
25. Robert McIintock, *The Meaning of Limited War* (Boston: Houghton Mifflin, 1967) p. 199.
26. Charles Ackley, *The Modern Military in American Society: a study in the nature of military power* (Philadelphia: Westminster Press, 1982) pp. 287-8.
27. William Carlton, 'Ranking armies before the Civil War', *Current History* (June 1968) p. 327.
28. Donald F. Bletz, *The Role of the Military Professional in US Foreign Policy* (New York: Praeger, 1972) p. 236.
29. Roger Hillsman, *To Move a Nation: the politics of foreign policy in the administration of John F. Kennedy* (New York: Doubleday, 1967) pp. 441-67.
30. Bernard Brodie, *Strategy in the Missile Age* (Princeton, NJ: Princeton University Press, 1959) p. 313.
31. Walter Millis, *Arms and Men: a study in American military history* (New York: Putnam, 1956) pp. 22-4.
32. Ackley, *The Modern Military, op. cit.*, p. 24.
33. Andrew Goodpaster, *West Point: the army and society – American institutions in constellation*, in Gary Ryan and Timothy Nenninger, *The US Army and the American People* (Washington DC: National Archives, 1987) p. 7.
34. Daniel Berringer, *They Call Us Dead Men* (London: Macmillan, 1966) pp. 172-3.
35. Most of the Vietnam War films, in fact, reflect the very vices they attempt to portray. Perhaps, the most notorious *Apocalypse Now* illustrates the point better than any other. Based loosely on Conrad's *Heart of Darkness*, it was really designed to show the ethical dilemmas of a war 'by remote control', in which 7 million tons of bombs were dropped by plane and 7 million tons by ground weapons, not to mention 72 million litres of defoliants and 577

kilograms of ammunition per head of population. And what of the film? In one shot 1,200 gallons of petrol were burned in 90 seconds. For another shot over 500 smoke bombs and 100 phosphorous sticks were used, together with 1,750 sticks of dynamite and more than 2000 rockets, and traces all at the cost of $31 million. See 'Evading the war: the politics of the Holywood Vietnam film', *History*, 73:238 (June 1988) p. 252.
36. John Mueller, 'Reflections on the Vietnam anti-war movement and the curious calm at the War's end', in Peter Braestrup (ed.), *Vietnam as History* (Washington DC: University Press of America, 1984).
37. Frances Fitzgerald, *Fire in the Lake: the Vietnamese and the Americans in Vietnam* (1972); *America Revisited* (1982).
38. Leonard, *Above the Battle, op. cit.,* p. 96.
39. Corelli Barnett, 'The outsider's input into military thinking', Part 2, *RUSI Journal* (June 1982) p. 7.
40. Mark Falcoff, 'Let's be honest about Vietnam', *American Spectator* (December 1987).
41. Ironically the Left stumbled upon the truth by accident. Noam Chomsky defended Hanoi's intervention in the war by arguing that only the Vietcong and the United States insisted that South Vietnam should remain a separate state, despite the fact that in South Vietnam's own constitution Vietnam was described as a single country. Hence if the entire North Vietnamese Army were to enter the South it would be guilty not of aggression, only insurrection or 'subversion' (*American Power and the New Mandarins*, op. cit., p. 243).
42. William Fulbright, 'The Great Society is a sick society', *New York Times* (20 August 1967).
43. Robert Utley, *Frontier Regulars: the US army and the Indians 1866-91* (New York: Macmillan, 1973) p. 530. See also James P. Tate (ed.), *The American Military of the Frontier: Proceedings of the 7th Military Historical Symposium*, US Airforce Academy 1976 (Washington DC: USGPO, 1978).
44. Harry Summers, *On Strategy: a critical analysis of the Vietnam War* (Presidio: Dell, 1982).
45. Thomas Schelling, *Arms and Influence* (New Haven: Yale University Press, 1966) pp. vi, 20.
46. Neil Sheehan, *A Bright Shining Lie: John Paul Vann in Vietnam* (New York: Random House, 1988).

5. Living with Caliban: The United States and the Third World

'To travel from California, south, suggested a journey from an existing future into a living past.'

    Patrick Markham, *So far from God . . . a journey to Central America*

'We have been offering the Asian nations the wrong kind of help. We have so lost sight of our own Past that we are trying to sell guns and money alone, instead of remembering that it was the quest for the dignity of freedom that was responsible for our own way of life'

    William Lederer and Eugene Burdick, *The Ugly American* (1961)

'There is no use dissembling. We might as well call it imperialism and not be befuddled by words.'

    Carl Becker

In his seminal work *The Imperial Republic* the French sociologist and political philosopher Raymond Aron discussed whether the United States could be described as an imperial or imperialist power. His distinction between the two was a simple one: an imperial power is one with a global network of interests which do not necessarily require defending by force; an imperialist power is a country which can only defend its world interests by the threat or use of coercion. Aron believed the United States to be the former; the Soviet Union to be the latter. For him there was a clear distinction, which far from being merely semantic, was very real in real life.[1]

There was a time when historians like Henry Feis could be self-confidently dogmatic in arguing that US foreign policy was neither 'imperialist in design, in fact or in temper'.[2] It has now become a received wisdom that the United States is an imperial power, which has managed on the whole with great skill a Pax Americana since 1945. Two conservative writers, Robert Osgood and George Liska, both accept that the term imperial is as good a description as any of the power the United States has become. Although Tucker wrote a book to refute the left-wing revisionist thesis that the United States had exploited the developing world, he accepted the word imperial as a useful epithet, that the United States had become a counter-revolutionary power whenever its position in the world, or the imperial order it managed, were seriously under threat.[3]

The questions that need to be asked are: What kind of imperial order are we discussing? Is it a crude outlet for US capital? Or is it a political environment in which the United States can not only survive, but thrive?

The word environment was first used in this context by Kennedy's National Security Adviser Walt Rostow, in an address to the graduating class of the US Army's Special Warfare Center on 28 June 1961. It has a much older provenance, however, among eighteenth-century writers who believed that if the trouble with Europe was its history, the creation of the United States would give it another chance by removing the historical constraints on individual aspirations. To an age which subscribed to the psychology of Locke and saw a causal connection between elevated foliage and the neck of the amiable giraffe, 'the environment was everything':

Society itself was the cause of all crimes; the perfectability of truth was a truth of practical and universal importance; the individual was perfectible by education . . . 'nations are educated like individual infants. They are what they are taught to be'.[4]

Although it would be a mistake perhaps, to take such views as an exclusive point of reference by which to explain American behaviour, Louis Hartz observed 30 years ago that 'an absolute national morality is inspired either to withdraw from "alien" things or to transform them; it cannot live in comfort consistently by their side'.[5]

If we use the environment, then we might ask whether it is necessarily a capitalist one. Is US foreign policy a shorthand for the policy of General Motors? Is what is good for General Motors of necessity good for the United States?

The Left in the person of Robert Gilpin have talked of a Pax Americana based on foreign investment, similar in many respects to the Pax Britannica which was based on free trade. At one point Gilpin cites in his defence the Peterson Report of 1971 which actually concluded that the United States' position in the world was relative to its investment in manufacturing industry.[6]

It is a thesis which has a specious plausibility. By 1973 187 US companies with subsidiaries in at least five foreign countries accounted not only for three-quarters of total US investment abroad, but also for half of its exports and one-third of the sale of manufactured goods in the US market. Their influence in finance was especially significant, given the size of their short-term disposable funds – more than twice the reserves of the world's central banks and its various international monetary institutions. A 2 per cent shift in their liquidities would have been enough to have provoked an acute monetary crisis anywhere in the world, according to the report of a Senate committee.[7]

Superficially, there is plenty of evidence to suggest that the Pax Americana has been largely commercial in inspiration. We can cite Dean Acheson's testimony when he was Assistant Secretary of State before the Congressional Committee on Post War Economic Policy in November 1944 – namely that unless the United States had access to overseas markets it would have to consume what it produced. Bretton Woods was designed to prevent the United Kingdom and France from retreating behind an imperial tariff regime as they had done in the 1930s, and as both contemplated doing in 1944. The Marshall Plan was popular with US businessmen whose profits from overseas sales depended entirely in the late 1940s on reviving the European market.

In that respect, as Gilpin argued, US imperialism was from the start self-defeating. Having told Japan to export or die, the Japanese proceeded to take the United States at its word and make the country their largest single market. The second defeated power Germany had already reached 140 per cent of its pre-war production by 1952, as the United States began to see its percentage of world manufacturing output gradually fall.

If we choose Acheson's statement, however, to illustrate a point, why not cite the Truman Doctrine in which capitalism is not mentioned once. Even Acheson's testimony needs to be studied very carefully. If the US economy needed to export so that expanding markets overseas could absorb 'its unlimited creative energy', Acheson's purpose in appealing to US industry and its interests was largely to elicit broad support for a policy pursued for primarily quite different reasons.[8] In the Truman Doctrine the key phrase was guaranteeing 'alternative ways of life', or as the Defense Secretary James Forrestal entered in his diary at the time, 'to channel revolutionary energies into different paths'.

That was the central theme of US policy in the Third World: to make the world safe for change, for 'democracy' or 'diversity', a phrase which became popular after 1963. As Eugene Rostow wrote in 1968, all the United States asked of the Soviet Union was acceptance of evolutionary change, and an organised pattern of peace.[9] Fifteen years later Alexander Haig was of exactly the same opinion, even if his domestic politics differed markedly from Rostow's: 'Our objective remains simple and compelling: a world hospitable to our society and our ideals.'[10]

The United States believed not only that it could live with change in a way that the Soviet Union could not, it actually believed in change for its own sake. The Pax Americana was firmly grounded in the belief that trade produced change and socialised regimes, even the most militantly Communist, in much the same way that the Pax Britannica had been based on the belief that free trade brought enlightenment, and with enlightenment liberty.

That is not to say that it has ever been an objective of US policy to assist its own companies to break into foreign markets, to bludgeon their way through a closed door, to convert at the point of the sword. We shall only make this mistake if we suppose that US investment in a developing country is as important to the United States as it is to the country concerned, which has never been the case. Instead US investment overseas since 1960 has been declining as a percentage of foreign investment, and is now down to 15 per cent. In 1968 US companies earned less than $5 billion from overseas income ($3 billion from the Third World, or 3 per cent of the income generated by US corporations inside the United States, or, put even more graphically, only 0.33 per cent of GNP for that year).

It would be wrong, on the other hand, to maintain that action against US corporations has not been important. It has played a significant role in formulating US attitudes, although not quite in the way that the conspiracy theorists choose to imagine. In short – if US companies lobby Washington to support them, they can expect precious little sympathy short of traditional expressions of regret, unless nationalisation is taken as conclusive evidence that the host society in question has ceased to be an open society, that it is becoming impervious to US ideas and choices, and that the environment is changing not for the better but for the worse. As John Kennedy told Guyana's radical leader in 1962, the United States was not engaged in a crusade to force free enterprise on the part of a world where it was not 'relevant'; it was engaged in a crusade to maintain national independence.[11]

Let us look at three examples: Guatemala (1954), Cuba (1961) and Chile (1973), each of which is trotted out time after time to illustrate the predatory nature of US 'imperialism'.

(1) In Guatemala the United Fruit Company lost most of its land (or 70 per cent of the country) in 1952 when the government decided it needed to raise revenue through nationalisation for land reform. Encouraged by Eisenhower's declaration in his first State of the Union Address that one of the most important purposes of his foreign policy would be to encourage 'a hospitable climate for investment' around the world,[12] the company asked the administration to intervene, if necessary with force. To its surprise it received the answer that US companies could no longer expect to operate as they had done in the 1930s, that new governments in a new era had to introduce land reform programmes if Communism was to be contained and defeated.

Unfortunately, the Guatemalan government committed one fatal error. Faced by opposition to the Agrarian Reform Law from the church, landowners and business, it felt it necessary to bring the Communist Party into a coalition government. Eisenhower immediately accused President Arbenez of treating the Communists as an 'authentic political movement' rather than part of a 'Soviet conspiracy'. It may well be true that Foster Dulles's law office had drawn up the company's agreements with Guatemala in 1930 and 1936, that the Assistant Secretary for Inter-American Affairs was a major UFC shareholder, and that Allen Dulles, the director of the CIA had once been the company's President.[13] It may also be true – to quote a former UFC official – that the corporation 'was involved at every level' in planning the coup,[14] but its executives neither authorised nor carried it out. The decision to unseat Arbenez was taken by Eisenhower for purely political, rather than commercial reasons.[15] Only by addressing those reasons are we likely to find out what we need to know instead of answering the questions we have traditionally asked.

(2) A similar story can be told about Cuba. Originally Castro had no greater admirer than the young Senator John F. Kennedy. Like Arbenez, the United States came to terms with Castro quite early. Batista had not been worth supporting because he was so corrupt. A government that could not be helped was clearly undeserving of US support. As a report on Cuba concluded in April 1961 the Cuban Revolution could not have succeeded on the basis of guerrilla action alone; it succeeded because of the rejection by thousands of civilians behind the lines of a regime that was beyond salvation, a rejection which had undermined the morale of Batista's superior military forces and produced a collapse from within.[16]

By 1961 however, Kennedy was to be found constantly berating Castro for 'betraying' his own revolution; for pursuing radicalism at the expense of reform. From that moment the writing was on the wall. What changed the situation so radically from one year to the next?

At the outset Castro had tried to finance his reform programme by increasing the price of the annual sugar quota to the United States. When the United States refused to offer more attractive terms he nationalised all US property in the course of a day. The Kennedy administration chose to interpret the move as final proof that Castro had moved from liberal socialism to out-and-out Communism. In his speech on 20 April 1961 justifying the Bay of Pigs Kennedy accused Communists of exploiting legitimate political grievances for their own ends, only to betray popular expectations once in power. Kennedy's hagiographer Arthur Schlessinger later tried to exonerate the President for the Bay of Pigs débâcle by arguing that the United States was 'under no obligation to defend Castro from the Cuban people',[17] although the *émigrés* who took part in the attempted invasion hardly constituted an 'opposition' at all.

The tragedy of 1961 was that the United States might have avoided a breach with Castro had it agreed to increase the quota or pay more for existing imports; if it had agreed to buy off a revolution, to ensure that it was not provoked into intervening, a price that was doubtless too high for its own sense of *amour propre*. Ironically as Regis Debray revealed in his book *Revolution Within a Revolution* Castro had only nationalised US companies because of the UFC's role in the Guatemalan coup seven years before. Nationalisation had been intended as a gesture to show that the United States could no longer hope to destabilise the regime from within, only overthrow it from without. Never expecting that Kennedy would choose the latter option, Castro seems to have expected the United States to increase the quota as he had demanded. Instead, his actions precipitated the very crisis he had hoped to pre-empt.

(3) The same issues were involved in Chile in the period 1970-3, a country in which the first Communist Party came to power in Latin America elected on a free vote. In 1973 it was toppled in a military coup which brought to power General Pinochet, a man who embarked upon what Richard Nixon was later to call 'a daring gamble . . . to turn the country into a laboratory for free market economics'.[18]

Like Arbenez and Castro, Allende chose to pay for his political reforms by expropriating US companies, especially Anaconda and Kennecott, the two largest corporations involved in exploiting the country's copper resources. Ananconda suffered particularly adversely since its stock dropped 60 per cent in value. It was promised only $500 million indemnification, a sum its board considered derisory.

As it happened Nixon had tried to prevent Allende from coming to power by spending $750,000 in covert operations and bribes. Writing many years later C. L. Sulzberger was convinced Nixon would have supported a military coup in 1970. He certainly welcomed it in 1973, but took no direct part when it actually happened. In a very American way Sulzberger found that Nixon was deeply committed to reform in Chile, but not Communist reform. Revealingly he subtitled his chapter on Chile: 'Waiting for Jefferson'. It was a Jeffersonian revolution the United States wanted, not a Communist programme of reform.[19]

The nationalisation of companies after the event – after Allende's election, barely aroused Nixon's interest. What the US government was not prepared to do was subsidise the nationalisations as it had in Brazil. When ITTC (the International Telephone and Telegraphic Corporation) had its assets expropriated in February 1962, the State Department had persuaded the government to pay the company the price it demanded by agreeing to reimburse the Brazilian government out of the funds earmarked for the Alliance for Progress. There was no such encouragement for ITT which worked closely with the Chilean army in 1973 to oust Allende, as the economy lurched into a recession and spiralling inflation. Convinced that instead of holding another election he could not possibly win, Allende would mount his own pre-emptive coup the Nixon administration made it known to the Chilean military that it would not stand in the way of Allende's removal.

In the end a nation with a past but no history was oblivious to the history of its neighbours. In its relations with Latin America the United States was patronising and insensitive. Kennedy's wish to save the Cuban people from Castro and Nixon's from Allende differed very little in fact from Woodrow Wilson's promise 'to teach the South American republics to elect good men'.[20]

Having perfected their own government, the Americans clearly believed they had a mission to face the monster Caliban, still slumbering in his cave. In the end all the United States could issue were declaratory exhortations, and veiled warnings that it might intervene if things did not improve. For the rest its weapons like Prospero's Phantoms 'were all spirits and/ are melted into air'. 'When thou cam'st first/ Thou strok'st me/ and made much of me,' Caliban complains. His complaint has a peculiar resonance today as Latin America retreats into its cave, unwilling to be patronised or tamed in the name of the 'eternal truths' God saw fit to reveal first to America, a name the United States arrogated for itself on the first possible occasion.[21]

The intellectual poverty of basing a policy entirely on anti-Communism was captured most perceptively, perhaps, by the English conservative writer Patrick Markham. Being told by his travelling companion Dr Blitzer when in Central America that the Americans had no imperial policy – unlike the British before them – because they were a moral people he begged to differ. Blitzer's analysis on one level held a perceptive truth. A distaste for Communism did not amount to a policy. A policy suggests a preference, a distinct national interest and a preferred means of serving it. But the reason why the United States had no national interest went deeper than Dr Blitzer's observation about morality: 'There is no distinct US national interest in Central America because there is no distinct US nation. Too much US energy and ability spends itself in attempting to decide what sort of nation the US should be' (p. 129).

Central America may be nearer to the United States than to God. But despite its very proximity, far from being swallowed up by America's past which has defined its international responsibilities, it has denied the Americans a convincing present: a precise definition of the kind of nation they wish to create. Perhaps too this is one of the 'ironies' of American history.

A MUDDLED PROGRESS: THE UNITED STATES AND THIRD WORLD DEVELOPMENT

'The American image too, will take care of itself, if we get on with what we have to do in, as our great-grandfathers would have said, the station to which it has pleased God to call us'

Dean Acheson, Grapes from Thorns (1972)

So much for one part of the equation; the use of economic coercion. What of the other: the use by the United States of its economic power to shape the world in its own image. 'It lies within our power', Dean Rusk once observed, 'to apply to the world community the lesson of our unique national experience.'[22] Hans Morgenthau believed that the process of decolonisation might provide a unique opportunity for the United States to realise the American dream, a chance for the United States itself to make 'a new beginning', one which offered an emotional, and psychological retreat from the unpleasant reality that Eastern Europe and the Soviet Union were politically and temperamentally unreceptive to the US message.[23]

The creation of the Peace Corps offered emancipation from the sterility of containment. It appealed in particular to public-spirited, naïve young men like the Americans who were discovered by a group of English travellers in the depths of Amazonia in 1910, men who 'bore themselves with the easy assurance of the favoured heirs of Adam'.[24] For Theodore Sorensen the Corps was one of America's 'unarmed forces', which would help convince the world that the United States intended to meet its international responsibilities, as well as its obligation to defend the world from Soviet Communism.[25] The limit of two years for each Peace Corps volunteer (with a slightly longer limit for full-time staff) recalled the diplomatic style of a much earlier generation, the era of Jacksonian democracy, when diplomats were expected to serve no more than two years in each post.[26]

The Peace Corps, in retrospect, can be seen as a typical US delusion, a decision to send out 'underdeveloped youngsters to underdeveloped countries' with an enthusiasm which moved Graham Greene to criticism and John Updike to derision. It was one of the idylls of Camelot, a typical Kennedy initiative, whose *naïveté* fitted the age only to turn sour by the time the Kennedy myth had become not a little tarnished.

Even so, the Corps' own self-assessment of 1981 makes amazing reading:

PC volunteers make things happen . . . they leave behind creativity. They leave a better sense of how to make the best of finite resources. They leave techniques which will help the Third World shape itself long after the volunteers go back home.[27]

The reality, alas, was rather different. The PC did not spark off 'a sweeping surge of development' which turned 'traditionally listless areas of the world into seething cauldrons of change'.[28] The reality, the American dream turned into grand guignol, or nightmare, was caught savagely by John Updike in his novel *The Coup* (1978), in his vivid description of a naïve, yet totally well-meaning USAID worker who is despatched to a Sahelian state suffering from an appalling drought, not with water but everything else from corn flakes to powdered milk. Is he unaware, the country's ruler asks him, that his own government's cattle vaccination programme had increased the size of the country's cattle herds even as the water of the region had begun to dry up? Is he unaware that the deep wells which had been drilled by foreign governments had disrupted nomadic conditions so that deserts were created with wells at their centre? As he sets light to the food mountain, which becomes a funeral pyre for the American trapped at the top, the country's ruler, whose political works the young American had read so avidly in his Science Pol. course at Yale, concludes that he must have been trained for martyrdom, that he must have had some 'marginal religious preparation' since the last look on his face is not one of reproach but surprise.[29]

For the United States foreign aid offered an opportunity to redeem the developing world from the evils of colonialism and its own torpor. Truman often used to refer to aid workers as 'technical missionaries'.[30] In 1953 a State Department official answered his own question of how a Christian should look at Truman's Point 4 Aid Programme with the biblical injunction: 'Verily, I say unto you in as much as ye have done it unto one of the least of my brethren ye have done it unto me.'[31] Even the great critic of foreign aid Eugene Castle, the author of such classic works as *Billions, Blunders and Balloney* and *The Great Giveaway*, supported the principle of foreign assistance; all he wanted to do was to cut $2 billion off the 1958 aid appropriations (or practically the entire aid budget).[32]

Aid appealed to a people who had a historical mission to redeem the redeemable. Did they wish to be taxed to provide more? No, a survey found in 1943, but it also discovered that 80 per cent of the respondents were willing to remain on a system of rationing for a further five years to help feed the starving, to realise one of Roosevelt's four freedoms: freedom from want.[33] Foreign aid remained popular throughout the 1950s. In the opinion of one government official the Point 4 Programme (technical aid to the less developed countries) was even more popular with the public than Marshall Aid had been.[34]

Disillusionment rapidly set in in the late 1960s, when the Third World – Kennedy's 'people in the huts and villages of half the globe struggling to break the bonds of mass misery' – chose to become neither more 'American' nor more democratic. As Geoffrey Gorer had predicted, a year after the Point 4 Programme had been introduced, if the 'universal aspiration towards Americanism' did not manifest itself in the developing world the United States' sense of rejection might lead it to abandon the countries concerned.[35]

In fact, the situation was somewhat more complex. Truman had believed that the Point 4 Programme could raise the standard of living of the rest of the world by 2 per cent. Kennedy had sought to propel half the world into self-sustained growth by increasing the foreign aid budget to $4 billion a year.[36] By the time Reagan had been installed in the Oval Office no one in

America thought it possible to save the world by one's exertions, only by one's example. As Reagan himself reminded the developing countries, 'no American contribution can do more for development than a growing prosperous US economy.'[37] Every 1 per cent reduction in US interest rates improved the balance of payments of the LDCs by $4 billion. Adverse changes in interest rates had an even more immediate impact than high oil prices. By boosting its own growth the United States promised to produce a 'new era of sustained non-inflationary growth and prosperity'. The United States could force the world into recession, it could no longer pull it out unaided. Redemptionism, perforce, gave way to exemplarism as the 1970s came to a close.

Perhaps, nothing disabused the United States more about the efficacy of foreign aid than Kennedy's Alliance for Progress, which was described by Arthur Schlessinger some years later as an attempt 'to transform the 1960s into a historic decade of democratic progress'.[38] It was a brave dream considering that the amount appropriated for the programme between 1961 and 1972 amounted to less than $5 billion, a fact which served to reveal not so much the nature of US redemptionism, but the strength of the United States commitment. By the end of the 1960s the dreams had faded, only the rhetoric remained. Johnson in his last foreign aid application insisted that the United States must save the Third World 'because we are a nation founded on the ideals of humanitarian justice and liberty for all men'.[39] But rhetoric apart, the 1969 budget presented to Congress was the smallest request for a foreign aid programme since 1949.

The Alliance failed for several reasons, some marginal, others more profound. The United States underestimated opposition to the programme from the church (which resisted land reform in El Salvador), as well as industry (which wanted rapid economic growth in Brazil without any substantial redistribution of income). In a word, most Latin American governments were far less radical than the United States. Kennedy may have called the Alliance 'a crucible of revolutionary ideas', but most governments were highly suspicious of ideas which they saw as politically destabilising. Within four years of the Alliance's launch seven governments had been toppled by military coups. As Nixon was forced to conclude, 'foreign assistance is not a panacea for international stability, for political development, or even for democratic progress.'[40]

A more profound problem was encapsulated in Schlessinger's summing up of the Alliance as a 'very American effort to persuade the developing countries to base their revolutions on Locke rather than Marx'.[41] Locke, of course, has always had a particular attraction for Americans. 'In the beginning all the world was America', he wrote in his *Second Treatise on Civil Government*. In *The Liberal Tradition in America* Hartz argued that Lockean liberalism had become so embedded in American life that it had become a political ideology.[42] US foreign policy has been criticised alternately for being too economically driven and imperialist, too moralistic and interventionist, too utilitarian and isolationist. All paradoxically are true, 'for the concern with wealth, power, status, moral virtue and the freedom of mankind were successfully transformed into a single set of mutually reinforcing values by the paradigm of Lockean liberalism'.[43] A Lockean revolution offered Latin America not even the promise of a major rethink of traditional assumptions about the relationship with the United States, only the promise of a return to traditional American idealism.

The ultimate indictment of the initiative was that its proponents appeared to have learned nothing from the mistakes of the past. In short, they had nothing new to offer. In the end, the Latin Americans had to trust to their own traditions, to fight shy of the nostrums peddled by US academics and politicians who spent the better part of two generations denying them self-respect in the name of their own somewhat recondite understanding of economic progress and freedom.

The collapse of the Alliance for Progress has left the Americans with a belief in their own society which is probably as deeply rooted as ever. The contrast between the post-colonial states, which present a depressing landscape of military regimes and corrupt officialdom, and the early development of the United States has opened the way for the reaffirmation of a peculiar cultural chauvinism which makes it possible even for liberal conservatives like George Kennan to compare the history of their own country favourably with that of others, while at the same time retaining their confidence that one still has something to say to the other. Kennan's point of departure is his picture of Wisconsin in the 1850s:

I am moved to recall that the Wisconsin of that day was very much what we today would call an underdeveloped country. Well, those people worked hard . . . and Wisconsin prospered . . . under their administration. Had the Wisconsinities been a lazy, violent people devoted more to war than to industry – had we wasted what little substance we had on civil strife of one sort or another . . . would we today be seen as the possessors of a peculiar virtue *vis-a-vis* the more developed countries, entitling us to put claims on their beneficence and to demand of them that they exert themselves to promote their development? And is no credit whatsoever to be given in this modern world for the old fashioned American virtues of thrift, honesty, tolerance, civil discipline and hard work?[44]

It is an analysis which justifies Kennan in making some very critical judgements, in particular that the Third World has largely itself to blame for its own underdevelopment. There is of course a striking difference between the Third World and the United States which Kennan grudgingly concedes, that the former is much poorer in resources, some countries to a far greater degree than others. But nowhere does he allow this qualification to alter the force of his initial conclusion. In putting forward the thesis that the United States offers the only example of how to escape from the underdevelopment trap, Kennan takes a romantic view of US history which hardly accords with the facts. Worse still, he is not sufficiently rigorous in his historical analysis to appreciate how irrelevant that experience may be to the Third World condition. Much of what he writes derives from a historical myth which sits somewhat uneasily on the unhistorical nature of his thinking.

While Kennan's appeal to history might mean something to an American audience for whom the image of a settler society still offers a seductive and plausible version of the past, it means nothing at all to a Third World audience. It is one thing to argue that the United States was totally underdeveloped when the first settlers broke into the Great Plains; it is quite another to neglect to mention the economic and social differences between the world of the 1850s and that of 1979. If the Americans were pioneers they were pioneers in a land of abundance.[45] They were also pioneers in a land without a sizeable population.

Or to be more precise, as Steele Commanger once observed, although it is a popular hobby horse of the Americans to berate the Spanish for their treatment of the Amerindians, they tend to overlook the fact that the latter survived; for the most part, the United States' own Indians did not.[46] The United States as a 'frontier zone' was at the bottom of A. P. Usher's three levels of historical demography, with a population which was confronted with a space which had hardly been developed by man.[47]

In his best-selling *Introduction to Contemporary History*, which was published in the mid-1960s, ten years before *The Cloud of Danger*, Geoffrey Barraclough also made a plea for the study of historical periods 'when the problems which are actual in the world today first took visible shape'. Even so, he thought that the United States was an absurd example of a pre-industrial, underdeveloped economy. It was not over-populated in the 1850s, it was not pre-industrial, it was not 90 per cent agricultural, underresourced or its population largely illiterate.[48] As Geoffrey Elton, another historian, argued at the time, 'when some writers can treat pre-industrial England, the economically most advanced society in Europe of its day, as though it was like tribal Africa . . . understanding is destroyed not assisted'.[49]

The fact that the lessons of the open frontier are irrelevant to a country in the throes of economic development has not, alas, prevented other American writers from propagating the American myth. In his book *African Realities* Kenneth Adelman paints a stark picture of a continent in which absolute poverty, instead of declining, is steadily gaining ground, in which seven out of ten countries are sinking even deeper into poverty. As he graphically points out many African states cannot even be described as developing countries; many are not developing at all.

Like Kennan, Adelman clearly stands outside the culture he is attempting to describe. Both men are imperfectly fitted to mediate between the two. Both are patently uncomfortable in any society but their own. Adelman is unusual in being prepared to admit that his own prescriptions for development, rooted as they are in the United States' own experience, may have little relevance to the developing world. Yet he is critical of the liberal intelligentsia for trying to encourage Africa to adopt indigenous solutions to its own problems:

It is one thing to claim (with a good measure of truth) that Africa will not soon adopt traditional Western values, but quite another to say that Africa should not adopt them, and further that the United States should not even promote its goals.[50]

Unfortunately, the United States' values, like its historical experience, are as foreign to Africa as they are to the rest of the Third World. They may have useful application in the United States; they do not, however, have universal significance and validity.

To argue otherwise is to take refuge in a form of cultural determinism that seems more like an attempt at evasion than explanation. Adelman betrays his real concern towards the end of his book when he notes that 'traditional African religions are entirely void of notions such as "fate" or the "forces of history" marching towards progress and redemption.'[51] In arguing that the United States should set an example that others can follow he is really arguing that only the United States can redeem societies suffering from a spiritual vacuum. Such premises only serve to obscure rather than illuminate an understanding of the developing world. Indeed, they have so distorted American perceptions that Adelman and Kennan, and others like them, have failed to appreciate how little their own conceptions actually conform to the reality they are trying to describe.

INGROWING THOUGHTS

'To have doubted one's own first thoughts is the mark of a civilised man'
                                                            Oliver Wendell Holmes

If the United States is a radical country why does it find itself so vilified by the Third World? It is a criticism which is not always taken lightly. Many Third World countries are genuinely at a loss to understand the motivating force behind US action, the belief that virtue is its own reward, that violence is entirely unacceptable. As Henry Wallace warned in 1947, 'once America stands for opposition to change we are lost. America will become the most hated nation in the world.'

The United States, of course, is not a status quo power, far from it, but as the principal defender of the present international order it still puts a premium on order rather than justice. In the world of the present, violence is seen as the principal threat. The United States will support radical governments, never violent ones.

Unfortunately there are few examples, if any, of non-violent revolutions, non-violent land reform programmes or non-violent experiments in political reform. In that respect, the United States is hopelessly tied to its own past, or rather a historical myth perpetuated by de Tocqueville. 'The great advantage of the Americans', he wrote, 'is that they have arrived at a state of democracy without having to endure a democratic revolution.' As it happened Tocqueville – for once – was a hopeless historian. The United States was not born free; it had to fight for its freedom. The rebellion of 1776 was not a war of independence but a revolution, more socially disruptive, in fact, than any similar uprising before the October Revolution of 1917.

The United States has fallen victim to a paradox of history. The paradox is not that the United States has been handicapped by its happy history, as Samuel Huntington maintains,[52] but that the Americans have been a turbulent people who have happened to live in a stable society since 1865.[53] The idea that the United States was born free, that its history is relatively bloodless persists to this day. An editorial in *The New Republic* in 1984 opined, 'America began free; its struggles were never to become free, but stay free ... history in other words has made Americans ... the least understanding people in the world.' The appeal of US isolationism and the awkwardness of US interventionism, it concluded, arose from unfamiliarity with political oppression and social injustice that is the common experience of the rest of the world. 'Out national consciousness of freedom has equipped us badly for the spreading of it. That may be history's bad joke on the American century.'

It is also a perverse joke at the United States' expense. For the main result of rewriting of history has been to advocate reforms without understanding the kinds of pressures which have proved effective in getting reforms on the statute book.[54] How does one measure the violence of a revolution against the violence of the regime that preceded it? There is no way of measuring the price of historical victories; there is no way of deciding whether a decisive social or political gain is worth a particular loss. Robert Heilbroner only knew that the way in which the United States normally kept 'the books of history' was probably wrong.[55]

The two seminal events in the United States' modern development, the Revolution of 1776 and the Civil War of the 1860s, were both revolutionary episodes. As Barrington Moore writes, 'The American civil war broke the power of a landed elite that was an obstacle in the way of democratic advance, in this case one that had grown up as part of capitalism.'⁵⁶ Charles Beard thought the Civil War important enough to merit the description 'the second American revolution'. Moore preferred to call it the first because he believed the rebellion against Britain had promoted no fundamental change in the structure of society.⁵⁷ He was wrong. He too was a victim of de Tocqueville's historical myth.

The axiom that the Revolution was not, in fact, revolutionary is an old one. George Bancroft writing in 1879 called it a 'revolution achieved with such benign tranquility' that even conservatives could find little to censure.⁵⁸ The liberals, naturally, found much to censure in the failure of the Revolution to reward poor farmers with expropriated land, or to abandon property qualifications for office-holding. The conservatives were reassured when the Convention of Philadelphia (1787) rallied to the propertied class and put the radical drift into reverse.

In the 1950s in the era of McCarthyism and the Cold War many historians were encouraged to see the rebellion as a purely anti-colonial struggle, a war of independence which involved few if any major social changes. It was John Quincy Adams who translated the first of many tracts comparing the French and American Revolutions – in this case one by Friedrich Gentz in 1800.⁵⁹ Gentz cited the US example as a conservative defence of established rights against the British challenge. The merit of his essay, wrote Adams in his introduction, was that it rescued 'the revolution from the disgraceful imputation of having proceeded from the same principles as the French'.⁶⁰

In 1955 the same essay was reprinted for mass distribution with a forward by Russell Kirk, a publicist of the 'new conservatism'. During the height of the Cold War no one wished to admit that the Revolution had marked a radical break with the past, that 24 *émigrés* per 1,000 of population had chosen to leave the thirteen colonies rather than live under the new order, compared with five for every 1,000 Frenchmen after 1789. The French *émigrés* chose to return after 1795; the Americans did not. The fact that there was a real conflict between Americans, that the Revolution was a civil war as well as a rebellion against Britain, was speedily forgotten. The American consensus rested on eliminating entirely from the national consciousness a once significant, even numerous element of dissent.⁶¹

It also rested on a reluctance to admit that violence was once considered an American birthright. As Jefferson acknowledged, the revolution had been conceived in violence and carried through with arms. He could not deny the right to protest, even if that right involved violent action. As he wrote to d'Ivernois in 1795, 'It is unfortunate that the efforts of mankind to recover the freedom of which they have been so long deprived, will be accompanied with violence, with error and with crime. But while we weep over the means, we must pay for the end.'⁶²

The upshot of all this is that the Americans have used a radical language which has a peculiar resonance for them in terms of their own past, but none at all to those outside it. That is the meaning of the title of Robert Brunstein's book *The Revolution as Theatre* (1971), for most Americans are incapable of taking foreign radicalism on its own terms.

Dean Rusk might express the conviction that the ideas which inspired the American Revolution were among 'the most powerful forces at work in the world today'.[63] Cyrus Vance in his first major speech as Secretary of State might claim that 'the cause of human liberty is now the one great revolutionary cause.'[64] The former, however, was appealing to a potent historical myth; the latter used the world revolution in a way that would have met with Bancroft's approval.

Perhaps, John F. Kennedy came closest to the truth when he accused Castro of betraying the Cuban Revolution. For what he was doing, in effect, was blaming him for pressing ahead with a revolution, rather than a programme of reform. As Woodrow Wilson once said, 'revolutions always put things back, and [postpone] sensible reforms.'[65] That explains why the United States is a radical but deeply unrevolutionary state, a victim of a manufactured past which betrays its own origins, a country that has chosen to treat the dilemmas of the Third World as if, to quote Hancock, they were not moral dilemmas at all but 'rather simple problems in applied ethics.'

Constantly retreating into the past, Americans have acted as if non-violence were its own reward. Their fascination with violence suggests a wish for self-forgetfulness, for a temporary abeyance of the internal conflicts which are its identity as a nation. As Niebuhr warned almost 40 years ago, one of the ironies of American history is that the United States could not have remained virtuous and have survived. If it had really been as innocent as it liked to believe, it would have had to have forsaken sin; in short, it would have had to have escaped from its own history into a fantasy world of its own imagination.[66]

Another reason why the United States has fallen foul of the Third World is that it seems to have applied a set of double standards towards non-Communist regimes compared with those which are Communist. It appears to have found nothing particularly traumatic about the violence of right-wing regimes; it has merely looked the other way. Left-wing governments are quite another matter.

When Suharto massacred 300,000 alleged Communists in Indonesia in the 1960s there was practically no mention of the event in the US press. When the Indonesian government began the systematic massacre of the people of East Timor in the late 1970s the same indifference was notable. The killing fields of Cambodia or the plight of the boat people in Vietnam were another matter altogether. Occasionally this dual standard has backfired badly. Ironically, in Central America the Contras accused

President Reagan of making them a joke by referring to them as the 'moral equivalent of the Founding Fathers',[67] while describing their armed struggle against the Sandinistas as being 'in the best traditions' of the American Revolution.[68] The need for balance is sometimes too important to ignore altogether.

The United States has never opposed revolution as such. It was the spectre of Communism which so alarmed successive US administrations in the past. As Johnson told the American people in May 1965 after the invasion of the Dominican Republic: 'Revolution in any country is a matter for that country to deal with. It becomes a matter for hemispheric action only when the object is the establishment of a communist dictatorship.'[69] Perhaps, Johnson's predecessor John F. Kennedy had put the matter most succinctly a few years earlier when discussing whether to remove the Trujillo family from Dominica. There were three possibilities, he told his colleagues: democratising the island by force; keeping Trujillo in power or allowing the Communists to take over. The United States should aim for the first option, but could not afford to renounce the second as long as the third remained theoretically possible.[70] In its more recent manifestation this thinking emerged in a memorandum leaked to the press in 1981. Human rights are not advanced, the Reagan administration noted, by replacing bad regimes with worse ones, or corrupt dictators with zealous Communists.[71]

In the 1960s the fear of Communist subversion was so great that it reached bizarre proportions. It was only a small step from identifying a world Communist conspiracy against the United States to seeing one at work in the United States itself, when Hubert Humphrey declared that 'the international communist movement [had] organised and masterminded the peace demonstrations' against the war in Vietnam.[72] Lincoln Gordon, the US ambassador in Rio, had earlier congratulated the Brazilian military for the 1964 coup which was to leave them in power for the next fifteen years. The coup, he told the Military College in Rio, was one of the 'major turning points' in recent history, equal in its significance for the world to the Berlin airlift, the Korean War and Kennedy's resolute stance during the Cuban missile crisis.[73]

It was this kind of thinking which inspired the Rockefeller Report of 1969, which was commissioned by Richard Nixon to look into the possibilities of revolution in Latin America. The report eventually identified all radical change as a threat to US interests. It was one of the most conservative documents the United States ever produced.[74]

Ever since then the United States has been plagued by having to support corrupt regimes against the threat of Communism. It is not necessarily a dilemma of its own making, but it is one to which the lessons of its own past afford no escape. Whether or not regimes like Mobutu's in Zaïre are deserving of Western support, both liberals and conservatives face the same dilemma. Liberals would prefer to distance themselves from a government that clearly shows little regard, if any, for democratic norms of behaviour; conservatives, while equally disapproving of its behaviour, are clearly wary of throwing over self-professed allies for fear the United States may find itself without any. Over the years hypocrisy has become a common refuge for liberal and conservative politicians alike.

The United States' fear of Communism, is not essentially military in inspiration; it is deeply cultural. Of course, the situation is not quite as bad as it was in the 1960s when it attempted to adjust to major changes in the international system over which it exercised little control, or even comprehension. It took many years for the United States to realise that nothing had really changed; that the new countries of the Third World would continue to remain prisoners of the economic order the Western powers had created at Bretton Woods; that neo-colonialism had enabled a country such as France to translate successfully a system of formal control in West Africa into a system of informal influence.

The post-war world, however, was still very much an age of transition. Some periods of history like the pre-1914 world create illusions of permanence; others like the inter-war years expectations of doom, what Jung detected in the 1930s as a 'faint whiff of burning in the air'. The problem with the world the United States occupied as a superpower was that everyone knew it was a period of transition, but no one knew what the future held. Was the United States likely to ride the 'wave of the future', or be swamped by it?

Kennedy was not the first politician to use the phrase. It had been popularised ironically by Charles Lindberg who had seen Fascism as the wave of the future in the 1930s and wanted the United States to identify with it before it was too late.[75] In the 1960s, however, it soon became a peculiarly American obsession. As Heilbroner wrote in 1967, the rise of Communism in the Third World might lead the rest of the world to conclude that Communism, not liberal capitalism, represented the future. As Kissinger told an audience in Dallas in March 1976, if the United States did not resist Communism everywhere it manifested itself, the world would inevitably and rightly accommodate itself to what it perceived to be the predominant ideology of the time.[76]

The dilemma has not vanished with the reversals, some of them significant (Afghanistan), others not (Grenada), which Communism has suffered in the last few years. As a country whose past mandates a role, the Americans are determined still to ride the wave, not be swamped by it. In his memoirs Brzezinski described Carter's human rights programme as a recognition of 'the historical inevitability of our times'. The programme was central to 'the relevance of' the United States in a changing world. 'Human rights was the wave of the present. It was the central form in which mankind is expressing its new political awakening and it was essential for the United States to be identified with it'.[77] Before Carter, Kennedy predicted that unless the United States adjusted to the 'revolutionary changes' in the world, the United States would be doomed to 'slide downhill into dust, dullness and decay'.[78]

Unfortunately, the Americans are still a desperately anxious people. As one of the critics of US liberalism has noted, the United States seems to have moved from a period of confidence that history is on its side to suspicion that it is not. It is facing 'an historic inability to cope with the modern world'. One of the reasons why liberal politicians have proved so unconvincing in the foreign policy platforms they have put before the electorate is that they have felt themselves to be 'cornered by events' not of their own making.[79] One of the reasons why conservatives have dominated the political agenda has been their willingness to return to the verities of the Founding Fathers, to use a language the electorate not only knows, but with which it can identify, and claim as its own.

The final reason why the United States has lost its way is that the world has become a deeply disturbing place; the pace of change has been too rapid to adjust to. It was disturbing that in Bolivia in 1965 300 guerrillas led by Che Guevara could seek to challenge the state. As Guevara maintained, it was not necessary to wait until all the conditions for making a revolution obtained; an insurrection could create them.[80] It was a flawed proposition, of course, one which was to lead to his own death, but it appealed to the Fidelista/Guevarist radicals of the 1960s whose brand of Marxism was anything but 'scientific'.

From an American perspective the world is still a deeply disturbing place. It is disturbing that a master sergeant can seize power in Liberia, the state in Africa with which the United States has had the closest and longest association. It is even more disturbing that a flight lieutenant in Ghana can seize power, not only once, but a second time as well.

In the 1960s the United States' fear was heightened by the fact that it saw all guerrilla wars or struggles for national liberation as part of a global Soviet conspiracy. It was particularly disturbed by the Three Continents Conference which convened in Havana in 1966 at the Soviet Union's expense, and which was attended by 82 different national liberation movements.

The United States remained true to the Truman Doctrine's insistence that the notion could not permit changes in the status quo which were brought about by 'such methods as coercion, subterfuge or political infiltration'. It did not help that the Pentagon's *Dictionary of US Military Terms* (1972) defined subversion as 'primarily communist inspired, supported or exploited'.[81] It was an unhelpful definition because it drew attention away from the causes of unrest. Instead it focused it on the aims of national liberation movements, rather than the means they had for realising them. The latter, after all, might amount to no more than Guevara's 300 men in Bolivia who were in the end captured and shot, betrayed by the very revolutionary theory they so enthusiastically espoused.

If the United States is no longer so obsessed by Communist conspiracies it still finds much of the Third World deeply unstable. Political instability is what the United States finds the greatest threat of all. For the Soviet Union instability still represents an opportunity to exploit; for the United States it still represents a threat, not even a challenge to which it might rise by displaying greater imagination.

One of the ironies of the situation, of course, is that much of the instability it faces has been created by contact with the United States itself, by accepting its economic maxims (the removal of food subsidies, for one, which produced rioting on the streets in Egypt in 1977 and Tunisia in 1981), or its political programmes, most of all the vision of the future derived from the United States' supposed past. For many countries the arrival of USAID teams, or Peace Corps workers, has had an effect similar to that of the visitors to Axel Heyst's remote island in Conrad's *Victory* whose appearance, Heyst felt, was 'like those myths current in Polynesia, of amazing strangers who arrive at an island, gods or demons, bringing good or evil to the innocence of the inhabitants – gifts of unknown things, words never before heard'.

In the end, the United States has taken the easy way out; propping up existing orders, rather than forging new ones; defending *anciens régimes* whenever it has been forced to. That is why it is possible to see the United States as a counter-revolutionary power, a role it has retained to this day. The problem with counter-revolutionary powers is that almost by definition they are in decline, countries that have lost confidence in themselves, societies that having turned their backs on the future, are sustained only by a fading vision of the past.

NOTES

1. Raymond Aron, *The Imperial Republic* (Englewood Cliffs: Prentice Hall, 1974).
2. Henry Feis, 'Is the United States imperialist?', *Yale Review* 61:1 (Autumn 1951) p. 13.
3. Robert W. Tucker, *The Radical Left and American Foreign Policy* (Baltimore: Johns Hopkins University Press, 1971) p. 61. See also George Liska, *Career of Empire* (Baltimore: Johns Hopkins University Press, 1978); Robert Osgood, *Retreat from Empire?* (Baltimore: Johns Hopkins University Press, 1973). Even Hans Morgenthau rather surprisingly identified with the Left on the issue of

economic imperialism. Noting that Wilson had wanted to bring order to the Old World by exporting the United States' democratic institutions, he argued that his own contemporaries wanted to bring wealth and prosperity to the rest of the world through the export of US capital (Morgenthau, *The Purpose of American Politics* (New York: Knopf, 1960) p. 190).

4. Joel Barlow, *Advice to the Privileged Orders*, vol. 2 (London: D. I. Eaton, 1795) pp. 90–1. Cited in James Field, *America and the Mediterranean World 1776–1882* (Princeton, NJ: Princeton University Press, 1979) p. 12.
5. Louis Hartz, *The Liberal Tradition in America: an interpretation of American political thought since the revolution* (New York: Harcourt Brace Jovanovich, 1955).
6. Robert Gilpin, *US Power and the Multinational Corporation: the political economy of foreign direct investment* (New York: Basic Books, 1975).
7. Fernand Braudel, *Civilisation and Capitalism*, vol. 3: *The Perspective of the World* (London: Collins, 1984) p. 622.
8. For two compelling criticisms of the US economic imperialism school see William Tabman (ed.), *Globalism and its Critics* (Lexington: Heath, 1973); and John Swomley, *American Empire: the political ethics of twentieth century conquest* (New York: Macmillan, 1970).
9. Eugene Rostow, *Law, Power and the Pursuit of Peace* (New York: Harper & Row, 1968) p. 44.
10. Cited in Richard Feinberg, *The Intemperate Zone: the Third World Challenge to US foreign policy* (New York: W. W. Norton, 1983) p. 193.
11. Robert Packenham, *Liberal America and the Third World: political development ideas in foreign aid and political science* (Princeton, NJ: Princeton University Press, 1973) p. 80.
12. Harry Magdoff, *The Age of Imperialism* (New York: Monthly Review Press, 1969) p. 126.
13. Ross and Wise (eds), *The Invisible Government* (New York: Bantam Books, 1965) pp. 116–21.
14. Cited in Tom Barry, Beth Wood and Deb Preusch, *Dollars and Dictators: a guide to Central America* (London: Zed Press, 1983) p. 119.
15. For a typical left-wing view see Stephen Kinzer, *Bitter Fruit: the untold story of the American coup in Guatemala* (London: Sinclair Brown, 1982).
16. John Girling, *America and the Third World: revolution and intervention* (London: Routledge & Kegan Paul, 1980).
17. Arthur Schlessinger, *A Thousand Days: John F. Kennedy in the White House* (London: André Deutsch, 1965).
18. Richard Nixon, *The Real War* (New York: Warner Books, 1980) p. 350.
19. C. L. Sulzberger, *The World and Richard Nixon* (New York: Prentice Hall, 1987) pp. 54–74.
20. Cited in E. Stillman and W. Pfaff, *Power and Impotence* (New York: Random House, 1966) p. 27.
21. The word 'America' has not always been held in high esteem. In Flaubert's *Dictionary of Received Ideas* in which he recorded the clichés, platitudes, the borrowed and unquestioned ideas with which the 'right thinking' swaddled their

minds, the entry for America reads: 'Famous example of injustice: Columbus discovered it and it is named after Amerigo Vespucci. If it weren't for the discovery of America, we should not be suffering from syphilis and phylloxera. Exalt it all the same, especially if you have not been there. Lecture people on self-government' (Gustave Flaubert, *Dictionary of Received Ideas*, trans. Jacques Barzun (London: New Directions, 1967) pp. 14–15).

22. Ernest K. Lindley (ed.), *The Winds of Freedom: selections from the speeches and statements of Dean Rusk* (Boston: Beacon Press, 1963) p. 21.
23. 'Morgenthau's foreign policy', *World Issues* 5:2 (December 1977).
24. Cited in V. G. Kiernan, *America: the new imperialism: from white settlement to world hegemony* (London: Zed Press, 1978) p. ii.
25. Theodore Sorensen, *The Kennedy Legacy* (London: Weidenfeld and Nicolson, 1970) p. 186.
26. Michael O'Leary, *The Politics of Foreign Aid* (New York: Atherton Press, 1967) p. 14.
27. *Peace Corps: the toughest job you'll ever love* (Washington DC: GPO, 1981) p. 2. For one of the many critical studies of the corps see David Hapgood, *A Close Look at the Peace Corps* (Boston: Little & Stead, 1968).
28. Robert Ellsworth and Kenneth Adelman, 'Foolish Intelligence', *Foreign Policy* 36 (Fall 1979) p. 149.
29. John Updike, *The Coup* (1978). For another literary invention of the American abroad at loose in the developing world see Saul Bellow, *Henderson: the Rain God* (1952).
30. O'Leary, *Politics of Foreign Aid*, op. cit., p. 93.
31. *ibid.*,
32. David Baldwin, *Economic Development and American Foreign Policy* (Chicago: University of Chicago Press, 1966) p. 262.
33. O'Leary, *Politics of Foreign Aid*, op. cit., p. 13.
34. *ibid.*, p. 14.
35. Geoffrey Gorer, *The American People* (New York: Norton, 1948) p. 225.
36. Packenham, *Liberal America*, op. cit., pp. 114–5.
37. Remarks at the 1981 annual meeting of the World Bank and IMF, *Press Release No. 3* (29 September 1981).
38. Schlessinger, *A Thousand Days*, op. cit., p. 204.
39. *The Budget of the United States Government Fiscal Year 1969* (Washington DC: USGPO, 1968) p. 27.
40. *Congressional Quarterly* (20 February 1970) p. 534.
41. Schlessinger, *A Thousand Days*, op. cit., pp. 588–9.
42. Donald Devine, *The Political Culture of the United States* (Boston: Little, Brown, 1972); see also Herbert McClosky and John Zaller, *The American Ethos: public attitudes toward capitalism and democracy* (Cambridge, Mass.: Harvard University Press, 1984).
43. Edward Weisband, *The Ideology of American Foreign Policy: a paradigm of Lockean liberalism* (Beverley Hills: Sage, 1973), p. 62.
44. George Kennan, *The Cloud of Danger: some current problems of American foreign policy* (New York: Little, Brown, 1979) p. 112.

45. David Potter, *People of Plenty: economic abundance and the American character* (Chicago: University of Chicago Press, 1954).
46. Henry Steele Commanger, 'A historical look at our political morality', *Saturday Review* (10 July 1965) p. 17.
47. Fernand Braudel, *Civilisation and Capitalism*, vol. 1: *The Structures of Everyday Life* (London: Collins, 1979) p. 61.
48. Geoffrey Barraclough, *Introduction to Contemporary History* (London: Penguin, 1965) pp. 9–24.
49. Geoffrey Elton, *Practice of History* (London: Pelican, 1969) p. 48.
50. Kenneth Adelman, *African Realities* (New York: Crane, Russak, 1980) p. 132.
51. *ibid.*, p. 136.
52. Samuel Huntington, *Political Order in Changing Societies* (New Haven: Yale University Press, 1968) pp. 5–7. See Hugh Graham and Ted Robert Gurr *Violence in America: historical and comparative perspectives* (New York: Bantam Books, 1969) p. 799.
53. *New Republic* (30 April 1984). The idea that the United States has a blameless past is an old one. In a best-seller in 1846 an American visiting the dungeons of an English castle observes, 'Better the past should be blank than be written over with such bloody hieroglyphics as these. When I consider these records and reflect upon the deeds of this crime stained land I look upon our young nation as an innocent child' (David Lowenthal, *The Past as a Foreign Country* (Oxford: Oxford University Press, 1985) p. 110).
54. Albert Hirschman, *Journeys towards Progress: studies of economic policy making in Latin America* (New York: Twentieth Century Fund, 1963) p. 260.
55. Robert Heilbroner, 'Counter-revolutionary America', *Commentary* (April 1967) p. 34.
56. Barrington Moore, *The Social Origins of Dictatorship and Democracy: lord and peasant in the making of the modern world* (London: Penguin, 1966) p. 426.
57. *ibid.*, p. 112.
58. Robert Palmer, *The Age of the Democratic Revolution: a political history of Europe and America 1760–1800*, vol. 1: *The Challenge* (Princeton, NJ: Princeton University Press, 1969).
59. *ibid.*, p. 187.
60. *ibid.*, p. 188.
61. *ibid.*, p. 190.
62. Cited in Saul Padover (ed.), *Thomas Jefferson on Democracy* (New York: New American Library, 1939) p. 30. See also Jefferson's response on hearing the news of Shay's revolt which was put down bloodily by Washington. 'I hold it that a little rebellion now and then is a good thing and is necessary in the political world as storms in the physical.' Cited in Charles Wiltise, *The Jeffersonian Tradition in American Democracy* (Chapel Hill: North Carolina Press, 1935) p. 86.
63. Cited in Carl Deger, 'The American past: an unsuspected obstacle in foreign affairs', *American Scholar* 32:2 (Spring 1963) p. 192.
64. Cyrus Vance, Athens, Georgia (30 April 1977).

65. Cited in William Appleman Williams, 'Wilson', *New York Review of Books* (2 December 1971) p. 4.
66.
    Reinhold Niebuhr, *The Irony of American History* (New York: Charles Scribner, 1952) p.23.
67. *New York Times* (28 March 1985).
68. *New York Times* (30 October 1988).
69. Ronald Steel, *Pax Americana, op. cit.,* p. 232.
70. Schlessinger, *A Thousand Days, op. cit.*
71. *New York Times* (5 November 1981).
72. Michael Parenti, *The Anti-Communist Impulse* (New York: Random House, 1969) p. 13.
73. Packenham, *Liberal America, op. cit.,* p. 171. Gordon was an implacable opponent of the Alliance for Progress.
74. See George Lodge, 'US aid to Latin America: funding radical change', *Foreign Affairs* 47:3 (April 1969).
75. Lionel Gelber, *America in Britain's place: the leadership of the West and Anglo-American unity* (London: George Allen and Unwin, 1961) p. 31n.
76. Henry Kissinger, *DSB* (March 1976).
77. Zbigniew Brzezinski, *Power and Principle: memoirs of the National Security Adviser 1977–81* (London: Weidenfeld and Nicolson, 1983) p. 127.
78. Schlessinger, *A Thousand Days, op. cit.,* pp. 872–3.
79. Paul Goldstone, *The Collapse of Liberal Empire: science and revolution in the twentieth century* (New Haven: Yale University Press, 1977) p. 72.
80. Che Guevara, *Guerilla Warfare* (London: Penguin, 1969) p. 13.
81. John Girling, *America and the Third World, op. cit.*

6. Intimations of mortality: is the United States in decline?

'Let us remember that we shall . . . fall into the decline and infirmities of old age'

John Quincy Adams (1787)

'Our Past has become unpredictable'

Editor of *Znamia* (1988)

According to some writers the United States has been in decline for much longer than even the most pessimistic analysts would contend. In 1942 Joseph Schumpeter predicted that the United States' entrepreneurship would be destroyed by mechanisation, which would in turn rob businessmen of their spirit of adventure and deprive the economy of dynamic management. His *cri de coeur* about the passing of America's entrepreneurial vitality on the eve of the nation's rise as a superpower bears a striking similarity to Arnold Toynbee's theory that Rome's decline could be traced to the Second Punic War, which destroyed the political ecology of the Italian peninsula and thus the base of the Roman Empire, whose decline and eventual fall six centuries later were to be captured so vividly by Edward Gibbon.[1]

Twenty-five years later the pessimists were dealing a stronger suit. Had the American century come to an end? One writer felt that the century had passed in the closing days of the Second World War, that the United States had lost its status as a superpower by the late 1960s, that its history 'as a nation [was] coming to an end'.[2] Writing a few years earlier Ronald Steele contended that the curtain had run down on the Pax Americana faster than it had on the Pax Britannica, which had been relegated to the scrap-heap of history within 25 years of the fall of Singapore in 1942.[3]

In the mid-1960s as the United States found itself mired in the Vietnam War Donald Brandon concluded that 'America must come of age', that it must escape its political adolescence if it was ever to reach maturity.[4] By 1973 it seemed too late. As the Vietnam War came to an ignominious end the noted political columnist, Henry Brandon confidently wrote of *The Retreat of American Power,* claiming that its 'design' had already been delineated; only its pace and extent remained a matter of speculation.[5] Throughout the early 1970s the American public may have been bewildered and bedazzled at turns by the artful statecraft of the master illusionist Henry Kissinger, whose brilliant diplomatic illusions seemed to compensate for any loss of power the United States had incurred in Indo-China. Yet it was Kissinger, the ultimate apologist of Bismarckian politics, who defined diplomacy in the same period as the 'art of restraining the exercise of power',[6] conscious of how little real power the United States enjoyed.

In addressing the whole subject it is not clear whether the peddlers of doom are talking about national decadence, imperial retreat or the passing of an era – the American century – a historical concept first propagated in 1942 by the writer Henry Luce. In such circumstances it is hardly surprising that modern scholars should have encountered such difficulty in defining what, if anything, constitutes the decline they are trying to describe. Its nature and causes have remained contentious for 25 years and will doubtless continue to defy precise definition for the foreseeable future. The popularity of Paul Kennedy's book *The Rise and Fall of the Great Powers*, together with the hostility with which its publication was greeted, illustrated how difficult it is to phrase the problem of America's decline in a manner conducive to rational discussion.[7]

Obsessed with the need to escape relegation to the sidelines of history, from which no country has ever regained centre-stage, different interest groups have defined the problem in different ways, each offering the patient dubious nostrums which may yet prove more fatal to recovery than the disease itself.

Politicians appealing to their own constituencies have been eager to communicate their particular concerns to the widest possible public. The Democrats may have been remarkably short of political ideas during the 1988 Presidential campaign but they were quick enough to attack their opponents for overseeing the largest budget and trade deficits in the country's history. 'As a nation' remarked New York's Governor Mario Cuomo in March 1989, 'we are increasingly unwilling to forgo anything that involves the smallest sacrifice.'[8] For many, America's 'intellectual deficit' is the most worrying of all.

Academics wishing to strike a chord with the 'attentive public', to articulate a popular fear or even a populist vision have also been forced to cut their cloth to the prevailing political fashion. Their's is an even more narrowly based trade than the politicians. If their works are to escape relegation to the shelves of university libraries, if, instead, they are to be discussed and debated by the informed public to whom they would like to appeal, their theories have to be universal in application. Their role inevitably has its critics. 'We appear to be living in yet another age', writes

Robert Nisbet, 'in which "failure of nerve" is conspicuous not in the minds of America's majority, but in the minds of those who are gatekeepers for ideas and intellectuals.'[9] Years earlier Spiro Agnew, Nixon's colourful first Vice-President, had also lambasted the 'nattering nabobs of negativism',[10] in keeping with the administration's belief that everything in Vietnam would be all right but for the manifest *traison des clercs*.

Certainly, Kennedy's book had an impact beyond the significance of the 30 or so pages which he devoted to a discussion of the decline of the United States. An earlier article in *The Atlantic Monthly* had passed almost unnoticed the year before, evidence perhaps that 30 pages of footnotes added authority to a view which might otherwise have been dismissed as a journalistic *jeu d'esprit* on the part of a younger member of the profession, or a valedictory reprise in the case of a respected political commentator such as Henry Brandon.

Intellectual 'fashion' must run deep indeed when there is little real evidence that the United States is in decline, or the evidence is at best conflicting, or even self-fulfilling. It is in fact the popular mood – the attractions of decline for a nation weighed down by its international responsibilities – which has tended to preclude dispassionate analysis of the question.

Decline is a potent theme for a popular audience. Neo-conservatives find in it a warning for the nation against falling educational standards, the drug culture of the inner cities and the 'decadence' of 'permissive' liberalism. Liberal Democrats dubious of the Reagan 'renewal' have attacked the foundations of America's economic resurgence while exaggerating the extent to which any administration could arrest, let alone reverse, a country's decline. The story of US politics, after all, is of grand designs ineptly executed, of aspirations on the part of enthusiasts like President Carter who failed to understand or master the political system in time.[11]

Erich Heller has given expression to a mood which is widespread among the intelligentsia, that 'the history of the West since 1917 looks like the work of children clumsily filling in with lurid colours a design drawn by Oswald Spengler'. To some extent we are all Spenglerians, doomed to think in the same categories, perhaps even to use the same mental language, to believe no longer in progress, but the ineluctable moral decline of Western civilisation.

What, however, do American politicians, academics or the public at large mean by decline? Do they mean the decline of the Pax Americana or the United States itself, or are they referring instead to the passing of an era – the American century, an era which, to quote de Madariaga, has coincided with 'the birth of the world',[12] a world which emerged from the carnage of the First World War from which the United States itself emerged as the world's pre-eminent power?

A NATION AT RISK

The feeling of national decline obviously runs deep. As Carter reminded the American people in 1979 the most immediate threat to the United States' power was a crisis of confidence in their government, in their public institutions, but above all in themselves. It was a problem which de Tocqueville had foreseen in the nineteenth century when he forecast that in their anxiety to make their own fortunes, the Americans might lose sight of the private fortune of each other and the prosperity of all. The idea of self-interest at the heart of the American character, de Tocqueville wrote, was a curious one: 'the better to look after what they call their business they neglect their chief business which is to remain their own masters.'[13] Reagan's promise of renewal seems to bear this prediction out, as young capitalists continue to strip the assets of companies listed on Wall Street, as the country allows foreign interests to buy huge chunks of the US economy, as the administration persists in financing its defence spending by borrowing increasingly from the Japanese.

Apart from the economic crisis many Americans have seized upon a number of cultural factors to amplify what they see as the progressive 'closing of the American mind'. In a book which remained on the best-seller list for months Allan Bloom decried the fact that in their desire to free the United States from prejudice American liberal educationalists had allowed the country to lapse into a mire of cultural and moral relativism. The United States, he believed, had reached a stage where 'indiscrimination is a moral imperative because it is the opposite of discrimination.' For a modern nation founded upon the principle of reason 'a crisis in the university, the home of reason, is perhaps the profoundest crisis they face.'[14]

Bloom's voice is not an isolated one. E. D. Hirsch's *Cultural Illiteracy*, which proved to be another best-seller, confirmed a prevailing mood of cultural *Angst*. In 1983, four years before Bloom put pen to paper, the Reagan administration issued a report with the dramatic title of *A Nation at Risk*, which diagnosed a 'rising tide of mediocrity' in US schools. Already 10 per cent of Americans are illiterate, the highest percentage in the industrial world. The National Geographic Society commissioned a survey in August 1988, which found that half of college students could not find Vietnam on a map. Perhaps, most disturbing of all is the knowledge of mathematics, in which the United States for once trails behind even the Soviet Union. Today students still read Silvester Thompson's *Calculus Made Easy*, as part of a two semester college course. When Thompson wrote the book in 1919 it was intended for 16-year-old adolescents.

Citing more examples would be valueless. The problem of ignorance after all is hardly new. Even at the height of the Vietnam War only 25 per cent of Americans were aware that mainland China was under Communist rule.[15]

During a visit to the United States before the First World War Rupert Brooke discovered that the students at Harvard were labouring under the impression that Matthew Arnold was still alive. 'I couldn't bring myself to tell [them] that even in Rugby we had forgiven that brilliant youth his iconoclastic tendencies some time ago and that as a matter of fact he had died when I was eight months old.'[16]

The critical difference between the past and the present, however, is marked. Something more profound than declining educational standards appears to be at work. Just as the printing press transformed language and behaviour (especially political consciousness) 300 years ago, so the electronic information revolution seems to have produced a nation whose attention span is strictly limited. American youth appears to have little patience for formal education and therefore fails to read or reason productively. Once they have left school 60 per cent of all American high school children never read another book.

IMPERIAL RETREAT?

We can also find structural signs of decline in the Pax Americana. The US empire in a sense created the seeds of its own decline by reviving the economies of Western Europe and Japan, while stimulating its own dependence on foreign trade and fixed investment. American scholars on the Left have been preoccupied for so long by Latin America's dependency that they have ignored the signs of the United States own dependence on an external economy it once dominated. Between 1946 and 1949 the country's national income doubled; by the late 1950s Germany and Japan were both growing faster than the United States. At the same time the United States mortgaged its future by running up vast defence budgets, initially to encourage its allies to rearm.

There is nothing especially 'new', therefore, about the United States' economic problems. When in the late 1960s a rumour that peace was at hand in Vietnam led to a rally in the stock market, it was clear that even those who were committed to the War believed the United States needed to curtail its international commitments to deal with such pressing domestic problems as inner-city renewal.[17]

Government policies seem merely to have compounded the problem. Carter's Presidency was important for a dramatic shift from unilateral reflation to agreement at the Bonn economic summit (July 1978) to ease up on domestic expansionary policies which were held responsible for high inflation. Reagan's tax cuts and regulatory reforms produced a massive budget deficit and a burgeoning trade imbalance with the rest of the world, which provoked the October 1987 stock market crash. The budget deficit was financed by high interest rates which made the United States an attractive market for foreign investment. In just two years (1983-5) the United States' capital position switched from that of a leading creditor to leading debtor nation. In relation to its export earnings the United States is going into debt faster than any major developed country since 1945, even faster than the average of the seven major developing country debtors on the eve of the debt crisis.[18] As *The Washington Post* observed some years ago, America was fortunate that there are no debtors prisons for nations, for the Reagan administration's policies had in a very real sense forced the country to mortgage its future.[19]

In addition to the immediate effects on the US economy, the Bretton Woods system which the United States had put in place in 1944 no longer seems to serve its own interests. By the time the Japanese and Germans emerged as economic powers in their own right the United States had become dependent on the system itself. During the 1970s its import and export dependency doubled. Exports rose from 5.7 per cent of GNP (1970) to 12.9 per cent (1980), imports from 4.6 per cent to 12.1 per cent. In 1970 foreign loans amounted to 7.6 per cent of all bank lending; by 1980 they had risen to 26 per cent. US companies have had to become more competitive simply to survive. By 1980 one in every six jobs in manufacturing industry depended on overseas markets; one in every 3 acres of farmland produced crops for export; $1 in every $3 of corporate profit derived from exports or foreign investment.[20]

Despite the forecasts of economic Cassandras, however, the fascination with statistics is in itself highly suspicious. The preoccupation with foreign reserves, trade balances and deficits reflects a more profound loss of confidence in economics itself. One set of figures can always be offset by another. Historically the US share of world manufacturing output in the year of the Munich agreement in 1938 was lower than at any time since 1910. The United States share was lower in 1938 than it had been on the eve of the Great Depression (1929). On this basis it could have been argued at the time that the United States would eventually be displaced by the Soviet Union, whose share of manufacturing output trebled between 1929 and 1938, that its displacement as the dominant economic power was not only inevitable, but also not very distant.[21]

In 1981 the United States still accounted for one-fifth of global production and 50 per cent of the world's exports (in dollar terms). As the world's major reserve currency the dollar was still the medium of exchange for 80 per cent of non-Communist trade and still represented 75 per cent of central bank reserves.[22] The United States is still able to borrow on its own currency, forcing its creditors to carry the exchange risk when lending to Washington. At the same time they are exposed to an exchange risk on their uncovered portfolio of dollar-denominated debt issued by other countries, which was estimated to be $800 billion in 1984.[23] We should never forget that as the world's principal reserve currency the dollar still provides the United States with what de Gaulle once called 'the exorbitant privilege' of being able to finance its balance of payments deficits with, what are in effect, IOUs rather than its own reserve assets.

Even after the 1987 crash the merchants of doom, in losing confidence in the US economy, tended to lose their heads. Kenneth Galbraith, whose progress to economic depression had been reflected in the titles of his two most important books, *The Affluent Society* and *The Years of Uncertainty*, predicted another Great Depression. Why? Because after the stock market had soared to a historic height of 250 per cent, it dropped by 22 per cent in the course of a day. What Galbraith ignored was the underlying strength of an economy that had produced sixteen million more jobs in 64 consecutive months (1982–8); boosted manufacturing productivity to 4.5 per cent a year, the highest rate since 1945, and increased manufacturing output by a factor of four since the late 1970s.

Galbraith, of course, was not alone. At the height of the recession Albert Bressand wrote of the Williamsburg economic summit (1983) that an administration that was neither all-powerful nor internationally minded could hardly expect to command the type of legitimacy which the Pax Americana had originally conferred.[24] Yet the United States' recovery from the recession illustrated the extent of the world's dependence on its economy, in particular its interest rates. In the words of the former President of the Bundesbank, the world saw a 'return to the Pax Americana'.[25]

It is true that the United States' economic weakness was relative to that of its allies, not its enemies. If between 1969 and 1979 the Soviet Union devoted almost as great a share of its national product to investment as did Japan, its economy grew at less than half the rate. In the late 1970s Soviet growth was stagnant. By comparison the US share of Gross World Product (GWP) may have declined since 1945 yet it still remains larger than that of the Soviet Union and Japan combined, and only marginally smaller than that of the European Community. Far from falling behind Japan in every sphere of economic activity the United States has managed to hold its own. Since 1982 US industrial production has been 5 per cent higher than Japan's; its competitiveness in manufacturing has been higher still, which is one reason why the Japanese now manufacture so many of their own cars in the United States. Labour costs are much lower. US productivity, which was lower even than that of Britain throughout the 1960s and 1970s now stands 29 per cent higher than in 1981, the most prolonged rise in the nation's history. Ninety per cent of all new jobs created in the Western world since the world came out of the recession have been created in the United States.

The United States, in fact, is not even a creditor nation if we value its foreign assets correctly. The 'net debt' position reported by the Department of Commerce is based on valuing all investments at book, not market values, a measurement which substantially undervalues the majority of US assets which are more than 30 years old. Assuming a 5 per cent rate of return on investment the current market value of US holdings abroad exceeds that of foreigners in the United States by $400 billion.[26] In 1986 when the United States supposedly became the largest debtor nation in the world, its income from overseas investment ($20.8 billion) was greater than US payments to foreign creditors and investors. Income earned by Americans on their foreign investments may no longer exceed the income derived by foreigners from their total holdings in the United States, but foreign direct investment (FDI) is still growing faster than world trade (by a margin of 25 per cent or more).

Trade flows, it is true, may still be larger than FDI but such a comparison is a deceptive indicator of a nation's economic performance. A large share of trade is FDI related, representing goods shifted between parent companies and their foreign subsidiaries. For six out of the United States' ten largest trading partners the local sales of US-owned companies were larger than US exports to the countries in question.[27]

What of the much-discussed budget and trade deficits? These too have been grossly exaggerated. The decision by US bankers to reduce their foreign lendings from $110 billion a year to less than $2 billion in 1985 turned a net creditor nation into a net debtor nation overnight, in the process providing a sudden stimulus for a trade deficit which was not quite as serious as it appeared.[28] As for the budget deficit, which is considered more serious still, that could be eliminated by a marginal increase in direct or indirect taxes. The United States runs it not because its governments are profligate, nor because they are irresponsibly funding public expenditure on welfare entitlements and defence through public borrowing, but because the deficit is not that expensive to run.[29]

It is not, of course, economic decline alone which preoccupies so many Americans. 'The history of the rise and fall of the leading countries in the Great Power system since the advance of Western Europe in the sixteenth century', writes Paul Kennedy, 'shows a very significant correlation over the longer term between productive and revenue raising capacities on the one hand and military strength on the other.'[30] US expenditure certainly has been marked by a colossal expenditure on arms accompanied by a rising tide of consumption, fuelled most recently by substantial tax cuts:

It is as though the intercontinental missile and the colour television set reside in the same area of economic expansion. In the modern age you can't keep the two kinds of ingenuity apart – the lethal and the allegedly life enhancing. Indeed, its possible to sum up part of the age in terms of a synthesis of the two . . . the cosy television evening with the Vietnam war as part of the chromatic entertainment.[31]

What we are dealing with in the US military however is not an industrial complex, but a political community which enables the political leadership in the United States to manage the transatlantic bargain in the face of growing opposition from Congress and public opinion. The Seventh Army provides a cultural underpinning of the US commitment to Europe's defence. It is the Army which permits the transmission of ideas favourable to Atlanticism, a community which is not only congenial to both sides, the European elite as well as the American, but which on the part of the former has bred an unwillingness to share power and on the part of the latter an unwillingness to seek a greater degree of independence. The collapse of NATO would be a double catastrophe for it would not only spell military disaster for the Europeans, but cultural disintegration for those Americans who still wish to transcend narrow political horizons and isolationist values.

Moreover, is the United States overstretched as Kennedy maintains? 'Imperial overreach' is the most-quoted phrase from Kennedy's book, one whose popularity is easily explained 'given that it combines neatly the idea that the United States has an "empire" and that military spending should be cut'.[32] Yet the argument is only acceptable if one believes that the United States lives in a security environment conducive to its survival and well-being, one in which the Soviet Union has ceased to pose a threat, in part because it is in a state of terminal decline. Unfortunately, declining powers tend to be more dangerous than aspiring ones. A country confident it could 'bury' the United States economically by 1980 felt equally confident to cut its armed strength by a million men. A country overtaken in terms of total GNP by Japan in 1986 (and possibly much earlier) has increased its defence spending from 14 per cent to 18 per cent of GNP.

Unlike Great Britain in the 1930s it may well be the case that the United States finds itself at the head of a coalition of powers, among the wealthiest in the world. The problem is not that the United States spends too much on defence but that it spends too little given that 55 per cent of GDP is accounted for by welfare entitlements and food stamps, not to mention the 15 per cent or more which is needed every year to service the country's debt. The real problem is that the United States has not derived a proper return on its expenditure because it has spent money with no particular strategic end in mind, in the belief that throwing money at a problem will somehow solve the problem itself. Now that it has engaged on four years of bloodletting to reduce defence spending as a percentage of GNP still further, two questions arise: over its response to burden-sharing with its allies, and more important perhaps, its view of its own role in the 1990s.

About the first question the United States remains deeply schizophrenic.

On the one hand, it wishes to share its burdens: 'We hear it said', declared Reagan in his inaugural address, 'that we live in an era of limits to our powers. Well then let it also be understood there are limits to our patience.' On the other hand, the United States is unlikely to look with relish on a destiny it has to share with others – as Pericles reminded the people of Athens during the Pelopennesian War, 'you cannot decline the burdens of empire and still expect to share its honours.'[33] Even in the 1960s Americans were unwilling to confront this reality. William Fulbright might have complained of 'the arrogance of power', but his commitment to the defence of Europe was firmly linked to the need to ensure that 'the critical decisions that lead to war and peace are not removed beyond our influence and responsibility'.[34] 'To conceive destiny as exterior to ourselves . . . a vast cycle of failures is requisite', argued E. M. Cioran.[35] That may be unavoidable for a small European power such as Cioran's Romania, but what of a power that has never relied on anyone else for its survival or fulfilment of its designs?

When Jefferson attributed to Washington the plea for the United States to avoid 'entangling alliances' for fear the republic would be drawn into conflicts not of its own making, he could not foresee a time when allies might instead prevent the republic from acting on behalf of its own interests. Through its close association with the United States Europe feels it necessary to caution it against adventurism or the use of force; through association allied public opinion occasionally feels it necessary to engage in emotional spasms, to demonstrate against US actions such as the bombing of Tripoli in 1986 or the invasion of Grenada in 1983. By comparison the invasion of Afghanistan in 1979 drew hardly any protest on the part of European opinion at all.

An adversary's actions invite far less comment. The need to reassure friends is a far more onerous task than deterring enemies. As Ibsen warned, 'the trouble with friends is not what they can do for you, but what they prevent you from doing for yourself.' As early as 1980 Henry Kissinger was already complaining that the United States' military spending no longer bought friends, or kept them on board, and certainly no longer promoted a world in which the United States could feel confident about its own future.[36]

Had Christian Herter's Atlantic community been realised the United States might have lived with this dilemma, and even transcended it. Unfortunately, we may expect further anxiety in the United States as the burden-sharing debate gathers momentum. We can interpret it in different ways: we may see it as a failure on the part of the United States to adjust to changing circumstances; or we may see it as the failure of an alliance created by the United States and Britain to adjust to new political realities. What we do know is that the United States is in danger of losing its autonomy in domestic economic problems, now that it relies on a capital inflow of $150 billion to pay its foreign bills and service its debt. Such a reversal in roles from the days of Marshall Aid suggests it may not be too long before the allies preach to their main protector, not the other way round. If the United States should forfeit its authority in the alliance, if its leadership is questioned, will it lose its 'vocation' as well?

In its rite of passage from a superpower to a great power the United States will have to transform its relations with its allies and enemies alike. In NATO it will not only have to revise the transatlantic bargain by shedding the burdens of empire where it can, it may also have to share power with its European and Japanese allies, to allow them to voice their own opinions and express their own misgivings more forcefully than they have in the past. It was Walter Lippmann who once suggested that the value of alliances was that like manacles they stopped one's hands from shaking. If the alliance is seen as a fetter restraining the United States energies, the analogy is unlikely to appeal even to a generation which has been encouraged to subscribe to an inverted Catholic litany that preaches that hope is the greatest sin of all. As Irving Kristol has argued quite persuasively, while power may indeed corrupt, in the world that exists, rather than the world we might prefer, powerlessness may be far more corrupting and demoralising.[37]

AMERICA *AGONISTES*, OR THE PASSING OF THE AMERICAN CENTURY

In all the noise and smoke of battle, most Americans seem to have lost sight of the fact that for most non-Americans decline is a peculiarly American obsession, which says more about a preoccupation with the past than fear about the future.

Of the three schools of decline which can be identified with confidence, none are more revealing than the feelings of the post-war generation. 'My theory has always been' wrote Jefferson in 1817, 'that if we are to dream the flatteries of hope are as cheap and pleasanter than the gloom of despair'.[38] The Americans have dreamed ever since, of new frontiers to be reached, and new obstacles to be overcome. For many Americans decline threatens nothing less than the need to come to terms with the concept of limited action. Indeed, one suspects that many Americans find the whole concept anathema for no other reason that that. It is a theme which for once finds both Left and Right in agreement. Most Americans seem to find the need for a mission critical in defining themselves, and their relationship to their own country. They are not alone. As one of Pasternak's characters remarks in *Dr Zhivago*, the Communist leadership isn't 'happy with anything unless it is on a grand scale. For them the transitional periods, worlds in the making, are an end in themselves . . .'. It is better to travel than to arrive, for fear of what one may find at one's destination.

In that sense, the United States and the Soviet Union are remarkably alike. As Arnold Rappoport once noted, most of the other states of the world evolved. Only the United States and the Soviet Union were 'declared into existence, each by a group of men . . . who had definite ideas about the nature of the state they were creating'.[39] Others may have been less impressed. Dada saw Bolshevism as 'Marx plus electricity'. In 1900 the Uruguyan writer José Enrique Rodo described the United States as a soulless 'equation of Washington and Edison'. Yet for the American and Soviet people the sense of mission is still very strong. In the late 1970s two Soviet historians argued that neither superpower should allow itself to be distracted from fulfilling its 'truly historical tasks' by unscrupulous and vested interests.[40] It is a position that Karl Popper would find deeply historicist. The father of historicism, of course, was Hegel. Walt Whitman, for one, was always amazed that the German philosopher 'whose vastness and multiplicity and vitality only America could comprehend' had been born in the Old World at all.

Such parentheses aside, America's Providential mission has remained a seductive vision since the Founding Fathers first told the Americans that they were 'unique', the first people to whom God the Educator had revealed those 'eternal truths' that were self-evident to no one else. Many Americans would still sympathise with the conclusions reached by a group of social scientists in 1957, who laid much of the groundwork for the Development Loan Fund: 'if we continue to devote our attention in the same proportion to domestic issues as in the past we run the danger of becoming a bore to ourselves and the world.'[41] Thirty years on Richard Nixon, who had been Vice-President in the 1950s still preferred to think in causes greater than the nation itself, in the belief that when a society becomes obsessed with its own material well-being to the exclusion of everything else it is 'destined for decline and decay.'[42]

The problems and complaints raised about America's 'retreat from power' are by no means exclusively American, but the burden of unrealised ambitions as one of its principle themes is felt most acutely by the generation that created the post-war world, the generation that with Dean Acheson were 'present at the Creation'.

The theme that emerges most clearly from the memoirs of George Ball is one of opportunities lost, a glimpse of a world that might have been, the aspirations of an elite that felt duty bound to make the world 'safe for democracy', or to push the developing world into an era of 'self-sustained economic growth'. Reflecting on his life at the age of 80 Ball recognised that the American people had become so introverted that they no longer displayed the ebullience and *élan* of a nation confident of its destiny – or even of its desired destination.

The importance of such reflections arises not from the number of ex-policymakers who express them, but from the fact that those who do are members of an educated, talented, sensitive and conscientious group of men who provided leadership and direction to the causes they espoused so strongly, only to see their achievement fall short of their hopes. Their fear is that if the United States turns its back on its destiny, its providential mission, it will pass into history with its tasks left unfinished, its debts unpaid, its accounts in disorder, in short, its image as a redeeming nation not a little tarnished, if not unmade.

Such an outcome would represent a decline, a decline anticipated, not described – a self-fulfilling prophecy. It was de Tocqueville, after all, who forecast that the United States would probably end not with the collapse of its democratic government but the expiry of its energy. Ultimately, he feared not for its want of boldness, but 'the mediocrity of its desires'. Ambition would lose its vigour, passions would abate, society would become less aspiring.

In one respect this has already happened. As we have seen, gone are the days when George Kennan could remark that the 'thoughtful observer' would find no 'cause for complaint in the Soviet threat', instead that he would thank Providence for providing the United States with such a challenge.[43] Not even the most hawkish member of the Committee on the Present Danger was prepared to join John Foster Dulles in condemning arms control for relieving America from 'harrassment' and thus denying it a 'historical role'.[44]

If the language has become more muted, however, the ambitions still remain. Even George Bush, during the 1988 election campaign saw SDI as an 'exit' from mankind's fear of annihilation. Even the Governor of Massachusetts, Michael Dukakis, promised to free Latin America from the debt trap, enthused with a sense of obligation to America's less fortunate neighbours which he had discovered on a walking trip in Peru and a visit to Mexico in his youth. Their promises notwithstanding, it is clear that a number of Americans now have less faith than ever that the dream can be exported, or worse still that America has anything to say to the world in which it lives. The American century which opened with such explosive confidence in the late 1940s looks like ending in a sense of despair, a glimpse of what it is to be merely mortal.

Another school of though, of course, is fascinated with the concept of decline for quite a different reason. Men like George Kennan have always believed that the emergence of the United States as a superpower in 1945 heralded not a new awakening, but a false dawn. For the architect of containment and those who like him think the end of America's innocence, through its entanglement in corrupting alliances, marked its true decline, its fall from grace. To that extent its 'present' decline, far from representing a threat, offers the promise of renewal.

Through his writings Kennan clearly reveals a veneration for a Jeffersonian past that vanished with the coming of the Cold War. What distinguishes him from the other members of the post-war generation with whom he served until 1950 is that his retreat into the past represented a subconscious refusal to understand the age in which he lived. True to the traditions of the Founding Fathers, Kennan has chosen to contemplate a republic which had never existed, a fantasy world similar to the Castile depicted by Cellorigo on the eve of Spain's rise as a great power 'a republic of bewitched beings living outside the natural order of things'.[45]

For the radicals, the period when the United States was last in control of its own destiny was 1917, *before* it aspired to become a great power. Whether one reads the speeches of Senator Taft or the polemics of former President Hoover, their message at the time was not one of too many commitments, but commitments which should never have been undertaken. Hoover opposed America's membership of NATO because it could distort the nation's economic development; Taft because of his belief that crusades had no place in the modern world. Protected by high-tarriff walls, and fortified by neutrality, Taft argued in his debate with Eisenhower that the struggle against Communism could be pursued with equal vigour at home.

For today's critics of 'empire' the prospect that the United States might surrender the status of a superpower offers what Donald Brandon hoped for in the mid-1960s – a chance to escape its adolescence, an opportunity to 'come of age'.[46] As Graham Greene wrote in *The Power and the Glory*, 'there is always a moment in childhood when the door opens and lets the future in', the future with all its betrayals, petty compromises and glimpses of lost innocence. The theme of maturing conjures up not John Quincy Adams' prediction that the United States would eventually 'decline into the infirmities of old age', but the promise that it will at last escape from pursuing a world role in the name of its Providential destiny, that it may soon become 'an ordinary country' spared the pain of obligation.

It is a sentiment that was given expression, perhaps, most forcefully, by Daniel Bell, writing in the year of America's bicentennial anniversary, 1976. Bell concluded that having aged, the United States was at last free for the first time in its history to choose its role: 'There is no longer a manifest destiny or mission. We have not been immune to the corruption of power. We have not been the exception . . . Our mortality now lies before us'.[47] It is not mortality, of course, but the discovery of adolescence which informs the radical fascination with decline, the hope that the United States has at last come of age. Put another way, the American Adam having left Eden of his own volition has been offered an opportunity to return by withdrawing from the world altogether.

What is of interest to the outside observer is that this last school of thought may have inadvertantly captured a popular mood, or tapped into a populist well of feeling which has remained largely hidden from America's leaders and allies alike. It is, in fact, the popular mood – the attractions of decline for a nation weighed down by its international responsibilities – which has invested the debate about America's decline with a political significance which the facts themselves do not merit. Governments notoriously reluctant to respond to public demands are anxious enough to lead public opinion, whenever they recognise the danger that leading a crowd and being pursued by it can be disconcertingly slight. There may be few, if any, examples of governments voluntarily denying themselves power, but history can furnish examples of political abdication by a public which has preferred to forfeit political influence, or refused to pick up the bill in order to spare itself the responsibilities which the exercise of power entails.

In 1964 the US Congress responded to an attack on a warship in the Gulf of Tonkin – an incident in which not a single life was lost, nor was the ship – by authorising President Johnson to begin the bombing of North Vietnam. In 1937 it had chosen to respond to an attack on the gunship *Pannay* in the Yangtse river, an incident in which the ship was sunk with the loss of several lives, by insisting that the administration withdraw all American warships from Chinese waters.

The perversity of Congress' shifting moods is of account only to the extent that it reflects public opinion. As late as 1981, when the American people narrowly voted in Ronald Reagan, four out of five Americans still believed that the United States had 'a special role to play in the world'.[48] Today, nine in ten Americans are willing to renounce the status of superpower, in the hope of sharing the burdens of power with allies against whose success they have begun to measure their own decline.[49] Will the popular perception of decline ultimately be the most important of all? As a concept, whether 'real' or not, it may have something not altogether superficial to say to an age trying to make a style out of despair.

For America's allies the question is more than one of passing interest. As its power relative to that of its allies continues to diminish, the United States will undoubtedly try to find an option, hopefully a *via media* between 'manic interventionism and depressive withdrawal'.[50] The possibility of withdrawal, however, cannot be discounted. Years before Paul Kennedy put pen to paper William Fulbright argued that the United States was at a turning point in its history, a point at which other powers by 'an overextension of effort' had declined and then fallen.[51] Writing as early as 1950, Gabriel Almond had remarked that any underlying doubt in its own strength that was allowed to surface would leave America with the feeling of being over-extended, a belief that might bring to the fore 'a need for contraction, for consolidation, for withdrawal'.[52] The most recent polls do not show any return to isolationism, but they do reveal that compared with 25 years ago when a majority of Americans wished the United States to remain 'the most looked up to nation in the world',[53] a remarkable number now wish it to remain 'uncommitted'.[54]

Is the United States ready to make the adjustment? The problem is the choice the American people will make. They can look back or they can look forward; they can retain a sense of mission or become an 'ordinary country', they can enter history for the first time, or stand outside it, looking on.

Decline, as the Mexican writer, Ocatvio Paz argues, is the Americans' gateway to history; for it 'offers them what they have always sought: historical legitimacy': 'The United States would like to be outside the world, but it is in the world – it is the world. Hence the contradiction of contemporary American society . . . having been founded against history, yet being itself history.'[55]

Just as the Soviet Union has been forced to come to terms with its own inability to play the role of a historical agent, giving history a push, as Suslov used to put it, so the United States has begun to question the role conferred on it by the Founding Fathers; the role of an actor outside history, an example to some, a crusader to others, a country which would ultimately redeem Twain's 'damned human race'. It is perhaps, significant that even so pragmatic a politician as Zbigniew Brzezinski should have concluded his memoirs with an observation by the Russian philosopher Pytor Chaadaev, writing in the 1820s:

We are one of those nations which do not appear to be an integral part of the human race, but exist only in order to teach some great lesson to the world. Surely the lesson we are destined to teach will not be wasted; but who knows when we shall rejoin the rest of mankind and how much misery we must suffer before accomplishing our destiny.[56]

For two centuries the United States has seen itself as a country once removed from the historical constraints within which others have had to manoeuvre for advantage or survive by cunning. For 40 years the United States has tried to make history, or seek various ways of escaping from it. None has succeeded. Neither containment in the 1950s nor isolationism in the 1920s secured its future. The attempt to help the Third World escape the poverty trap ended only in mutual recrimination, in the not entirely undeserved caricature of Greene's *Quiet American*.

The question for America's allies is whether the United States will contract into history at the expense of its friends? The danger of becoming an ordinary country is that the transformation may generate fears that are more acute than real, that are magnified, not muted; a sense of collective despair which may make political abdication preferable to political responsibility.

As the Romanian philosopher Cioran once wrote, a man lives by fictions;

the man who unmasks them renounces his own identity and in a sense himself.

> How much more so this applies to a civilisation which vacillates as soon as it exposes the errors which permitted its growth and its lustre, as soon as it calls into question its own truths ... When the sceptic no longer extracts any active virtue from his problems and interrogations, he approaches his denouement, indeed seeks it out.[57]

That is the danger of the American people feeling betrayed by their political leaders, their historians, and everyone else who has called for sacrifices to be made to redeem the world from Communism or poverty, or both, in the name of America's 'mission'. The intellectual crisis which lies at the heart of the debate about America's decline is far more profound than the endless disputes over trade statistics, or the largely sterile debate about burden sharing in NATO.

If the Cold War is not yet over, if new battles still need to be fought, it is essential that the United States should not feel itself an 'ordinary country'. Confronted with the need to maintain the American people's confidence in themselves, the American government might be well advised to ban books like Paul Kennedy's, or even burn them. It might be wiser still to follow the sound advice of the poet Heine, who suggested that every state should imprison its prophets of doom until such time as their prophecies came true.

NOTES

1. Joseph A. Schumpeter, *Capitalism, Socialism and Democracy* (New York: Harper & Row, 1942) pp. 131-9. For Toynbee see *Hannibal's Legacy*, vol. 2: *Rome and her neighbours after Hannibal's Exit* (Oxford: Oxford University Press, 1965) p. 90. 'In fact the after effects of the Hannibalic bout of the Romano-Carthaginian Double War were not solely military; they were economic, social and religious as well. This was the price of Rome's subjugation of the western end of the old world-oikoumene. It was a price that condemned the Roman Empire in advance to be short lived.'
2. Andrew Hacker, *The End of the American Era* (New York: Atheneum, 1970) p. 230.
3. Ronald Steel, *Pax Americana* (New York: Viking, 1967) p. 45.
4. Donald Brandon, *American Foreign Policy: beyond utopianism and realism* (New York: Appleton and Century Croft, 1966) pp. 269-89.
5. Henry Brandon, *The Retreat of American Power* (New York: Doubleday, 1973) p. 360.
6. *ibid.,* p. 346.
7. Paul Kennedy, *The Rise and Fall of the Great Powers: economic change and military conflict from 1500 to 2000* (New York: Random House, 1987).

8. *The Times* (8 March, 1989).
9. Robert Nisbet, *History of the Idea of Progress* (New York: Basic Books, 1980) p. 197.
10. Cited in William O'Neil, *Coming Apart: an informal history of America in the 1960s* (New York: Quadrangle, 1971) p. 405.
11. For the best book on the Carter administration see Gaddis Smith's *Reason and Power: American diplomacy and the Carter years* (New York: Hill & Wang, 1986).
12. Salvador de Madariaga, *Americans* (Oxford: Oxford University Press, 1930) p. 3.
13. Alexis de Tocqueville, *Democracy in America*, vol. 2, trans. Phillips Bradley (New York: Alfred Knopf, 1945) p. 141.
14. Allan Bloom, *The Closing of the American Mind* (New York: Simon & Schuster, 1987). The issue of cultural literacy has been the subject of intense debate since the mid-1980s. Fuelling the national controversy is the question of what body of knowledge constitutes cultural literacy. For an alternative ethnic minority view see Rick Simonson and Scott Walker (eds) *Multicultural Literacy: opening the American mind* (Saint Paul: Graywolf Press, 1988). One is not reassured to read in the introduction Hirsch being taken to task for not including mastectomy, alcoholism, internment camps, El Salvador and Gabriel Marquez's important but hardly 'core' novel *One Hundred Years of Solitude* among the preliminary list of 5,000 words he believed an educated American should know (p. xii). A course designed to cater for such 'minority' groups as women, alcoholics, and Hispanics illustrates how knowledge itself could become an instrument of marginalisation, not an escape route into the mainstream culture. By the year 2005 one-third of all Americans will be non-white. A large part, however, will be Asians who, having taken America's present core culture to heart, are now the single most successful 'ethnic' group in the country, despite the fact that they are neither white, Protestant, nor even largely male.
15. Lloyd Free and Hadley Cantrill, *The Political Beliefs of Americans: a study of public opinion* (New York: Simon & Schuster, 1968) p. 50.
16. Rupert Brooke, *Letters from America* (Gloucester: Allan Sutton, 1984) p. 46.
17. Richard D. Challenger, 'The next President's foreign policy legacy', *University – a Princeton Quarterly* No. 69. (Summer 1976) pp. 11–12.
18. Stephen Marris, *Deficits and Dollars: the world economy at risk* (Washington DC: Institute for International Economics, 1985) p. 94.
19. *The Washington Post* (7 October 1985).
20. Fred Bergsten, 'The cost of Reaganomics', *Foreign Policy* no. 44 (Fall 1981) p. 36.
21. Owen Harries, 'The rise of American decline', *Commentary* 85:5 (May 1988) p. 32.
22. Robert Ayres, 'Breaking the bank', *Foreign Policy* no. 43 (Summer 1981) pp. 104–20.
23. Marris, *Deficits and Dollars, op. cit.*, p. 371.

24. Albert Bressand, 'Mastering the world economy', *Foreign Affairs* 61:4 (Spring 1982) pp. 761-2.
25. Cited in Sam Brittan, 'A very painful world adjustment', *Foreign Affairs* 61: 3 (1986) p. 547.
26. *National Review* (7 November 1988) p. 14.
27. *The Times* (17 November 1988).
28. Warren T. Brooks, 'The silent boom', *American Spectator* (August 1988) p. 18.
29. It is often suggested that were the United States to tax itself at a much higher rate it could ease the budget deficit quite speedily. Over time ideas change. It is possible, however, to ignore Madison and cite the note by Thomas Jefferson in de Tracy's *Treatise on Political Economy* (1817), which he recommended as a text-book for the University of Virginia. The note read: 'The use of taxing power to correct inequalities of wealth violates the first principle of society, the guarantee to everyone of a free exercise of his industry and the fruits acquired by it' (Frank Tariello, *The Reconstruction of American Political Ideology* (Charlottesville: University of Virginia Press, 1982) p. 13.
30. Kennedy, *Rise and Fall of the Great Powers, op. cit.,* p. 306.
31. Anthony Burgess, *1985* (London: Arrow, 1985) p. 63.
32. Harries, 'The rise of American decline', *op. cit.,* p. 34.
33. William Fulbright, *Prospects for the West* (Cambridge, Mass.: Harvard University Press, 1963) p. 57.
34. E. M. Cioran, *The Temptation to Exist* (London: Quartet, 1987) p. 70.
35. Nowhere in Washington's Farewell Address is the phrase 'entangling alliances' to be found. It was first introduced in Jefferson's inaugural address of 1801.
36. Henry Kissinger, 'Address before the annual Convention of American Society of Newspaper Editors', Washington DC (10 April 1980).
37. *The Wall Street Journal* (18 January 1979).
38. Cited in Saul K. Padover (ed.), *Thomas Jefferson on Democracy* (New York: New American Library, 1939) p. 29.
39. Arnold Rappoport, *The Big Two: Soviet-American perceptions of foreign policy* (Indianapolis: Pegasus, 1971) p. 9.
40. N. V. Suvachev and M. Yakoulev, *Russia and the United States: US-Soviet relations from the Soviet point of view* (Chicago: University of Chicago Press, 1979) p. 269.
41. Max Millikan and Walt Rostow, *A Proposal's Key to an Effective Foreign Policy* (New York: Harper & Row, 1957) p. 150.
42. Cited in *The Sunday Times* (London: 2 October 1988).
43. George Kennan (X), 'The sources of Soviet conduct', *Foreign Affairs* (July 1947).
44. Richard Goold-Adams, *The Time of Power: a re-appraisal of John Foster Dulles* (London: Weidenfeld and Nicolson, 1962) p. 80.
45. J. H. Elliot, 'The decline of Spain', in C. M. Cipolla (ed.), *The Economic Decline of Empires* (London: Methuen, 1970) p. 195.
46. Donald Brandon, *American Foreign Policy: beyond utopianism and realism* (New York: Appleton and Century Croft, 1966) p. 269.

47. Daniel Bell, 'The end of American exceptionalism', in Nathan Glazer and Irving Kristol, *The American Commonwealth – 1976* (New York: Basic Books, 1976).
48. Bruce Russert and Donald Deluca, 'Don't tread on me: public opinion and foreign policy in the 1980s', *Political Science Quarterly* 96 (Fall 1981).
49. Mellman and Lazarus, *Research Defining American Strength: results of a survey conducted for the World Policy Institute* (October 1987) p. 14.
50. Bruce Russert, *No Clear and Present Danger* (1980) p. 94.
51. William Fulbright, *The Arrogance of Power* (New York: Random House, 1966) p. 3.
52. Gabriel Almond, *The American People and foreign policy* (New York: Harcourt Brace Jovanovich, 1950) p. 65.
53. Lloyd Free and Hadley Cantril, *The Political Beliefs of Americans* (New York: Simon & Schuster, 1968) p. 92.
54. John Reilly, 'American opinion: continuity not Reaganism', *Foreign Policy* 50 (Spring 1982) pp. 86–104.
55. Octavio Paz, *One Earth, Four Worlds: reflections on contemporary history* (London: Carcanet, 1985) pp. 31–2.
56. Zbigniew Brzezinski, *Power and Principle: the memoirs of the National Security Adviser 1977–81* (London: Weidenfeld and Nicolson, 1983) p. 541.
57. E. M. Cioran, *The Temptation to Exist* (London: Quartet, 1987) pp. 55–6.

7. Present at the Fall, or the death of history

'True history comes long after us. That's when it will be decided whether or not we measured up and our greatness – or its lack – will be defined.'
'True history', said Hearst with a smile that was for once charming, 'is the final fiction. I thought even you knew that.'

Gore Vidal, *Empire*

'. . . No room is left
For antecedents, inference, nuance,
One escapes from all the anguish of this world
Into the refuge of the present tense.'

Anthony Hecht, *The Venetian Vespers*

As a country the United States has spent the past 40 years legitimising its actions by reference to a past which is more perceived than real. 'Truth is not constant; it is created', wrote George Kennan in his *Foreign Affairs* article of 1947 with reference to the role Communist ideology played in legitimising the Soviet government's actions. 'Every generation rewrites the past', claimed John Dos Passos on the eve of the United States' entry into the Second World War.[1] In the case of the United States every generation has drawn inspiration from one of three pasts which provide a parable as well as an operational code.

What one learns from a study of US foreign policy is how seldom the United States has taken the political initiative; how often it has responded to external challenges in defence of what it has taken to be its 'national interest' or security. In that respect the past has been important because it has helped to legitimise U-turns, changes in policy, and even changes in message. It helped Senator Vandenberg change from a fervent isolationist to a reluctant redemptionist. It justified Hans Morgenthau, who supported *détente* with the Soviet Union in the 1950s, in opposing Kissinger's attempt to implement it twenty years later. It even explains why John Foster Dulles, who as Chairman of the Commission on International Relations of the National Council of Churches supported the admission to the United Nations of the

People's Republic of China, did so only to throw up every obstacle in its path once in power.[2] If Emerson was right in claiming that consistency is the mark of little minds, US politicians have been giants.

Each of these men chose to search for the future by journeying back into the past. Each found himself divided from the United States' allies by myth and legend, by dreams that no one else shared. In inventing a new language to express their aspirations, whether manifest destiny or the new frontier, the Americans have been able to engage in a self-colloquy, a discourse unique in history. In a sense the rest of us have eavesdropped on a private conversation, as the myths have turned into B movie clichés, or the rhetoric has sounded increasingly hollow. The distinguishing mark of modern European culture is that it has lost confidence in itself, a point borne out by its use of language, its recourse to irony, and moral ambiguity. The language of US politicians has remained robustly one-dimensional. If at times the nation has been short of political ideas, its leaders have never lost the confidence to express them.

The past has served the United States well at certain times in its history especially in the last century, if we mean it has given coherence to US policy. Coherence also arose from physical isolation. The United States was separated from the Old World not only by choice, but also by geography until it was called in 1917 to intervene, to redress the balance of the Old World in favour of the New. In the 1930s the past sanctioned isolationism, when a true understanding of history would have revealed the policy as desperately irresponsible and nakedly self-serving, ultimately a dangerous form of escapism from the responsibilities of power.

After 1945 the past was harnessed to persuade the American people to accept its responsibility with good grace. Successive governments succeeded so well that the task soon became onerous. The United States soon found itself over-extended, fighting limited wars in the wrong place at the wrong time. The past also gave the United States a conception of the outside world which rapidly transformed itself into a complete incomprehension of the world outside it.

To add to the dilemma Americans remembered not one past but several. If we can quote Arthur Schlessinger's reversal of Santayana's aphorism, those who can remember the past are condemned to repeat it.[3] For Dulles it meant redeeming the Communist world by rolling back Communism; for Kennedy venturing out to the new frontier; for Carter renewing the United States' belief in itself by propagating respect for human rights. All of them struggled to find an appropriate voice, to justify a role that was distinct, if not always distinctive. In so doing they gave the impression of a 'muddled progress' through a world with which the United States was fundamentally ill at ease, performing a role that either was expected of it, or what it expected of itself. The past, in short, not only gave American policy coherence, but made it incoherent as well. 'There's an eagle in me and a mocking bird', cried Carl Sandburg.⁴ The eagle was the United States' past – its mission, its providential destiny. The mocking bird was what Niebuhr called 'the irony of American History'.

AN EMBATTLED ELITE

> 'Elastic as bark, and sure as roots, stretching and holding fast,
> Certain and conscious, rejecting nothing, the past
> Never a skin to slough but to wear unencumbered at last.'
>
> P. K. Kavanagh, *About Time* (1970)

The past has been critical, however, in allowing the elite to 'lead' the nation, to drum up public support for policies which at first glance have not always been self-evidently in the public interest. In the late 1950s Raymond Aron congratulated the United States that decision-making was 'the outcome not of popular passions or popular greed' but the measured opinions of a political elite.⁵ The past was the key. It created an ideology which motivated society and inspired its members. If it also demanded a suspension of personal identity, it also offered a great profusion of experiences by which identity is drawn: common origins or roles, a sense of purpose, particularly bereavement or fulfilment in time of war. As T. S. Eliot wrote in *Little Gidding* (1942), 'a people without history is not redeemed from time.'

History, however, exerts its own influence, as Eliot was the first to discover during the Second World War, a conflict which separated him by three centuries from his ancestors who had left East Coker for New England. Eliot himself had fled the United States to escape a history that seemed increasingly meaningless to him. Rootless, he clung to the few consolations of the English tradition so that by the time he wrote *The Four Quartets* he could write 'History is now and England' without a trace of self-doubt.

In 1940 the past served Churchill particularly well in his dialogue with the nation. He of all leaders could instil in those who listened to his radio broadcasts a sense of national destiny, which he constantly evoked to fortify the present. It was a sense of destiny shared by historians like Trevelyan who accepted Churchill's rhetoric as a dogma of their faith, and tried to convey it in their writings. Indeed, it was the last time they were able to do so. As J. H. Plumb noted in his book *The Death of the Past* there was something elegiac in the writings of Trevelyan and his colleagues in the years leading up to the war, a sense of despair in the future, a nostalgic respect for a past which was fast failing to capture the popular imagination, in part, because it could no longer disguise Britain's decline.⁶

In an earlier essay Plumb had written that the past was not history; it was merely an interpretation of events which generations of scholars, poets and even novelists had shaped to give a sense of meaning and purpose to the events in which they were involved. It was a highly usable commodity, of course, since it helped a political elite to formulate its ideas and regulate political decisions. One of the purposes of professional historians was to demonstrate the truth of the beliefs which they themselves had inherited.[7]

Unlike the United States the English had only one past: the Whig interpretation of history, which had been conveyed to them by Macaulay in his depiction of the Glorious Revolution of 1688. In 1940 Britain was more deeply conscious of and committed to the Whig interpretation than at any other time in the twentieth century, precisely because it forged a bond between the elite and the public in their hour of maximum need. Churchill was the last great voice of England's providential destiny. As a political figure, however, he was already irrelevant, his message obsolete, by the time he was re-elected in 1951.[8]

When Plumb wrote *The Death of the Past* the United States was suffering from its own moment of spiritual crisis – the Vietnam War. Writing at its height in 1969 he predicted that the American past would also lose its hold over the American imagination; that historical metaphors such as manifest destiny were already obsolescent, 'a threadbare refuge for the ageing rulers of a society . . . from which all strong emotion is rapidly draining away'.[9] As he looked forward to 'the death of the past', he conjured up an image of an ideology which had inspired, but also distorted American thinking in the interests of a political elite. 'The past has served the few', he wrote dismissively, 'perhaps history may serve the multitude.'[10]

By history Plumb meant the modern school of objective historians who would be able to reveal to the next generation of Americans the real nature of social change; the true history of their revolution; men who could paint the Founding Fathers as they were, not the stiff-necked eighteenth-century caricatures they were presented as in the political speeches of the time. Several years later Ernest May made a similar appeal to allow history a proper hearing, when he called for the appointment of 'court historians', like Herbert Feis who had been commissioned by Dean Acheson to write an authoritative history of the United States' relations with China, from which the true story of its 'loss to Communism' might emerge. May hoped to free politicians and public alike from a past which had 'imprisoned them' for so long.[11]

Plumb believed that history had much more to offer the American people than the social sciences, precisely because in place of laws and systems it offered only rigorous analysis. Unfortunately, his hopes that the historian would be 'unshackled' and the past overturned has not come to pass. Many politicians still have next to no understanding that US history has corresponded little to the idealised version they were taught in school, and which may well have inspired them to run for public office. In commissioning 'court historians' they have done so in the Camelot tradition, as iconographers, not biographers, whose sole commission is to recall the passing of the 'once and future' kingdom that the Kennedy era constituted for so many on the margins of political life.

There are three additional reasons for thinking that the situation will not change for the better, that history may never realise its promise, or may have nothing to offer but new myths and revised legends.

THE ROLE OF THE PROFESSIONAL HISTORIAN

The professional historians themselves must incur much of the blame. In the 1940s and 1950s they felt nothing of lifting history from the realm of scholarship so that it might be used as a political weapon. After 1945 the past took on an immediacy it had enjoyed only in the Civil War, in part because the period seemed to demand a sense of purpose and mission. In 1949 the President of the American Historical Association declared that US historians could not afford to be 'unorthodox'; that in a time of cold war they were no more free of their 'obligation to serve' the community than nuclear physicists were the government. The following year his successor Eliot Morison complained that the isolationist school of historians, of which Charles Beard had been the leading luminary, had left the younger generation 'spiritually unprepared for the war they had to fight'. Ten years later an American historian went on to suggest that any 'objective' study of Communism would be quite irresponsible, since it might be used by unscrupulous politicians to promote greater 'mutual understanding' between the two superpowers.[12]

Fortunately, that sense of political mission has been totally discredited. But as historians have eschewed politics for scholarship their scholarship has made them marginal to the political debate. Culturally American historians are still predisposed to treat history in a very American way – namely, pragmatically. Pragmatic history, alas, is fundamentally ahistorical since it denies the past any reality independent of present needs and requirements. By placing the past in the service of the present, they have abdicated any responsibility for providing an 'objective' account of events.[13]

The pragmatists' approach is highly Spenglerian. It was Spengler who used to argue that we cannot understand history if it is culturally out of tune with us. We may understand the revolution of the Gracchi because we are at a similar point in our historical development. One day, however, we will be unable to appreciate the music of Mozart because it will be culturally 'out of phase'. It is a view which renders history meaningless. If we cannot understand what is out of phase with us or what is out of style with us, then apparently we can only understand ourselves.[14]

The professional historians' ability to communicate to the public has also been increasingly restricted by their obsession with the quantitative approach to the subject. Like its generals, many of America's historians have fallen foul of the national preoccupation with technology. The computer was the great discovery of the 1960s, one which allowed Frederick Mosteller and David Wallace to analyse the average length of the sentences that Madison and Hamilton had written, by listing the percentage of nouns and adjectives they used in *The Federalist Papers*. Was the exercise worth it? Two mathematicians had already discovered that Hamilton's average sentence length was 34.55 words, Madison's 34.59, a difference so marginal that mathematically it was 'hopeless for discriminating between the two authors'.[15]

That is not to devalue the history books which have emerged in recent years, many of which have challenged the myths which still dominate the US political debate. There was a time when only a Marxist historian such as William Appleman Williams could suggest that, contrary to popular wisdom, the great bankers at the turn of the century had acted on three inter-linking premises: that the free market was a system, not a market in the true sense; a system driven by inherent contradictions and instability which could only survive through regulation.[16] Today it is encouraging to find authors on the Right such as Paul Weaver arguing that the Founding Fathers of corporate America were not Rockefeller, Vanderbilt, Carnegie, Mellon or Duke – the ruthless, rugged individualists of conservative tradition, but the enemies of Adam Smith's free market, or 'invisible hand', the prophets of state regulation with its cartels, trusts, private monopolies, government subsidies and land grants, the managers of the 'organised fiefdoms' of the modern era.[17]

Unfortunately, such exceptions apart, the historical debate in the United States has not captured the popular imagination. If historians' minds are often vigorous, they are often notoriously narrow. Their narrow focus is a source of strength. It encourages true scholarship, but it also cuts them off from a wider audience which has nowhere to turn but the social sciences. Today's historians with their carefully sanitised doctorates must look with envy at a generation which was inspired with enough confidence to write on the grand scale, whose members were able to understand history by creative imagination rather than the careful empirical treatment of facts – a process denounced by Spengler as mere plodding.[18] They were men who refused to be entirely detached from the period about which they were writing in the belief, to quote Carl Becker, one of the greatest of them all, that 'a really detached mind is a dead mind, lying among the facts of history like magnetised steel among iron filings, no synthesis ever resulting from one case or the other to the end of time.'[19]

THE REVISIONISTS' BETRAYAL

The second problem is that the US approach to history has survived, even if American interest has not. And where the approach has yielded different interpretations on the part of revisionist historians of the Left, it has not corrected the distortions of historical writing. Far from challenging the past, many left-wing *mal pensants* have merely tried to refashion it to serve a 'higher' purpose.[20] As Daniel Boorstein wrote in the early 1960s: 'What ails us most is not what we have done with America but what we have substituted for America ... we are haunted not by reality but by those images we have put in its place.'[21]

The shallowness of much left-wing criticism in the United States is astounding anyway, even outside the narrow field of history. The Depression in the 1930s produced few great writers except John Steinbeck, something which struck Gramsci while reading the novels of Sinclair Lewis and Upton Sinclair while in prison.[22] Even the Vietnam War, the second 'crisis' of the twentieth century after the Depression, failed to produce any major work comparable to the novels produced after the Second World War. For historians such as Gabriel Kolko the Vietnam War 'still surpasses the literary imagination'.[23] As Kolko goes on in his study *Vietnam: anatomy of a war* (1986, p. xi), 'The reader who personally saw the dust and heat of the war and its terrible destruction will immediately comprehend the limits of mere words. Those among the many millions for whom the war was a part of life, the cause of sorrow, hard choices and action, will also quickly grasp the difficulties of seeking to capture the elusive sense of reality.' Capture it, however, the historian must if he is to perform any useful role at all.

In Noam Chomsky this poverty of thought reached its nadir. Although a self-professed political scientist he has refused at times even to enter the minds of those about whom he is writing. In *American Power and the New Mandarins* he explains that he was disturbed to discover when reading about Nazi policy in the East that he had entered the arena of argument and counter-argument, that in discussing the technical feasibility of the Holocaust he had been in danger of losing his 'humanity'. A scholar writing about Vietnam runs a similar risk:

He degrades himself and insults beyond measure the victims of our violence and our moral blindness. There may have been a time when American policy was a debatable matter. This time is long past. It is no more debatable than the Italian war in Abyssinia, or the Russion suppression of Hungarian feeling. The war is simply an obscenity, a depraved act by weak and miserable men.[24]

In men like Chomsky the Left is looking as the Right did in the 1950s for a 'usable Past', to give direction over the future course of history, not to produce an understanding of the present by reference to the past. Poets almost Aristotelian in their belief that poetry offers a greater insight into history than the study of history itself, find history valueless. As William Carlos Williams argued, history 'portrays us in generic patterns, like effigies or the carving in sarcophagi which say nothing save, of such a man, that he is dead.'[25]

But the Left has also found in reinterpreting the past an escape from the present. As Stephen Spender argued at the time of the Vietnam War, the Left had questioned US policy only to re-emerge redeemed by their own understanding of what the past really sanctioned: non-intervention and Jefferson's ultimate hope of eliminating war. The trauma of Vietnam ironically enabled the Left to renew itself, even to rediscover its original innocence.[26] In seeing the real meaning of US history as a perpetual quest for the pursuit of happiness, the Left has reified happiness as an end in itself, a mission which if realised might well turn into H. G. Wells's nightmare fantasy *Men like Gods*, in which he describes a race whose only feature of divinity is that of growing taller and taller with every generation.

When Left-wing historians have tried to write history, they have tried to escape from the 'meaninglessness' of America's past by reintroducing a meaning 'if only in patches'. The phrase is Aldous Huxley's made in 1937.[27] The patches are works of history which pass for scholarship. Unfortunately, too many revisionist historians have also betrayed history as a subject by turning their backs on Schlessinger's plea to reinterpret it in accordance with the facts which have been obscured or suppressed, instead of trying to appropriate it in the name of their own values.[28]

When historians begin calling for a 'higher proportion of socially relevant, value motivated, action-inducing historical work' we should expect the worst. We would not be disappointed. According to Howard Zinn in a world plagued by war historians should write as human beings first, scholars second, instead of hiding behind 'disinterested scholarship' or such meaningless terms as 'objectivity'.[29] For William Appleman Williams history is merely 'a stockpile of facts to be requisitioned on the basis of what is needed to prove a conclusion decided upon in advance'.[30]

Zinn insists that our values should be determined by the questions we ask, not the answers we expect. To prove his point he has drawn up five rules for the historian to follow:

1. to sharpen our perception of how the majority of people have been history's victims, not its beneficiaries;
2. to expose the pretensions of governments to 'neutrality';
3. also to expose the ideology that pervades US culture;
4. to 'recapture those few moments in the past which show the possibility of a better way of life than that which has dominated the world so far'; and
5. to show how leaders betray their followers, rebels become bureaucrats and ideals become frozen as time passes.

Citing two historians who addressed the American Historical Association in December 1971, Zinn calls on his profession to adopt a 'radical non-objective peace research' programme, as well as 'a value inspired' history course. This is precisely what most history courses on campuses have been for the past 40 years. The only difference is that the values have been very different from those espoused by the revisionists.

Regrettably, many revisionist works too often invent facts, rather than distort them to prove a point. In dismissing the Katyn massacre as 'an exception to the rule' (Stalin's), Gabriel Kolko can be said to have violated the basic methodological rule formulated by Karp Popper, that one should try to falsify rather than verify hypotheses before adopting them.[31] Williams is even worse. Not only does he invent speeches allegedly made by Stalin at the first plenary session at Potsdam, he presents Molotov's remarks in a single conversation, which are taken from the notes of two separate meetings. As Robert Maddox has written of Williams' book *The Tragedy of American Diplomacy*, the real 'tragedy' was that it was taken seriously by those who should have known better.[32]

The effect of so many indictments of US foreign policy, many of them burdened with titles as pretentious as their themes,[33] is to leave the reader stranded in an echoing emptiness. Unlike more orthodox indictments by historians such as George Kennan whose writing is truly symphonic in scale, those like Chomsky's is essentially chamber music in its intensity, best communicated in the closed room of the imagination. Chomsky's massive tomes display a feeling that the real world can only be properly explained in an all-embracing fashion – that it needs elaboration rather than brevity, demonstration rather than obliqueness – the true mark of the political zealot.

HISTORY AND THE SCHOOLS

If neither the mainstream historians, writing their doctoral theses most of which, even if published, are rarely read, nor the outspoken revisionists have made any headway, the teaching of history is a more lamentable development of recent years. Back in 1962 Acheson received a letter from a child in the sixth grade at a school in Paramus, New Jersey, asking him what makes a great nation. In his published reply he invoked Milton, de Tocqueville and Thucydides.[34] Today it is doubtful whether most schoolchildren at any age would have heard even of de Tocqueville with his own definition of a great nation, one that 'perseveres in a great design'.

The historical illiteracy of the public, of course, is not a new phenomenon, much though the moralists of today may try to portray it as if it is. At the height of the Second World War 60 per cent of adult Americans could not locate one of the four members of the Grand Alliance, China, on the map.[35] Perhaps it is surprising they knew China was an ally at all when 3 per cent of Britons thought that the United States was still part of the British Empire.[36]

The situation, however, has deteriorated seriously ever since. A recent report by the National Endowment for the Humanities found that 68 per cent of high school children did not know in which century the United States had fought the Civil War, while 40 per cent had no idea when the Declaration of Independence had been drawn up. If anything knowledge of contemporary history is even worse. A Gallup poll commissioned by CBS and the *New York Times* found only 22 per cent of those polled had heard of the Panama Canal Treaty (1977) despite the 247 amendments the Senate insisted on adding before it agreed to its formal ratification. Twenty-two per cent could not name either of the two parties to the SALT 2 treaty which the Senate refused to ratify in 1979. Only 8 per cent in 1983 knew that the United States supported the Contras in Nicaragua – an issue Congress had chosen to make the main debating point between itself and the administration.

There are many explanations for the crisis in history teaching in the schools and campuses of the United States, but one deserves special mention. As the Council for Basic Education concluded in its report *Making History Come Alive* (1978) the subject had been subsumed in most schools into social studies – which may or may not require history as a separate course of study. Virtually no training in history is demanded of secondary school teachers. In one state teachers were asked to emphasise concepts that allegedly 'transcend' historical situations. In another state the educational authorities predicted that history would soon be supplanted by more 'relevant courses' such as ecology.

The great irony, of course, is that this is precisely what Charles Beard – one of the most revered of the United States' twentieth-century historians –

hoped would happen. By stripping the past of its myths he hoped to produce not 'objective' history, but a social imperative for action. Scientific history would provide the public with a real choice between political parties; their claim to objectivity would further increase their chance of creating 'a uniquely authentic American language'. Social science has indeed become the tool of the reformers with whom Beard was associated all his life.[37] For him history as an 'act of faith' demanded an ultimate act of faith – renouncing 'the diplomacy of the dollar, the navy and the marines'.[38] History of course can suggest the wisdom of renouncing such measures; only the past can transform them into *moral* absolutes.

The government is not oblivious to the disturbing fall of history standards in the United States. The study of history, as the Bradley Commission reported, helped students to understand themselves, as well as – in the dreadful vernacular of contemporary American culture – 'otherness', i.e. other people and cultures. History, the Commission reminded its readers, enabled students to question national stereotypes, to distrust simple answers, to recognise the fallaciousness of 'historical lessons', to recognise – most difficult of all for Americans – that not every problem necessarily has a solution.

Unfortunately, history is no longer part of the core curriculum beyond the eleventh grade. So much for Plumb's hopes that the American people would be able to liberate themselves from their past by discovering their real history. Instead, history is frequently considered 'irrelevant', or meaningless, part of the intellectual baggage of another era. Far from being 'irrelevant', of course, a knowledge of history is what is desperately needed to restore the quality of the American political debate, to challenge the Left's reluctance to find problems with Soviet power, or disarmament, or moral relativism, or the Right's reluctance to question covert operations, the arms race, or stereotyped attitudes to the Third World. 'If the centre is to hold', writes Paul Gagnon, 'as the founders held Philadelphia against the simplifiers of their day, we will need an audience prepared and willing to listen to complications.'[39]

It now looks as though the Centre will hold only if the past can be packaged and sold to the American people like a soap opera, or a bargain basement item. What the Americans want, claimed Barbara Tuchman, is not history, but news, 'history by the ounce'. To borrow a metaphor from Susan Sontag, the force of historical argument has become the force of collage.[40] It is a depressing prospect. 'No foreign policy – no matter how ingenious – has any chance of success if it is born in the minds of a few and carried out in the hearts of none.'[41] Kissinger may well be proved right for the wrong reasons. Traditionally policy has been conceived by the few, and communicated successfully to the many, by dressing it up in Clio's clothes, by appealing to the past for sanction. But what of a society where the past no longer conveys any resonance, or message, in which not even history can liberate informed opinion from its influence?

There is evidence that the former has already happened in the ghettos and backwaters of American life. In his youth, writes Theodore White, he accepted his father's past implicitly. Yet when he revisited the suburb in Boston in which he had spent much of his childhood he found nothing but a devastated society, with burnt out buildings, a typical picture of the urban decay which has disfigured the US landscape. 'It was retrospectively clear to me', he wrote on the last page of his book *In Search of History* (1978), that

the old English political culture had lost control over the other people who had filled America's vast spaces and clotted cities. The polyglot peoples of America had no common heritage but only ideas to bind them. ... what would really be at issue was whether America would be transformed in the name of opportunity simply into a Place, a gathering of discreetly defined and entitled groups, interests and heritages.[42]

As White noted twenty years earlier, 'when one is a stranger to oneself then one is estranged from others too.'[43] It would appear the United States may have to cling to its myths a little longer if it is to absorb its million immigrants every year, or the underclass which haunts its inner cities, the estranged foreigners in its midst.

IN CONCLUSION

'The sphinx must solve her own riddle'

Emerson, 'History'

There is still ground for optimism, of course. It was Lincoln who reminded the American people that for a policy to be tempered by scepticism does not mean that policymakers need be 'bereft of faith'. One can be sceptical of one's history, and still remain true to one's own values.[44]

The renunciation of exceptionalism, for example, need not involve renouncing the ideals it is supposed to embody. As one author observes, by understanding how much US diplomacy resembles the record of most nations in history, how the United States has stumbled into wars on the flimsiest of pretexts, the country might be able to shape policies in the future that actually reflect the promise of its idealistic rhetoric.[45]

Let us also not forget, moreover, that the past the United States has manufactured has imposed a strait-jacket on society by suggesting an end, not a process of age and rebirth. As George Ball once remarked of South Africa, the Americans have never understood the problem of apartheid because they 'have never known how the story will end'.[46]

In perpetually searching for the story's end, the United States has always found the quest frustrating. In his book *The Myth of the Eternal World*

(1954) Mircea Eliade entitled his last section 'The terror of history' precisely because the Americans appeared to live under sentence of a punishment or reward which has yet to be determined. Cyclical theories of history, such as Spenglerianism in the 1920s and Toynbeeism in the 1950s, were popular because they foretold what was going to happen. As Eliade wrote of the public's fascination with Toynbee at the time, 'The formulation, in modern terms, of an archaic myth betrays at least the desire to find a meaning and a transhistorical justification for historical events.'[47]

A country which has lost interest in history as such and which may no longer be influenced even by its past, may be freed from that particular sisphean labour. Unfortunately, it may also find itself adrift in the world. A society which craves instant news and pictorial images, whose attention span is too limited for historical lessons or analogies, may very soon lose its identity as well as its soul. The past may have run its course, history will continue, taking with it a nation that has lost its innocence, not through the forbidden pursuit of knowledge, but an inadvertent drift into ignorance, a nation which, having been present at 'the Creation', seems to be cooling its heels in the antechamber of history, anxiously awaiting the Fall.

NOTES

1. John Dos Passos, *The Ground We Stand On: some examples from the history of a political creed* (Boston: Houghton Mifflin, 1941) p. 3.
2. Kenneth W. Thompson, *Morality and Foreign Policy* (Louisiana State University Press, 1980) pp. 29-30.
3. Arthur Schlessinger, *The Bitter Heritage: Vietnam and American Democracy* (Boston: Houghton Mifflin, 1966) p. 91.
4. Cited in Paul N. Goldstene, *The Collapse of Liberal Empire: science and revolution in the twentieth century* (New Haven: Yale University Press, 1977) p. 79.
5. Raymond Aron, *Diversity of Words: France and the United States look at their common problems* (New York: Reynal, 1957) pp. 79-80.
6. J. H. Plumb, *The Death of the Past* (London: Penguin, 1972) pp. 149-50.
7. J. H. Plumb, 'Churchill as historian', in A. J. P. Taylor (ed.), *Churchill: Four Faces and the Man* (London: Allen Lane, 1969) p. 121.
8. *ibid.* Alan Taylor wrote of Churchill that he was 'the price the British people paid for reading history'. James Morris wrote of him: 'He spoke in imperial hyperboles, saw with an imperial vision and gave to the British themselves for the last time, the feeling that they were a special people with honourable duties of their own' (*Farewell the Trumpets: an imperial retreat* (London: Faber and Faber, 1978) p. 436).

    As for the *Whig Interpretation of History* itself, Butterfield wrote: 'We may believe in some providence that guides the destiny of men and may, if we like, read this into our history; but what our history brings to us is not proof of providence but rather the realisation of how mysterious are its ways, how strange its caprices. Our assumptions do not matter if we are conscious that they are assumptions, but the most fallacious thing in the world is to organise our historical knowledge upon an assumption without realising what we are doing, and then to make inferences from that organisation and claim that these are the voice of history. It is at this point that we tend to fall into what I have nicknamed the Whig fallacy' (*The Whig Interpretation of History* (London: Bell and Sons, 1968) pp. 22-3).

9. Plumb, *Churchill: Four Faces, op. cit.*, p. 36.
10. *ibid.*, p. 16.
11. Ernest May, 'A case for court historians', *Perspectives on American History* 3 (1969) pp. 413-39. Herbert Feis wrote *The Chinese Triangle* in 1953. See also Feis, 'The shackled historian', *Foreign Affairs* 45:2 (January 1967); and Francis Lowenheim (ed.), *The Historian and the Diplomat: the role of history and historians in American foreign policy* (New York: Harper & Row, 1967).
12. Stephen Cohen, *Rethinking the Soviet Experience: politics and history since 1917* (New York: Oxford University Press, 1984) pp. 13-24.
13. Richard Neustadt and Ernest May, *Thinking in Time: the uses of history for decision makers* (New York: Free Press, 1986).
14. William Dray, *Perspectives on History* (London: Routledge & Kegan Paul, 1980) p. 124.
15. Robin Winks (ed.), *The Historian as Detective: Essays on Evidence* (New York: Harper, 1968) p. 433; and Marcus F. Cunliffe and R. W. E. Winks (eds), *Past masters: some essays on American historians* (New York: Harper, 1975).
16. William Appleman Williams, *Empire as a way of life: an essay on the causes and character of America's present predicament* (Oxford: Oxford University Press, 1968) p. 12.
17. Paul Weaver, *The Suicidal Corporation* (New York: Simon & Schuster, 1988).
18. Michael J. Smith, *Realist Thought from Weber to Kissinger* (Baton Rouge: Louisiana State University Press, 1986) p. 194.
19. Carl Becker, *Detachment and the Writing of History* (ed.) P. L. Snyder (Ithaca, New York: Cornell University Press 1958) p. 24.
20. For left-wing critiques see Aileen Kraditor, 'American radical historians and their heritage', *Past and Present* no.56 (August 1972); James Weinstein and D. W. Eakins (eds), *For a New America: essays in history and politics* (New York: Random House, 1970); Barton J. Bernstein (ed.), *Towards a New Past: dissenting essays in American history* (New York: Chatto, 1970).
21. Daniel Boorstein, *The Image* (New York: Atheneum, 1962) p. 6.
22. Victor Kiernan, *America: the new imperialism: from white settlement to world hegemony* (London: Zed Press, 1978) p. 263.
23. Gabriel Kolko, *Anatomy of a War: the United States and the modern historical experience* (New York: Pantheon, 1985) p. xi
24. Noam Chomsky, *American Power and the New Mandarins* (London: Penguin, 1969) p. 12.
25. William Carlos Williams, *In the American Grain* (New York: 1925) pp. 188-9.

26. *Partisan Review* (Spring 1972).
27. Aldous Huxley, *Ends and Means* (London: Chatto and Windus, 1937) p. 274.
28. Arthur Schlessinger, 'The vital centre reconsidered', *Encounter* 35 (Spring 1970) pp. 88-92.
29. Howard Zinn, *The Politics of History* (1970) p. 36.
30. William Appleman Williams, *The Tragedy of American Diplomacy* (New York: Dell Publishing, 1962) p. 207.
31. J. L. Richardson, 'Cold War Revisionism: a critique', *World Politics* 24 (1972) p. 608.
32. Robert James Maddox, *The New Left and the Origins of the Cold War* (Princeton, NJ: Princeton University Press, 1973) p. 37.
33. See Noam Chomsky, *The Political Economy of Human Rights: the Washington connection and Third World Fascism* (Nottingham: Spokesman, 1979); and *The Political Economy of Human Rights: post-war Indo-China and the reconstruction of imperial ideology* (Nottingham: Spokesman, 1981).
34. Dean Acheson, *Fragments of My Fleece* (New York: Norton, 1971) p. 81.
35. Hadley Cantril and Mildred Strunk, *Public Opinion 1935-46* (Princeton, NJ: Princeton University Press, 1951) p. 265.
36. James Morris, *Farewell the Trumpets, op. cit.*, p. 474.
37. Raymond Seidelman, *Disenchanted Realists: political science and the American crisis 1854-1984* (New York: Albany State University Press, 1985) p. 84.
38. C. Ushing Strout, *The Pragmatic Revolt in American history: Carl Becker and Charles Beard* (New Haven: Yale University Press, 1958) p. 142.
39. Paul Gagnon, 'Why study History?', *Atlantic Monthly* (November 1988) p. 66.
40. Susan Sontag, *On Photography* (London: Penguin, 1986) p. 73.
41. Henry Kissinger, 'America's strengths and American purposes', Speech to the American Legion's National Convention 20 August 1974, *DSB* (16 September 1974) p. 377.
42. T. H. White, *In Search of History: a personal adventure* (New York: Harper & Row, 1978).
43. Cited in Ann Morrow Lindbergh, *Gift for the Sea* (1955).
44. Thompson, *Morality and Foreign Policy, op. cit.*, p. 1.
45. Melvin Small, *Was War Necessary: national security and US entry into war* (Beverley Hills: Sage, 1980) p. 304.
46. Cited in Kenneth Adelman, *African Realities* (New York: Crane Russak, 1980) p. 154.
47. Mircea Eliade, *The Myth of the Eternal World* (Princeton, NJ: Princeton University Press, 1954) p. 147.

Bibliography

GENERAL

Ambrose, Stephen, *The Rise to Globalism: American foreign policy in 1938-70* (Pelican, 1971).
Aron, Raymond, *Peace and War: a theory of international relations* (Weidenfeld and Nicolson, 1966).
——— *The Imperial Republic: the US and the world 1945-73* (Weidenfeld and Nicolson, 1975).
Bartlett, Christopher, *The Rise and Fall of the Pax Americana* (Elek, 1974).
Bloomfield, Lincoln, *In Search of American Foreign Policy* (Oxford University Press, 1974).
Brandon, Donald, *American Foreign Policy: beyond utopianism and realism* (Appleton and Century Croft, 1966).
Brandon, Henry, *The Retreat of American Power* (Doubleday, 1973).
Brown, Seymon, *The Faces of Power: constancy and change in US foreign policy from Truman to Reagan* (Columbia University Press, 1983).
Gardner, Lloyd C., *A Covenant With Power: America and the world order* (Oxford University Press, 1984).
Hacker, Andrew, *The End of the American Era* (Atheneum, 1970).
Hamilton, Michael, (ed.) *The American Character in Foreign Policy* (Eerdmans Publishing Co., 1986).
Harrington, Moria, *The Dream of Deliverance in American Politics* (Alfred Knopf, 1986).
Hartz, Louis, *The Liberal Tradition in America: an interpretation of American political thought since the revolution* (Harcourt Brace Jovanovich, 1955).
Hodgson, Geoffrey, *America from World War 2 to Nixon* (Macmillan, 1977).
Hoffmann, Stanley, *Primacy or World Order: American foreign policy since the cold war* (McGraw Hill, 1978).
——— *Dead Ends: American foreign policy in the new cold war* (Harper & Row, 1983).
Holsti, Ole and James Rosenau, *American Leadership in World Affairs: Vietnam and the breakdown of consensus* (Allen & Unwin, 1984).
Hunt, Michael, *Ideology and US Foreign Policy* (Yale University Press, 1987).
Kaplan, Morton A., *Global Policy: challenge of the 1980s* (Institute for Values in Public Policy, Washington, 1984).
Kegley, Charles, and Eugene Wiltkopf, *American Foreign Policy: Problems and Processes* (Macmillan, 1987).
Liska, George, *Career of Empire* (Johns Hopkins University Press, 1978).
McClosky, Herbert and John Zaler, *The American Ethos: public attitudes towards*

capitalism and democracy (Harvard University Press, 1984).

O'Neil, William, *Coming Apart: an informal history of America in the 1960s* (Quadrangle, 1971).

Osgood, Robert, *Retreat from Empire?* (Johns Hopkins University Press, 1973).

——— (ed.) *America and the World: from the Truman doctrine to Vietnam* (Johns Hopkins University Press, 1970).

Potter, David, *People of Plenty: economic abundance and the American character* (University of Chicago Press, 1954).

Rosenberg, Emily, *Spreading the American Dream* (Hill & Wang, 1982).

Rosencrance, Richard, *America as an Ordinary Country* (Cornell University Press, 1976).

Rostow, Eugene, *Peace in the Balance: the future of American foreign policy* (Simon & Schuster, 1972).

Steel, Ronald, *Pax Americana* (Penguin, 1977).

Stillman E., and W. Pfaff, *Power and Impotence: the failure of American foreign policy* (Random House, 1966).

Tucker, Robert W., *The Radical Left and American Foreign Policy* (Johns Hopkins University Press, 1971).

Weisband, Edward, *The Ideology of American Foreign Policy: a paradigm of Lockean liberalism* (Sage, 1973).

Whetten, Lawrence, *Contemporary American Foreign Policy: minimal diplomacy defence strategy and detente management* (Kentucky University Press, 1973).

Wildavasky, Golda, *US Foreign Policy: prospects and proposals of the 1970s* (McGraw Hill, 1969).

3 specialist books

Bleichman, Barry M., and Stephen Kaplan: *Force Without Arms: US armed forces as a political instrument* (Brookings Institution, 1978).

Krasner, Stephen, *Defending the National Interest: raw materials investment and US foreign policy* (Princeton University Press, 1978).

May, Ernest R., *Lessons of the Past: the use and misuse of history in American foreign policy* (Oxford University Press, 1973).

THE MAKING OF US FOREIGN POLICY

Allison, Graham, *Essence of Decision: explaining the Cuban missile crisis* (Little, Brown, 1971).

Bacchus, William, *Foreign Policy and the Bureaucratic Process* (Princeton University Press, 1974).

Campbell, Franklin, *The Foreign Affairs Fudge Factory* (Basic Books, 1971).

Destler, I. M., *Presidents, Bureaucrats and Foreign Policy: the politics of organizational reform* (Princeton University Press, 1972).

Fisher, Lewis, *Constitutional Conflicts between Congress and the President* (Princeton University Press, 1985).

Frye, Alton, *A Responsible Congress: the politics of national security* (Council for Foreign Relations, 1975).

Hass, Richard, 'Congressional power: implications for US security policy', *Adelphi* 153 (International Institute of Strategic Studies, 1979).
Hughes, Barry B., *The Domestic Context of American Foreign Policy* (Freeman, 1978).
Neustadt, Richard, *Presidential Power* (Wiley and Sons, 1960).
Rosenau, James, *National Leadership and Foreign Policy: a case study in the mobilization of public support* (Princeton University Press: 1963).
Rosenau, N., *Domestic Sources of Foreign Policy* (Free Press, 1967).
Schick, Allen, *Making Economic Policy in Congress* (American Enterprise Institute, 1983).
Sorenson, Theodore, *Decision Making in the White House* (Columbia University Press, 1963).
Turner, Kathleen, *Lyndon Johnson's Dual War: Vietnam and the press* (University of Chicago Press, 1985).
Yarmslinsky, Adam, *The Military Establishment: its impact on American society* (Harper & Row, 1971).

SIX SPECIFIC CASE STUDIES

for SALT negotiations: John H. Barton and Lawrence D. Weller (eds) *International Arms Control: issues and agreements* (Stanford University Press, 1976).
for the role of the military in crises: Richard Betts, *Soldiers, Statesmen and Cold War Crises* (Harvard University Press, 1977).
for CIA and defence evaluation: Lawrence Freedman, *US Intelligence and the Soviet Strategic Threat* (Macmillan, 1977).
for study of The White House: Herbert Schaudler, *The Unmaking of a President: Lyndon Johnson and Vietnam* (Princeton University Press, 1977).
for 'middle level' crisis policy-making: Dan Haendel, *The Process of Priority Formulation: US foreign policy in the Indo-Pakistan war 1971* (Westview Press, 1978).
for the Iranian crisis: Warren Christopher (ed.), *American Hostages in Iran: the conduct of a crisis* (Yale University Press, 1985) and Gary Sick, *All Fall Down: America's fateful encounter with Iran* (Random House, 1985).

US AND THE COLD WAR: ORIGINS

Davis, Lynn, *The Cold War Begins: Soviet-American conflict over Eastern Europe* (Princeton University Press, 1974).
Etzold, Thomas, and John Gaddis, *Containment: documents on American policy and strategy 1945-50* (Columbia University Press, 1978).
Feiss, Herbert, *From Trust to Terror: the onset of the cold war 1945-50* (Norton and Co., 1970).
Freeland, Richard M., *The Truman Doctrine and the Origins of McCarthyism 1946-8* (Alfred Knopf, 1972).

Gaddis, John L., *The United States and the Origins of the Cold War 1941-7* (Columbia University Press, 1972).
Gaddis, John, *Strategies of Containment: a critical appraisal of post-war American national security policy* (Oxford University Press, 1983).
Gardner, Lloyd, *Architects of Illusion: men and ideas in American foreign policy* (Quadrangle Books, 1972).
Kolko, Gabriel, *The Limits of Power: the world and US foreign policy 1945-54* (Alfred Knopf, 1972).
Korvig, Bennet, *The Myth of Liberation: East-Central European US diplomacy and politics since 1941* (Johns Hopkins University Press, 1973).
Lukas, Richard, *Bitter Legacy: Polish-American relations in the afternoon of World War Two* (Kentucky University Press, 1982).
Lundestad, Geir, *The American Non-policy Towards Eastern Europe 1943-7* (Humanities Press, 1975).
Masty, Votjech, *Diplomacy, Warfare and the Politics of Communism 1941-5* (Columbia University Press, 1979).
McCauley, Martin, (ed.): *Communist Power in Europe 1944-9* (School of Slavonic and East European Studies, 1977).
Muller, L. H., and R. Pruessen (eds): *Reflections on the Cold War: a quarter century of American foreign policy* (Temple University Press, 1974).
Paterson, Thomas, *Soviet-American Confrontation: post-war reconstruction and the origins of the cold war* (Johns Hopkins University Press, 1973).
Sherwin, Martin, *A World Destroyed: the atomic bomb and the grand alliance* (Alfred Knopf, 1975).
Siracusa, Joseph (ed.), *The American Diplomatic Revolution: a documentary history of the cold war 1941-7* (Open University Press, 1978).
Stoler, Mark, *The Politics of the Second Front: American military planning and diplomacy in coalition warfare 1941-3* (Westport Publications, 1977).
Wittner, Lawrence, *American Intervention in Greece 1943-9* (Columbia University Press, 1982).
Yergin, Daniel, *Shattered peace: the origins of the cold war and the national security state* (André Deutsch, 1978).
Zayas, Alfred M. de, *Nemesis at Potsdam: the Anglo-Americans and the expulsion of the Germans: background, execution, consequences* (Routledge & Kegan Paul, 1977).

FIVE PRIMARY SOURCES:

Acheson, Dean, *Present at the Creation* (Norton and Co., 1969).
Harriman, W. Averell, *America and Russia in a Changing World: a half century of personal observations* (Doubleday, 1971).
Bailey, Thomas, *The Marshall Plan Summer: an eyewitness report on Europe and the Russians in 1947* (Stanford University Press, 1978).
Djilas, M., *Conversations with Stalin* (Pelican, 1962).
Kennan, George (X), 'The sources of Soviet conduct', *Foreign Affairs*, 1947.

THE KOREAN WAR 1950-3

Caridi, Ronald, *The Korean War and American politics: the republican party as a case study* (University of Penn Press, 1968).
Cummings, Bruce, *Origins of the Korean War* (Princeton University Press, 1981).
——— (ed.), *Child of Conflict, the Korea-America relationship 1943-53* (University of Washington Press, 1983).
Heller, Francis (ed.), *The Korean War: a twenty-five year perspective* (Kansas University Press, 1977).
Henderson, Gregory, *Korea: the politics of the vortex* (Harvard University Press, 1968).
Lowe, Peter, *The Origins of the Korean War* (Longman, 1986).
Nagai, Yonosuke and Akira Iriye (eds): *The Origins of the Cold War in Asia* (Columbia University Press, 1977).
Paige, Glenn D., *The Korean Decision* (Free Press, 1968).
Simmons, Robert, *The Strained Alliance: Peking, P'yongyang Moscow and the politics of the Korean civil war* (Collier Macmillan, 1975).
Whiting, Allen, *China Crosses the Yalu: the decision to enter the Korean war* (Macmillan, 1977).

Two primary sources:
Eisenhower, Dwight D., *The White House Years* (vol. I, Mandate for change 1953-6, Doubleday, 1963).
Khruschev, Nkita, *Kruschev Remembers* vol. I (André Deutsch, 1971).

US AND THE SOVIET UNION 1945-86

Abel, Elie, *The Missile Crisis: the Cuban Missile Crisis* (Lippincott, 1966).
Devine, R. (ed.) *The Cuban Missile Crisis* (1971)
Edmonds, Robin, *Soviet Foreign Policy 1962-73: the paradox of a super power* (Oxford University Press, 1975).
Eubank, Keith, *The Summit Conference 1919-60* (University of Oklahoma Press, 1966).
Gaddis, John Lewis, *Strategies of Containment: a critical appraisal of post-war American national security* (Oxford University Press, 1982).
Gillingham, Arthur, *Cuban Missile Crisis: a selected bibliography,* Political issues series 2:6 (University of California Press, 1976).
Hoffmann, Erik (ed.), *The Conduct of Soviet Foreign Policy* (Butterworths, 1971).
Holbraad, Carsten, *Super Powers and International Conflict* (St. Martin's Press, 1979).
Kennedy, Robert, *Thirteen Days* (Macmillan, 1969).
Lafeber, Walter, *America, Russia and the Cold War 1945-80* (Wiley, 1980).
Liska, George, *Rethinking US-Soviet Relations* (Basil Blackwell, 1987).
Rappoport, Arnold, *The Big Two - Soviet-American Perceptions of Foreign Policy* (Pegasus, 1971).
Rozsarenc, Edwin and Kenneth Lindfors, *Containment and the Origins of the Cold*

War (Heath & Co., 1951).
Schick, Jack, *The Berlin Crisis 1958-62* (University of Philadelphia Press, 1971).
Seabury, Paul, *The Rise and Decline of the Cold War* (Basic Books, 1967).
Slusser, Robert, *The Berlin Crisis of 1961: Soviet-American relations* (Johns Hopkins University Press, 1973).
Stoessinger, John, *Nations in Darkness: China, Russia and America* (Random House, 1971).
Tanter, Raymond, *Modelling and Managing International Conflict: the Berlin crisis* (Sage, 1974).
Ulam, Adam, *Expansion and Co-existence: the history of Soviet foreign policy 1917- 67* (Praeger, 1968).
——— *The Rivals: America and Russia since world war two* (Viking Press, 1971).
Wesson, Robert G., *Soviet Foreign Policy in Perspective* (Homewood, 1969).

GEORGE KENNAN AND CONTAINMENT

Kennan, George, *American Diplomacy 1900-50* (University of Chicago Press, 1951).
Kennan, George, *Russia, the Atom and the West* (Reith Lectures 1957) (Oxford University Press, 1958).
Kennan, George, *Democracy and the Student Left* (Hutchinson, 1968).
Kennan, George, *The Cloud of Danger: some current problems of American foreign policy* (Little, Brown, 1979).
Urban, George (ed.), *Encounters with George Kennan: the great debate* (Frank Cass, 1979).

DULLES AND CONTAINMENT

Beal, John R., *John Foster Dulles* (Harper & Row, 1959).
Berding, Andrew (ed.), *Dulles on Diplomacy* (Princeton University Press, 1965).
Dulles, John Foster, *War, Peace or Change* (Harper & Row, 1939).
Goold-Adams, Richard, *A Time of Power, a Reappraisal of John Foster Dulles* (Weidenfeld & Nicolson, 1962).
Heller, Dean and David, *John Foster Dulles: soldier for peace* (Holt, Reinhart, 1960).

DÉTENTE AND HENRY KISSINGER

Bell, Coral, *The Diplomacy of Détente: the Kissinger era* (Macmillan, 1977).
Brandon, Henry, *The Retreat of American Power: Nixon and Kissinger's foreign policy and its effects* (The Bodley Head, 1973).
Caldwell, Jan (ed.), *Henry Kissinger: his personality and policies* (Duke University Press, 1983).
Hirsch, Ernest and Tony Thomas, *Angola: the hidden history of Washington's war* (Pathfinder Press, 1976).

Kissinger, Henry, *The White House Years* (Weidenfeld and Nicolson, 1979).
Liska, George, *Beyond Kissinger: ways of conservative statecraft* (Johns Hopkins University Press, 1976).
Morris, Roger, *Uncertain Greatness: Henry Kissinger and American foreign policy* (Quartet Books, 1977).
Sheldon, Della, *Dimensions of Détente* (Praeger, 1978).
Smith, Michael J., *Realist Thought from Weber to Kissinger* (Louisiana University Press, 1986).
Stoessinger, J., *Henry Kissinger: the anguish of power* (Norton & Co., 1976).

CARTER AND CONTAINMENT

Brzezinski, Zbigniew, *Power and Principle, Memoirs of the National Security Adviser (1977-81)* (Weidenfeld and Nicolson, 1983).
Rosati, Jerel, *The Carter Administration's Quest for Global Community: beliefs and their impact on behaviour* (University of South Carolina Press, 1987).
Smith, Gaddis, *Morality, Reason and Power: American diplomacy and the Carter years* (Hill & Wang, 1986).

THE VIETNAM WAR (1956-1975)

Austin, Anthony, *The President's War* (Lippincott, 1971).
Berman, Larry, *Planning a Tragedy* (Norton and Co., 1982).
Braestrup, Peter (ed.), *Vietnam as History* (University Press of America, 1984).
Charlton, Michael and Anthony Moncrieff: *Many Reasons Why: the American involvement in Vietnam* (Penguin, 1978).
Chomsky, Noam, *American Power and the New Mandarins* (Penguin, 1969).
Cooper, Chester, *The Lost Crusade: America in Vietnam* (Dodd Mead, 1970).
Galluci, Robert, *Neither Peace nor Honour: the politics of American military policy in Vietnam* (Johns Hopkins University Press, 1975).
Gelb, Leslie and R. Betts, *The System Worked: the irony of Vietnam* (Brookings Institutions, 1979).
Goldman, Alan, *The Tragedy of Lyndon Johnson* (Alfred Knopf, 1969).
Goodman, Allan E., *The Lost Peace: America's search for a negotiated settlement of the Vietnam War* (Stanford University Press, 1978).
Haley, Edward, *Congress and the Fall of South Vietnam and Cambodia* (Association University Presses, 1982).
Hamilton, Michael P. (ed.), *The Vietnam War: christian perspectives* (Eerdmans, 1967).
Herring, George C., *America's Longest War: the United States and Vietnam 1950-75* (Wiley, 1979).
Isaacs, Arnold, *Without Honour: defeat in Vietnam and Cambodia* (Johns Hopkins University Press, 1983).
Kolko, Gabriel, *Anatomy of a War: Vietnam, the United States and the modern historical experience* (Pantheon, 1985).

Manning, Robert and Michael Janeway (eds): *Who We Are: an Atlantic chronicle of the US and Vietnam* (Little, Brown, 1969).
Popkin, Samuel L., *The Rational Peasant: the political economy of rural society in Vietnam* (University of California Press, 1979).
Porter, Gareth, *A Peace Denied: the US, Vietnam and the Paris Agreement* (Indiana University Press, 1975).
Race, Geoffrey, *War Comes To Long An: revolution and conflict in the Vietnamese village* (University of California Press, 1972).
Schlessinger, Arthur, *The Bitter Heritage: Vietnam and American democracy* (Houghton Mifflin, 1966).
Shawcross, William, *Kissinger, Nixon and the Destruction of Cambodia* (André Deutsch, 1979).
Sheehan, Neil, *A Bright Shining Lie: John Paul Vann in Vietnam* (Random House, 1988).
Summers, Harry, *On Strategy: a critical analysis of the Vietnam war* (Dell, 1982).
Thompson, W. Scott and Donaldson Frizzel, *The Lessons of Vietnam* (Macdonald, 1977).
White, Ralph, *Nobody Wanted War: misperceptions in Vietnam and other wars* (Doubleday, 1970).

Original Sources:

Elsberg, Daniel (ed.), *The Pentagon Papers: the Defence Department History of US decision making in Vietnam* (4 vols) (Beacon Press, 1971).
Johnson, Lyndon B., *The Vantage Point: perspectives on the Presidency 1963-9* (Reinhart and Winston, 1971).
Kissinger, Henry A., *The White House Years* (Little, Brown, 1979).
Westmoreland, William, *A Soldier Reports* (Doubleday, 1976).

THE AMERICAN WAY OF WARFARE

Ackley, Charles, *The Modern Military in American Society: a study in the nature of military power* (Westminster Press, 1982).
Bletz, Donald F., *The Role of the Military Professional in US Foreign Policy* (Praeger, 1972).
Huntington, Samuel, *The Soldier and the State: the theory and politics of civil-military relations* (Harvard University Press, 1957).
Leonard, Thomas, *Above the Battle: war-making from Appomattox to Versailles* (Oxford University Press, 1978).
Luttwak, Edward, *The Pentagon and the Art of War* (Simon & Schuster, 1985).
McLintock, Robert, *The Meaning of Limited War* (Houghton and Mifflin, 1967).
Millis, Walter, *Arms and Men: a study in American military history* (Putnam & Sons, 1956).
Osgood, Robert, *Limited War: the challenge to American strategy* (University of Chicago Press, 1957).
——— *Limited War Revisited* (Westview Press, 1979).
Small, Melvyn, *Was War Necessary? national security and US entry into war* (Sage, 1980).

van Horne, Winston, and Thomas V. Tommesen (eds), *Ethnicity and War* (University of Wisconsin, 1984).

US AND THE ATLANTIC ALLIANCE

Bell, Coral, *The Debatable Alliance: an essay in Anglo-American relations* (Oxford University Press, 1964).
Duroselle, Jean-Baptist, *France and the United States* (University of Chicago Press, 1978)
Fox, W. and A. Fox, *NATO and the Range of American Choice* (Columbia University Press, 1967).
Gardner, R., *Sterling/Dollar Diplomacy* (McGraw Hill, 1969).
Hoffmann, Stanley, *Gullivers Troubles or the Setting of American Foreign Policy* (McGraw Hill, 1968).
McGeehan, Robert, *The German Re-armament Question: American Diplomacy and European Defence* (University of Illinois Press, 1971).
Morgan, Roger, *The US and West Germany 1945-73: a study in alliance politics* (Oxford University Press, 1974).
Neustadt, Richard, *Alliance Politics* (Columbia University Press, 1970).
Newhouse, John, *De Gaulle and the Anglo-Saxons* (André Deutsch, 1970).
Porte, A. W. de, *Europe Between the Super Powers: the enduring balance* (Yale University Press, 1979).
Richardson, James L., *Germany and the Atlantic Alliance* (Harvard University Press, 1966).
Schaetzel, J. Robert, *The Unhinged Alliance: America and the European Community* (Harper & Row, 1975).
Sulivan, Marianna, *France's Vietnam Policy: a study in French-American relations* (Greenwood Press, 1978).
Turner, A. C., *The Unique Partnership: Britain and the US* (Pegasus, 1971).
Waltz, Kenneth, *Foreign Policy and Democratic Politics: the American and British experience* (Longman, 1968).
Williams, Geoffrey, *The Permanent Alliance: the European-American partnership 1945-82* (Macmillan, 1985).
Williams, Phil, *The Senate and US Troops in Europe* (Macmillan, 1985).

US RELATIONS WITH CHINA

Barnds, William (ed.), *China and America: the search for a new relationship* (Council for Foreign Relations, 1977).
Cohen, Warren, *America's Response to China: an interpretative history of Sino-American relations* (Wiley, 1971).
Dixon, Joseph (ed.), *The American Military and the Far East* (USGPO, 1980).
Gungaru, Wang, *China and the World Since 1949* (Macmillan, 1977).
Hsiao, Gene, *Sino-American Détente and its Policy Implications* (Praeger, 1964).

Lawrance, Alan, *China's Foreign Relations Since 1949* (Routledge & Kegan Paul, 1975).
MacFarquhar, Roderick, *Sino-American Relations 1949-71* (Praeger, 1972).
Moorstein, Richard, *Remaking China policy: US China relations and government decision making* (Harvard University Press, 1971).
Rossay, Koen, *The China Lobby in American Politics* (Macmillan, 1960).
Tucker, Nancy, *Patterns in the Dust: Chinese-American relations with the recognition controversy, 1949-50* (Columbia University Press, 1983).
Wilcox, Francis (ed.), *China and the Great Powers: relations with the US, Soviet Union and Japan* (Praeger, 1974).
Yahuda, Michael, *China's Role in World Affairs* (Croom Helm, 1978).

THE US AND THE THIRD WORLD

Baldwin, David, *Economic Development and American Foreign Policy* (University of Chicago Press, 1966).
Feinberg, Richard, *The Intemperate Zone: the third world challenge* (Norton & Co., 1983).
Gilpin, Robert, *US Power and the Multinational Corporation: the political economy of foreign directive investment* (Basic Books, 1975).
Girling, John, *America and the Third World: revolution intervention* (Routledge & Kegan Paul, 1980).
Hapgood, David, *A Close Look at the Peace Corps* (Little & Stead, 1968).
Kiernan, V. G., *America: the new imperialism: from white settlement to world hegemony* (Zed Press, 1978).
Magdoff, Harry, *The Age of Imperialism* (Monthly Review Press, 1969).
O'Leary, Michael, *The Politics of American Foreign Aid* (Atherton Press, 1967).
Packenham, Robert, *Liberal America and the Third World: political development ideas in foreign aid and political science* (Princeton University Press, 1973).
Parent, Michael, *The Anti-Communist Impulse* (Random House, 1969).
Swomley, John, *American Empire: the political ethics of twentieth-century conquest* (Macmillan, 1970).
Tabman, William (ed.), *Globalism and Its Critics* (Heath, 1973).

THE US AND THE MIDDLE EAST

Mangold, Peter, *Super Power Intervention in the Middle East* (Croom Helm, 1977).
The Middle East and the international system Part I: the impact of the 1973 war. Papers from the 16th IISS Annual Conference, Adelphi Paper 114 (ISSS Spring 1975).
Quandt, William, *Decade of Decision - American Policy Towards Arab-Israeli Conflict 1967-76* (University of California Press, 1978).
Rubner, Michael, *Conflict in the Middle East: a selected bibliography* (Political issues series 4:4 (University of California Press, 1977).

Spiegel, Steven, *The Other Arab-Israeli Conflict: making America's Middle East policy from Truman to Reagan* (University of Chicago Press, 1985).
Whetten, Lawrence L., 'The Arab-Israel dispute: great power behaviour', *Adelphi Paper* 128 (IISS, Winter 1976/7).

THE US AND ASIA

Barnds, William, *India, Pakistan and the Great Powers* (Pall Mall, 1972).
Cohen, Warren, *New Frontiers in America – East Asian Relations* (Columbia University Press, 1983).
Gordon, Bernard, *Towards Disengagement in Asia: a strategy for American foreign policy* (Prentice Hall, 1969).
Jackson, Robert, *South Asian Crisis: India, Pakistan and Bangladesh* (Chatto and Windus, 1975).
May, Ernest and James Thompson: *America–East Asian Relations* (Harvard University Press, 1972).
Nam, Koo Hong, *America's Commitment to South Korea: the first decade of the Nixon doctrine* (Cambridge University Press, 1986).
Osgood, Robert, *The Weary and the Wary: US and Japanese security policies in transition* (Johns Hopkins University Press, 1972).
Watts, William, *The United States and Asia: changing attitudes and perspectives* (Kentucky University Press, 1982).

THE US AND AFRICA

Adelman, Kenneth, *African Realities* (Crane Russak, 1980).
Coker, Christopher, *The United States and South Africa 1968–86: constructive engagement and its critics* (Duke University Press, 1986).
Hance, William, *Southern Africa and the United States* (University of Columbia Press, 1968).
Lake, Anthony, *The Tar Baby Option: American policy towards southern Africa* (University of Columbia Press, 1976).
Mahoney, Richard, *JFK: ordeal in Africa* (Oxford University Press, 1984).
Marcum, John, *The Politics of Indifference: Portugal and Africa – a case study in American foreign policy* (University of Syracuse Press, 1972).
Mayall, James, *Africa, the Cold War and After* (Elek Books, 1971).
Mazrui, Ali, *Africa's International Relations: the diplomacy of dependency and change* (Heinemann, 1977).
Nielsen, Waldemar, *The Great Powers and Africa* (Pall Mall Press, 1969).
Shepherd, George W., *The United States and Non-aligned Africa* (University of Denver Press, 1970).
Uttley, Garrick, 'Globalism or regionalism? US policy towards southern Africa', *Adelphi Paper* 154 (IISS, Winter 1979/80).

THE US AND LATIN AMERICA

Barry, Tom and Beth Wood, *Dollars and Dictators: a guide to central America* (Zed Press, 1983).

Black, Jan, *US Penetration of Brazil* (University of Pennsylvania Press, 1977).

Blasier, Cole, *The Hovering Giant: US responses to revolutionary change in Latin America* (University of Pittsburgh Press, 1976).

Cotter, Julio and Richard Fagen (eds): *Latin America and the United States: the changing political realities* (Oxford University Press, 1974).

Crawley, I., *Dictators Never Die: a portrait of Nicaragua and the Somoza dynasty* (1979); revised as *Nicaragua in Perspective* (St. Martins Press, 1984).

Gleijeses, Piero, *The Dominican Crisis 1965: constitutional revolt and American intervention* (Johns Hopkins University Press, 1979).

Hirschman, Albert, *Journeys Towards Progress: studies of economic policy making in Latin America* (Twentieth Century Fund, 1963).

Kinzer, Stephen, *Bitter Fruit: the untold story of the American coup in Guatemala* (Sinclair Brown, 1982).

Markham, Patrick, *So Near to God: journey through central America* (Penguin, 1985).

Martin, John, *US Policy in the Caribbean* (Westview Press, 1978).

Parker, Phyllis, *Brazil and the quiet intervention 1964* (Texas University Press, 1979).

Parkinson, F., *Latin America, the Cold War and World Politics 1945-73: a study in diplomatic history* (Sage, 1974).

Slater, Jerome, *Intervention and Negotiation: the US and the Dominican Republic* (Harper & Row, 1970).

THE US AND THE UNITED NATIONS

Beichman, Arnold, *The Other State Department: the US mission to the UN* (Basic Books, 1970).

Bloomfield, Lincoln, *The UN and US Foreign Policy: a new look at the national interest* (Little, Brown, 1967).

Fasulo, Linda, *Representing America: experiences of US diplomats at the UN* (Praeger, 1985).

Finkelstein, Lawrence (ed.): *The US and International Organisation: the changing setting* (MIT Press, 1969).

Goodrich, Leland M., *The UN in a Changing World* (University of Columbia Press, 1974)

Haas, Ernest, *The Web of Interdependence: the US and international organisation* (Prentice Hall, 1970).

Kay, David (ed.): *The Changing UN: options for the US* (Academy of Political Science, 1977).

Moynihan, Daniel, *A Dangerous Place* (Secker and Warburg, 1979).

Riggs, Robert, *US/UN Foreign Policy and International Organisation* (1971).

Russell, Ruth, *The UN and US Security Policy* (Brookings Institution, 1968).

Weiler, Lawrence, *The US and the UN: the search for international peace and security* (1967).

THE US AND HUMAN RIGHTS

Bozeman, Ada, *Rights and Responsibilities: international social and individual dimensions* (University of Southern California Press, 1980).
Graebner, Norman, *Humanitarianism and Foreign Policy* (University of Virginia Press, 1977).
Kaufman, Natalie, (ed.), *The Dynamics of Human Rights and US Foreign Policy* (Transition Books, 1982).
Lefever, Ernest, *Ethics and US Foreign Policy* (University Press of America, 1986).
——— *Ethics and US Foreign Policy* (University Press of America, 1986).
Mail, Kenneth (ed.), *The Moral Dimensions of American Foreign Policy* (Transition Books, 1984).
van Dyke, Vernon, *Human Rights, the United States and the World Community* (Oxford University Press, 1970).

THE US AND DECLINE

Bloom, Allan, *The Closing of the American Mind* (Simon & Schuster, 1987).
Free, Lloyd and Hadley Cantrill, *The Political Beliefs of Americans: a study of public opinion* (Simon & Schuster, 1968).
Fulbright, William, *Prospects for the West* (Harvard University Press, 1963).
——— *The Arrogance of Power* (Random House, 1966).
Glazer, Nathan, and Irving Kristol, *The American Commonwealth – 1976* (Basic Books, 1976).
Goldstene, Paul N., *The Collapse of Liberal Empire: science and revolution in the twentieth century* (Yale University Press, 1977).
Marris, Stephen, *Deficits and Dollars: the world economy at risk* (Institute for International Economics, 1985).
Montgomery, John, *Aftermath: tarnished outcomes of American foreign policy* (Auburn House Publishing, 1986).
Paz, Octavio, *One Earth, Four or Five Worlds: reflections on contemporary history* (Carcanet, 1985).
——— *The Tragedy of American Diplomacy* (Dell Publishing Co., 1962).
Williams, William Appleman, *Empire as a Way of Life: an essay on the causes and character of America's present predicament* (Oxford University Press, 1968).

THE UNITED STATES AND HISTORY

Backer, Carl, *Detachment and the Writing of History*, ed. P. L. Snyder (Cornell University Press, 1958).

Bernstein, Burton J. (ed.), *Towards a New Past: dissenting essays in American history* (Pantheon, 1968).
Boorstein, Daniel, *The Image* (Atheneum, 1962).
Cunliffe, Martin (ed.), *Past Masters: some essays on American historians* (1969).
Dickson, Peter, *Kissinger and the Meaning of History* (Cambridge University Press, 1976).
Dray, William, *Perspectives on History* (Routledge & Kegan Paul, 1980).
Eliade, Mircea, *The Myth of the Eternal World* (Princeton University Press, 1954).
Gay, Peter, *A Loss of Mastery: puritan historians and colonial America* (California University Press, 1966).
Kolko, Gabriel, *Anatomy of a War: the United States and the modern historical experience* (Pantheon, 1985).
Lowenheim, Frances (ed.), *The Historian and the Diplomat: the role of history and historians in American foreign policy* (Harper & Row 1967).
Maddox, Robert James, *The New Left and the Origins of the Cold War* (Princeton University Press, 1973).
Neustadt, Richard, and Ernest May, *Thinking in Time: the uses of history for decision-makers* (Free Press, 1986).
Niebuhr, Reinhold, *The Philosophy of History in Our Time* (Charles Scribner, 1949).
——— *The Irony of American History* (Charles Scribner, 1952).
Passos, John Dos, *The Ground We Stand On: some examples from the history of the political creed* (Houghton Mifflin, 1941).
Plumb, J. H., *The Death of the Past* (Penguin, 1973).
Schlessinger, Arthur, *The Cycles of American History* (André Deutsch, 1987).
Seidelman, Raymond, *Disenchanted Realists: political science and the American crisis 1854–1984* (Albany State University, 1985).
Strout, C. Ushing, *The Pragmatic Revolt in American History: Carl Backer and Charles Beard* (Yale University Press, 1958).
van Woodward, C., *American Attitudes Towards History* (Clarendon Press, 1958).
Weinstein, James, and David Eakins (eds), *For a New America: essays in history and politics* (Random House, 1970).
White, Theodore H., *In Search of History* (Harper & Row, 1978).
Winks, Robin (ed.), *The Historian as Detective: essays and evidence* (Harper & Row, 1968).
Zinn, Howard, *The Politics of History* (1970).

Index

Acheson, Dean 9–10, 12, 21, 37, 55, 64–5, 81, 106, 110, 139, 151, 157
Adams, James 20
Adams, John Quincy 12, 21, 118, 128, 141
Adelman, Kenneth 115–16
Auden, W. H., 2, 4, 11
Afghanistan, Soviet invasion of (1980) 77, 79, 121
Almond, Gabriel 142
Alliance for Progress 113–15
American Revolution
 exceptionalism 5–11
 happiness 6–8

Ball, George 9, 25–6, 29, 139, 159
 exemplarism 26–7
Barraclough, Geoffrey 115
Beard, Charles 5, 22, 74, 152, 157–8
Becker, Carl 154
Bell, Daniel 141
Benes, Eduard 43, 45, 48
Berlin Crisis (1948) 40, 51, 68
Berlin Crisis (1958) 68
Bloom, Allen 131
Brandon, Henry 128
Brodie, Bernard 95
Brzezinki, Zbigniew 2, 11, 28, 36, 71, 75, 79, 80, 82, 163
Bush, George 11, 17, 140

Cabot Lodge, Henry 89
Carter, Jimmy 21, 75, 131, 132
 redemptionism 13–14
Castro, Fidel 108
Chesterton, G. K. 7, 55
Chomsky, Noam 154–5, 156

Churchill, Winston 150–1
Cioran, E. M. 137, 143
Commanger, Steele 2, 115

Debray, Regis 108
de Tocqueville, Alexis 1, 38, 117, 131–2, 140, 157
Dickens, Charles 7
Dukakis, Michael 140
Dulles, Allen 107
Dulles, John Foster 12–14, 41, 64–9, 70–9, 82, 140, 148

Eisenhower, Dwight 12, 64–9, 70, 75, 81, 87, 107
Eliade, Mircea 159–60
Eliot, T. S. 8, 150

Fitzgerald, Frances 96
Ford, Gerald 72
Forrestal, James 37, 106
Freud, Sigmund 7, 11
Fullbright, William 13, 20, 98, 137

Galbraith, Kenneth 134
Greene, Graham 90, 111, 141, 143
Guevara, Che 122–3

Haig, Alexander 17, 106
Hamilton, Alexander 38, 50, 153
Hartz, Louis 82, 113
Herter, Christian 137
Hirsch, E. D. 131
Huntingdon, Samuel 117

Jefferson, Thomas 6, 25, 27, 50, 190, 118, 137–8, 141, 155

Johnson, Lyndon 18, 20, 55, 87–8, 89, 98, 106, 113, 120, 142
Jung 121

Kennan, George 73, 140–1, 148, 156
  exemplarism 23–5
  exceptionalism 8–9
  Third World 8–9
Kennedy, Paul 129, 130, 135–6, 142, 144, 148
Kennedy, John, F. 11, 28, 88–9, 95, 107, 108–9, 112, 119, 121, 122, 152
Kolko, Gabriel 154, 156
Korean War (1950–3) 37, 49, 61, 64–6, 96, 120
Kissinger, Henry 21, 56, 67, 69–75, 89, 93, 94, 121, 129, 137, 158
Kristol, Irving 94, 138

Lincoln, Abraham 21, 159
Lippmann, Walter 59–9, 61, 66, 71, 89, 138
Liska, George 80–1, 104
Locke, John 15, 105, 113–14
Luce, Henry 67, 129, 144

MacArthur, George 37, 60
Madison, James 20, 38, 153
Macmillan, Harold 41, 45
MacNamara, Robert 91–2, 94
Markham, Patrick 110
Marshall Plan (1947) 9, 13, 48–9, 58, 60–1, 89, 138
manifest destiny 9, 18, 149
Morgenthau, Hans 21, 111, 148
Moynihan, Patrick 8, 21

National Security Council 68 (NSC 68) 61, 68 74
Niebuhr, Reinhold 8, 14, 16, 94, 119, 150
Nietzsche 2, 81, 98
Nitze, Paul 39, 64–5
Nixon, Richard 17, 20, 65, 93, 96, 98, 109, 113, 120, 130, 139
  administration (1969–74) 69–75

Osgood, Robert 104

Paz, Octavio 143
Peace Corps 111–12, 123
Peterson Report (1971) 105
Plumb, J. H. 5, 150–1
Popper, Karl 64, 139, 156
Puritan tradition 14–18
Potsdam Conference (1945) 47, 156

Reagan, Ronald, 2, 4, 28, 56, 71, 120, 122–3, 131, 133, 137, 142
  administration (1981–8) 75–81
revisionism 154–6

Rockefeller Report (1969) 120
Rostow, Eugene 106
Rostow, Walt 105
Rusk, Dean 22, 64, 68, 111, 119

Sandberg, Carl 150
Schlessinger, Arthur 11, 36, 108, 113, 149, 155
Schultz, George 9, 76, 80
Schumpeter, Joseph 128
Sontag, Susan 25, 29, 96, 158
Spengler, Oswald 59, 73, 130, 152–3, 155
Stalin, Joseph 36–7, 45–6, 47–8, 51, 57
Steinbeck, John 1, 2, 154
Stimson, Henry 27–8
Strategic Defense Initiative (SDI) 80, 140

Taft, Robert 141
Tchephone Plan (1965) 99
Tet Offensive (1968) 98–9
Toynbee, Arnold 128, 159–60
Truman, Harry 37, 39, 51, 61, 112
Truman Doctrine (1947) 2, 13, 57, 59, 106, 122
Tuchman, Barbara 158

United Fruit Company (UFC) 107–8
United States
  aid to the Third World 112–16
  atomic warfare 37–41
  Central America 77–8, 119–20

Cold War 36–51
containment: Kennan and 58–63;
    Dulles and 63–9; Kissinger and
    69–75; Regan and 75–81;
decline: national 131–2; imperial
    132–8; intellectual 138–44;
exemplarism 20–3
investment in the Third World
    105–7
isolationism 21–2
Middle East 72, 76–8
past 1–5, 150–9
redemptionism 11–20
special relationship with Britain
    39–41
southern Africa 72–3, 78

Vance, Cyrus 119
Vann, John Paul 100
Vietnam War 87–100, 113, 154
Vietcong 97–9

Wallace, Henry 116
Webster, Noah 6
Weber, Max 16–17, 64
Westmoreland 9, 92, 96–8
White, T. H. 159
Williams, Willam Appleman 27, 153, 156
Wilson, Woodrow 42, 43, 119

Yalta Conference (1944) 36, 45

Zinn, Howard 155–6